OUR HOME IN MYANMAR

FOUR YEARS IN YANGON

JESSICA MUDDITT

CONTENTS

For Mum and Dad –
    thank you for everything.

And for Olivia and Claire –
    you are my world.

Our Home in Myanmar by Jessica Mudditt

www.jessicamudditt.com

© 2021 Jessica Mudditt

Hembury Press

Cover photo by Kaung Htet.

Cover design by Kirby Young.

Paperback ISBN: 9780648914228

Ebook ISBN: 978-0-6489142-3-5

ABOUT THE AUTHOR

Jessica Mudditt is a Sydney-based author and journalist whose articles have been published by *The Economist*, *BBC*, *CNN*, *GQ* and *Marie Claire*. She was accredited as a newspaper journalist in London in 2009 and spent a decade working in the UK, Bangladesh and Myanmar before returning to Australia in 2016. *Our Home in Myanmar* is her first book.

MAP OF MYANMAR

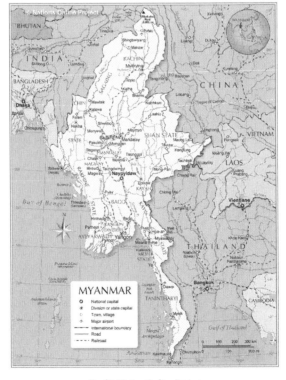

Credit: Nation Online Project

The tide was out. But when it came back in, the waves would lap at Daw Myint Shwe's house. Pointing towards the ocean, she told me the erosion was so bad that she'd been forced to move her bamboo shack four times, but could only ever move it a little further inland. She had lived in the area her entire life and was now in her sixties, but even so, she wished that she could start again in a safer place. The problem was that she didn't have the money. And every year, the Bay of Bengal crept closer in.

As my translator asked Daw Myint Shwe another question on my behalf, my eyes strained to make out the horizon behind her, so muted were the colours of the landscape. The hazy sky seemed to melt into the taupe mud flats, where shallow pools of water looked like shards of broken glass. Debris was scattered across the soggy sand on which the three of us stood: a ripped blue tarpaulin, cracked ceramic bowls, coconut husks and discarded fishing nets.

The next person the United Nations had lined up for me to interview was U Myint Swe, who lived slightly further inland.

Raising his voice to be heard over a noisy gust of wind, he told us that his main worry was for his three young children, who had to cross a river in a small boat to get to school.

'During the wet season, when the waters are high and rough, U Myint Swe worries that the boat will capsize,' my translator said. 'He says that no one in the fishing village can afford life jackets – not even if they all chipped in together to buy them.'

U Myint Swe's family was stuck in Labutta Township in the southern, low-lying Ayeyarwady Delta: the only jobs were there, near the coast. Even so, he only made about two American dollars a day as a fisherman.

'Nowadays the weather is often too foul to go out in – and on those days he earns nothing,' my translator said. 'But he says he is grateful for the weather warnings that are broadcast through speakers at the local monastery.'

In 2008, there had been no warning before Cyclone Nargis swept through the 115 villages in U Myint Swe's township and left 85,000 people dead in its wake. He told us several times that he was still haunted by the death and destruction he had seen, and I suspected that his current worries about his children were exacerbated by previous trauma.

But as arresting and poignant as these stories were, I was struggling to focus. My attention kept wandering from the people the United Nations had sent me to interview for a series of articles on climate change to my husband's visa situation. Sherpa is from Bangladesh and getting a visa for Myanmar – or anywhere, for that matter – had never been straightforward. But in the four years we had been living in Yangon and working as journalists, it had never taken as long as it was taking this time around. He had submitted his passport to the immigration department three months ago, but when his go-between, Aye Chan Wynn, started calling to find out whether the visa was ready, his contact at the department wouldn't return his calls. I was worried that Sherpa's passport had been lost, as nothing else seemed to explain the delay.

I spent the next day in a village on an island so remote that accessing it required a two-hour journey by longboat. I was anxiously hoping for an update on the visa, but my phone lost reception soon after we set off through the mangroves. The island had no electricity and supplies of clean water were limited. Stagnant water, however, was abundant: it pooled under the residents' shacks on stilts, so the mosquitoes bred incessantly. Later, I suspected it was our lunch in the village that gave me a painful and lasting bout of colitis.

While I was on the island, I met a young woman called May Thazin who worked at a prawn farm for fourteen hours a day. The work was seasonal, so she and her husband scavenged for crabs to get by in the off-months. She said that most of her friends had moved several hundred kilometres away to Yangon in search of a better life, but she was deterred by the bad stories she'd heard from those who couldn't make a go of it and were forced to return. Her only fun was watching Korean soap operas on a solar-powered television.

When I got back to the bare bones guesthouse at dusk, there was still no news on Sherpa's visa. He said that Aye Chan Wynn would keep trying to make contact and would go to the department in person if he had to. I lay in bed that night with an aching stomach, morosely thinking of my husband's uncertain visa situation and how vulnerable Myanmar was to climate change. The United Nations was working with the government to boost resilience in places like Labutta Township – including practical courses on what to do in an emergency situation – but I could see that the challenge was immense. Everyone I had met depended on agriculture for a livelihood, and the need to take out high-interest loans to rebuild homes and farmland following a natural disaster trapped them in a continuous cycle of poverty. The UN had hired me as a sort of in-house journalist to draw attention to the need for urgent action.

After doing an interview at a government department in the morning, I farewelled my translator and hopped back in the UN's oversized 4WD. With my completely silent driver at the wheel, I continued on to the drought-ravaged plains of Magway region in central Myanmar, where I heard harrowing stories of how a particularly terrible flood in 2010 swept entire families away in their beds one night. In the late afternoon, a surprise storm caused flash-flooding that almost made the road impassable on our way out. From there it was only a few hours to the capital city of Nay Pyi Taw, where I was scheduled to interview members of the environment ministry and work from the UN's office. I was on the tail end of a ten-day mission, and my loneliness was compounded by Nay Pyi Taw being a bizarre place without a heart or soul. A visit there always left me feeling blue.

The junta abruptly moved Myanmar's capital city to Nay Pyi Taw in 2006 and it was built in secret, possibly using slave labour. Nay Pyi Taw is the only place in Myanmar with 24-hour electricity and decent internet speeds. It is flat, deserted and massive: New York City is just a sixth of its size. But it wasn't a case of 'build it and they will come,' as not even the embassies could be convinced to move to the purpose-built city, which is nothing short of dystopian. It is divided into 'zones' for retail, government, hotels and so forth, and it has a zoo that cost a fortune to build but scarcely sees any children pass through its gates. There are also oddities like the restaurant in an aeroplane that is parked out the front of a palatial hotel.

As we sped along an empty twenty-lane highway, my phone pinged with a text message from Sherpa.

'Hey babe. Great news. My passport is ready to be collected.

Aye Chan Wynn will go to the immigration department now to pick it up.'

I was so relieved that I wanted to cheer. We pulled up at an enormous hotel that looked like a wedding cake. I checked in at the vast, empty lobby, then unpacked my things and took a shower, humming all the while.

I'd been enjoying the warm water for a couple of minutes when someone started violently banging on the door of my room.

'I'm in the—!' I began to shout, but was drowned out by a deafening roar. It sounded as if artillery was hitting the building, so my first instinct was to crouch. As the ground beneath me gave way, I realised it was an earthquake. I tried to grab the bath rail but missed: my hands were covered in soap suds and wet hair covered my face.

The shaking lasted maybe a minute, and it was the most terrifying minute of my life. When it stopped, I stood there dripping wet and praying that it wouldn't start again. With trembling hands I wrapped a towel around me, then I went online and discovered that the epicentre of the 6.8 magnitude earthquake was 250 kilometres away in Magway region, where I'd just been. Photos were appearing on social media of the moment the earthquake struck Bagan's thousand-year-old temples, leaving dozens of the ancient structures lying in the dust. One person was killed.

Still frightened, I called Sherpa. He listened to me recount the experience and said how sorry he was that he wasn't there to comfort me. And then he said he had something to tell me. I could tell from his tone that something was amiss.

'Aye Chan Wynn picked up my passport,' he said quietly. 'There was no visa inside. They wouldn't say why they didn't give me one.'

I felt unsteady on my feet all over again.

~

THREE DAYS LATER, I was back in Yangon and Sherpa and I were heading to the airport in a taxi through torrential rain. His plan was to get a visa from the embassy in Bangkok, while I would stay put in Yangon with our cat, Butters. But we were worried that he wouldn't make it out of Myanmar at all – and that he may even be arrested at the airport. Overstaying a visa by several months could be considered a crime under local laws. It didn't matter that it had been impossible for Sherpa to leave because the immigration department had his passport. We were scared and hadn't slept.

The taxi ride through the rain seemed to take forever, but we eventually pulled up out the front of the new international terminal. It had opened just the previous week after years of hype about its refurbishment. A small group of taxi drivers in grotty white singlets and *longyis*, a long sarong tied at the waist, stood out the front and spat red daubs of betel nut onto the freshly laid cement as they waited for a fare. One fanned himself with a newspaper as he stood there shooting the breeze with the others, his gut protruding like a balloon and his singlet rolled up above his nipples. It looked like he was wearing a cut-off sports bra.

Sherpa handed over 6000 kyat to our driver, which was about US$5, and we leapt out of the taxi. He hadn't any luggage, apart from the small backpack he took to work every day, into which he'd tossed a couple of t-shirts and his shaving gear. If he got out okay, it was only going to be a quickie visa run to Bangkok and back.

I shivered as a shot of icy air met us as we walked inside the terminal. The carpet was a sickly green with mustard-coloured swirls, but there was no denying that the place looked a lot more modern than it used to – the previous incarnation was more of a shed. The airport's bigger size made it seem emptier than usual, but I took the upgrade as a reassuring sign that Myanmar was eager to be part of the global community after decades of self-imposed isolation. I hoped that perhaps it wouldn't be heavy-handed in its treatment of outgoing foreigners like my husband.

Please just let him leave.

I squeezed Sherpa's hand one last time before reluctantly letting go. He looked edgy and unsure of himself, which I knew wouldn't bode well when he fronted up to the immigration counter. Our eyes locked for a second and we mouthed a quick 'I love you' – the most affection it was appropriate to show in the conservative Buddhist country. I wanted to run my hand through his mop of curly black hair but he was already walking away from me.

I crossed both my fingers behind my back and whispered 'please, please, please' under my breath as Sherpa approached the counter. *Please let luck come our way.* After all the time we'd spent in Myanmar, it was probably inevitable that its superstitious ways had rubbed off on me.

I watched on from behind a set of glass doors as Sherpa held up his green passport to the immigration officer, whom he was speaking to deferentially in Burmese. I held my breath. A minute passed, then two. Sherpa had his back to me and I couldn't read the officer's unchanging facial expression. He called another officer over. Another couple of minutes passed as they conversed. Just when I couldn't bear to watch on any longer, I saw Sherpa reach for his wallet to retrieve the wad of US dollars he had ready to pay in overstay fees. As he was waved through to passport control I breathed an enormous sigh of relief. The months of worry were over.

Sherpa turned back to look at me from where I stood in the

departures hall. His large brown eyes were lit up with happiness. I grinned back and made a stupid thumbs-up gesture, feeling giddy with relief.

I had no idea that this was the last time I'd ever see my husband in Myanmar.

1

THE NEW GIRL AT WORK

JULY 2012, FOUR YEARS EARLIER

I was wide awake long before it was time to set out for my first day as a sub-editor at *The Myanmar Times*. I'd woken at five and after tossing and turning in a futile bid to fall back asleep, I'd left Sherpa snoring softly beside me in our guesthouse room. I crept down the stairs and into the misty light of the new day. I sat on the front steps and lit a cigarette, and I smiled. Here I was in beautiful, beguiling Myanmar, and I wasn't merely passing through: I was about to start a month-long trial at Myanmar's best known newspaper, at a time when the country was beginning to take tentative steps in the transition from dictatorship to democracy.

I had wanted to see Myanmar with my own eyes for such a long time. Back in 2005, before I left my home in Melbourne for a year of backpacking through Asia, I went to a travel agency at my local mall and said that the first place I wanted to go to was Myanmar. The travel agent told me to wait while he went into the back room, and when he returned five minutes later, he had a sheepish look on his face.

'I hadn't heard of Myanmar so I had to ask my colleague for help. We looked it up in an atlas. You meant "Burma," right?'

Then he told me that there were several rules I would have to comply with on my visit, including flying into and out of Yangon from Bangkok. The flights would be costly and my time in Myanmar would be limited to a couple of weeks. I'd wanted my funds to last longer by travelling overland as much as possible, so I'd begun my journey in Cambodia instead. However, the yearning to visit Myanmar never left me.

As I thought once again how lucky I was to have finally made it to Myanmar, a posse of Buddhist nuns appeared from around the street corner. They were dressed in rose-coloured robes, with thick apricot sashes wrapped diagonally across their delicate shoulders and torsos. Their heads were shaved bare and they walked with a silver alms bowl tucked under an arm and velvet slippers on their feet. As they came closer, I saw that the only variation in their appearance was their height, with a couple of pint-sized nuns trailing up the back who may have been as young as six. They padded along silently and in single file, holding out their bowls to the half dozen shopkeepers who stood on the side of the road and spooned in rice and small handfuls of kyat, the local currency. The nuns kept their eyes downcast as they accepted the offerings. I'd seen photos of Myanmar's Buddhist nuns in guidebooks but I'd assumed that I'd have to visit a temple to see them – yet here they were in downtown Yangon, and it was only my third day in the country.

Back in our guesthouse room, Sherpa wished me well as he kissed me goodbye.

'Don't be nervous,' he added, tenderly tucking a loose strand of hair behind my ear. 'You will do great.'

The newspaper's offices were located at the upper end of Bo Aung Kyaw Street, which was named after a famous student leader who was murdered by British colonial officers a decade before Myanmar won its independence in 1948. It was less than ten minutes' drive from where I was staying, but the fact that I was mangling the pronunciation of *Kyaw* while trying to find a taxi was making the journey an impossible one.

'Bo Aung Kay-yore?' I asked a taxi driver who pulled up at the kerb, having no idea that the sound for *kyaw* is closer to 'jaw'.

He looked at me dumbfounded and drove off. So did the next two drivers. Some saw me but ignored me, perhaps unwilling to risk the hassle of dealing with a foreigner. Flustered, I tore a scrap of paper out of the notebook in my backpack and scrawled 379 BO AUNG KYAW STREET in large letters. I held it up to the next driver who pulled over and wound down his window. He couldn't read English; nor could the next one. The third driver grinned a betel-stained smile, held up three fingers and said, 'Three thousand.' Heaving a sigh of relief, I leapt into the back seat of the creaking vehicle, unaware that he'd charged me triple the usual fare.

By this time I was in danger of being late on my very first day, which was ironic, given how long I'd been up and ready to go. Mercifully, we sped past the teahouses and Chinese restaurants, a Hindu temple and an assortment of shopfronts half-covered with sliding grates, and I was dropped opposite the office with a few minutes to spare. Before crossing the road, I gazed up at my new workplace and took a couple of seconds to savour the moment. The tropical climate had taken a toll on the white paint covering the imposing three-storey art-deco building, which had a huge sign bearing the newspaper's name in the same bold typeface as that on its masthead. The building stood opposite a beautiful nineteenth-century cathedral built with blush-coloured bricks – the first and the fourth estates staring each other down in a country devoid of democracy.

I almost tripped as I raced up the wide timber steps, scarcely registering the carp that swam underneath in a pond with a broken fountain and lined with algae. I gave my name to a moon-faced receptionist and took a seat in the foyer while trying to catch my breath, still cursing myself for not setting out earlier. I was rummaging around in my bag for a tissue to wipe the sweat off my forehead when I heard my name called.

Tom was the news editor and a twenty-something Australian. I shook his hand, feeling self-conscious about mine being damp with sweat. We'd been in contact in the month leading up to my arrival, but his emails were brief and had given me no clues as to personality. He was short and slight and spoke so quietly that I could scarcely make out what he was saying over his shoulder as he led me through the newsroom. I think it was something about being short-staffed.

The office was an elegant loft conversion with exposed bricks, high ceilings and steel columns. There were bright modernist paintings on the walls. I thought it all looked fantastically cool. Through the centre of the newsroom ran a long row of tiny cornflower-blue desks for the Burmese reporters. Many of the journalists typing away were female, and unlike the majority of women I'd seen on the streets of Yangon, they mostly wore Western-style clothes rather than traditional Burmese dress, which consisted of a fitted blouse and ankle-length *longyi* skirt. One reporter even had a pixie haircut with streaky blonde highlights, which was such a contrast to the long, jet-black hair most Burmese women sported.

Tom and I stopped at a row of larger workspaces that flanked the church side of the newsroom. Each was divided by a bookshelf and had a large window.

'Geoffrey, this is Jessica. Jessica, this is our world news editor.'

A lanky middle-aged man with straggly ash blond hair glanced up from his keyboard and swivelled his chair round to face us.

'G'day,' he said.

There was the briefest flicker of a smile before it was snuffed out and Geoffrey's grey eyes returned to the screen. The window for me to say anything was shut before I'd even had time to utter a quick hello. I was taken aback by his brusqueness and looked at Tom, but his face registered no surprise.

We took three steps to the left and repeated the under-whelming welcome, this time with the American arts and culture editor, Douglas. He at least smiled and said hi, but was clearly busy. On my third introduction I was greeted with a grunt. I was so confused that I didn't register Tom telling me that we were going to meet the business editor until we'd reached his desk on the other side of the newsroom.

'Jess, Stuart. Stuart, Jess.'

'Hey there. Good to have you here,' Stuart said with a wide smile and a strong Aussie accent. He had ginger hair, green eyes and the strong arms of a sportsman. 'I've got plenty of stories that need subbing. I'll make sure to send them your way.'

This was better. I smiled and started gushing about how excited I was to be working at *The Myanmar Times*. Stuart stared at me a little incredulously before Tom changed the subject.

'If you're wondering why Stuart sits on the opposite side of the newsroom from the rest of the English language team, it's because he had an argument with the boss. Afterwards, Ross was so pissed off with him that he moved him to a desk where an elderly Burmese copy editor died a few months ago. Our Burmese staff think the area is haunted and there's a rat in the panelling that pops his head up every now and again. Quite the punishment, huh Stuart?"

'Don't mess with the boss or you'll cop it,' Stuart said with half a laugh. 'Seriously though – Ross can be a real arsehole.'

'Oh wow, okay ... That's good to know,' I said, not knowing what else to say. I wondered what the fight was about but wasn't game to ask.

The boss Stuart and Tom were referring to was the newspaper's co-founder Ross Dunkley, a Walkley Award–winning journalist from Perth and the person who had given me the job trial via a mutual friend. With the backing of an Australian mining magnate named Bill Clough, Ross had opened Myanmar's first privately owned newspaper in 2000, with his Burmese business partner Sonny Swe. It was a move that took a lot of guts, considering the country had been ruled by one of the world's most oppressive military dictatorships since 1962. Indeed, half of the duo was in prison. By the time I arrived, Sonny had been in his cell in Shan State for seven years, and he had another seven left to go. He had been retrospectively found guilty of bypassing censorship laws as the publisher of *The Myanmar Times* – meaning that his actions were not criminal at the time, but only deemed to be so after the event. His supposed crime was gaining approval for stories from the wrong censorship authority, and he was given a seven-year sentence for the English edition, and seven years for the Burmese. Everyone knew that the charges were politically motivated and had more to do with his father having made some powerful enemies while serving as a senior member of Military Intelligence. Sonny's dad was serving an unfathomable 146-year sentence.

Ross, on the other hand, wasn't prosecuted, and the newspaper was allowed to continue operating. *Vanity Fair* had recently published a profile of Ross that compared him with Hunter S. Thompson due to his colourful lifestyle and turn of phrase. Others dubbed him the Murdoch of Southeast Asia because he had at various times owned stakes in papers in Vietnam, Cambodia and Myanmar. Ross, while much younger than Rupert Murdoch, also resembled the publishing magnate physically, as both men were bald, slim and wore spectacles. I also knew that Ross had a reputation for being loved and hated in equal measure (clearly, Stuart was leaning more to the latter).

Ross was nowhere in sight that morning – Tom had told me that he would introduce us when he arrived, which was usually after eleven o'clock.

Tom ended the tour by introducing me to his wife, Moh Moh Thaw, the editor of the Burmese language edition. She had a lovely smile and was dressed in a chic green dress. Tom then showed me my seat, which was next to his and at a workstation that seated four people.

'You'll get to know everyone soon enough. Have a read of some of the articles on our website and I'll give you some raw copy to edit in a bit,' he said.

As my computer warmed up, I took in my surroundings a little more. Opposite me was a Burmese translator who was long in the jowls and appeared to be nodding off. The fourth member of staff at the workstation was Tim, who was studying journalism at the Ivy League Princeton University. He had arrived a couple of weeks earlier with another student from Princeton called Bill. Both of them had scarcely glanced my way.

The coolness from some of the editors was a shock. I'd assumed there'd be a strong sense of camaraderie borne out of the tough conditions journalists faced in Myanmar, such as the possibility of angering a notoriously brutal military regime. But perhaps they were simply on deadline and stressed out, or had just been dealt a blow by the censorship board, who made them submit every article for approval before it could be published – with the result being that around a quarter of all content was lost every week and had to be replaced with filler and fluff. Maybe they'd pop over later for a proper hello.

Midway through the morning, and without any further chitchat having ensued, Tom yawned and stretched his arms over his head before calling out, 'Douglas, fancy a cuppa?'

'Sure.'

Douglas popped his head into Geoffrey's workspace. 'Keen for a tea?'

'Oi, Tim, Bill, Ben – let's head out,' added Tom. 'Stuart says he will meet us there.'

No one had spoken my name, so I remained at my desk. As the other expat editors filed out past me, chatting away happily as though I didn't exist, I pretended to be engrossed in the story I was sub-editing. But the truth was that I was crushed. I'd so badly wanted to hang out with these experienced Burma hands; to hear their stories so I could retell them until I had my own. I noticed that Moh Moh Thaw was also still plugging away at her desk. *Is this a boys' club or something?* I wondered. I also found it strange that the expats appeared to hang out separately from the Burmese staff – it had never been this way at the newspapers I'd worked at in Bangladesh.

The friendliest person I met that first day was Nicky. I was taken aback when he came up to my desk and offered his hand for me to shake. Being a teenager, it seemed rather formal.

'I'm Nicky. My dad is Sonny Swe: he's in prison still. My grandfather is in prison too. But they are kept in different prisons so that they can't talk to each other.'

He had scarcely got this out when I saw a tear roll down his cheek. Without thinking, I stood up and hugged him. Nicky regained his composure and told me that he was doing an informal internship at the paper. I assumed it was Ross' way of being something of a stand-in dad to the young man.

By the end of my first week, I had just about given up on being invited to take part in the morning tea ritual. I tried telling myself that it didn't matter, but I blushed with humiliation every time the guys did the roll call and I was left out. Having lived overseas already for six years, I had taken it for granted that a fellow Australian could be relied on as a friendly face in a strange place. It was such bad luck to encounter these grumpy ones.

So I was pleasantly taken aback when Tom invited me not for tea one Friday morning, but to a party that night at the British Club. I excitedly agreed, seeing it as my chance to melt the ice with my new colleagues. And I would bring Sherpa as my trump card. Everyone liked Sherpa. And it may help that he was a guy.

YANGON HAD VIRTUALLY no bars or pubs, so I wasn't altogether surprised to see that a small queue had formed outside the British Club's towering iron gates when Sherpa and I arrived. The party was hosted by the embassy's social club and it was apparently the social event of the month for expats. We were waved inside the compound by a security guard in a crisp white shirt with the Union Jack embossed on his shoulder sleeve.

We were told to put our passports in a wooden box and in return we got a little square of laminated paper with a number on it so that we could collect them at the end of the night. Tom had told me that this was a condition of entry, and I was starting to become accustomed to taking my passport with me everywhere, as I often needed to produce it – for example, when changing money.

With a grin, Sherpa squeezed my hand before nipping off to the bar.

'Meet you outside,' he said.

I wandered out. It was a shock to see so many Westerners in one place. There must have been almost a hundred people there, and it was a parallel universe compared with the poverty of much of Yangon. Milling around the floodlit lap pool on the well-watered lawns were men in pastel shirts, linen shorts and loafers. An attractive blonde in a fitted white dress appeared to have dunked herself in fake tan, while a guy with a hand around her waist wore a pair of distressed Levi's that suddenly struck me as ridiculous when I thought of my trishaw driver's threadbare shirt with a missing sleeve.

Sitting around a picnic table with a folded shade umbrella at its centre were two young Burmese men in suit jackets and fitted white t-shirts. One lit a cigarette and took a sip from his tumbler of whisky. They were joined by a stunningly beautiful woman wearing a red satin blouse with her hair in a low chignon. I presumed the men, and possibly the woman too, were well-connected, wealthy businesspeople known as 'repats' – Burmese who had been exiled abroad but were returning as Myanmar began to open up.

Sherpa came over with the first of many rounds of gin and tonics. We were already pretty drunk, as we had started drinking at our guesthouse, Motherland Inn 2, after meeting some friendly American travellers in the common area.

Sherpa and I spotted Tom, Douglas, Tim, Bill and Geoffrey standing near the children's play equipment and we wandered over to them. Sherpa was in fine form, and he and my colleagues hit it off. Before I knew it, he was regaling them with stories of his tough childhood in Bangladesh, such as when he'd seen a dead cow hanging from a tree after a cyclone hit his home city of Chittagong. They asked me what it was like to work as a journalist in the capital city of Dhaka, and I'd explained how Sherpa and I first met out the front of a garment factory after I'd hired him as my translator, and that we got married just seven months later. The guys also told me a bit more about what Ross was like to work with. Difficult and unpredictable, it seemed.

'Just ignore any emails he sends you after 2 a.m.,' said Geoffrey. 'That's when he gets crazy ideas into his head. Sometimes he just forgets that he sent you the email anyway.'

I laughed and thanked him for the advice.

Sherpa vanished shortly after 10 p.m. I searched the club's grounds, casually at first and then with rising panic. As Geoffrey and Douglas had just gone home and Tim and Bill were mingling with others, I asked Tom if he could see whether Sherpa was inside the men's toilets. Tom obliged, and returned quickly.

'I knocked on the door of a locked cubicle but there was no response,' he told me with a shrug.

I followed Tom back inside the men's toilets, shielding my eyes from the urinals as I did so. When we finally managed to get Sherpa to unlock the door, we found him drenched in sweat and his t-shirt stained with vomit. He wasn't accustomed to heavy drinking sessions because alcohol is illegal in Bangladesh.

Sherpa was weak on his legs and muttering nonsensically, so it took a few minutes to get him out of the toilets. I wrapped his arm around my shoulder and gripped his waist, thinking how lucky it was that he had a lean physique. I was seriously drunk myself and I lost my balance just as we came out the doorway. Sherpa came crashing down on top of me. Tom didn't make a withering remark or anything, but he looked unimpressed – and remarkably sober. Ending the night on the floor with my boss looking on was a terrible impression to have made. It was basically the opposite of what I'd hoped would happen.

I WAS desperate to redeem myself at work, but I seemed set on a calamitous path. I was halfway through my third week of the trial when I decided to head out for my break a bit earlier than usual. I'd started the day by sub-editing a story about a conference held by some of Myanmar's ethnic groups, and I'd made a total mess of people's names and even the ethnic groups themselves. I muddled up Kayin and Kayah and omitted Kachin altogether, not realising it was something different. On top of that, I'd given the male honorific 'U' to a female speaker instead of 'Daw', as I hadn't realised she was a woman. Tom had explained the corrections he'd had to make and the conversation had left me feeling despondent about my abilities. It certainly wasn't the first set of mistakes I had made – my lack of confidence was causing me to make some really stupid ones. I was painfully aware of how little I knew about Myanmar, and I was overwhelmed by the steep learning curve ahead of me. Myanmar's political history was so complex and there were a staggering 135 ethnic minority names to learn: I wondered how I would ever get a handle on the basics. The spelling of names confounded me, because there seemed not to be any agreed conventions: for example, the name of a township could appear as one word or be split into three shorter ones, possibly using slightly different letters. That is to say, Mingala Taungnyunt Township could be Mingalar Taung Nyunt, and it was my job as a sub-editor to remember how *The Myanmar Times* preferred to spell it. I worried that I was too slow to turn around edited stories to Tom, who worked beside me with a quiet serenity I envied.

As I lit a cigarette on the footpath, I noticed that my hands were trembling. I felt a chill pass through my body, but I took a couple of drags and kept on walking, going past a row of electronics shops, a tailor, a convenience store and a narrow stairwell inhabited by a sleeping street dog. Suddenly my vision blurred and my knees buckled. I went down with a thud next to a tree with a gold-painted trunk. My face met its roots, which had burst through the concrete.

WHEN I CAME TO, I was shouting Sherpa's name. In my delirium I somehow thought we'd been together when I fell. I gazed up at the small crowd of women hawkers that had formed a circle around me. Their faces were smeared with a dried pale-yellow bark paste called *thanaka*, which is used as a sunscreen. I blinked. They looked like ghosts.

I put my hand to my head and withdrew it with a wince. My fingers were covered with blood. I lifted myself onto an elbow and saw that my trousers were ripped. I also had a banging headache.

The next thing I knew, I was lying on a stretcher in a dimly lit room that reeked of antiseptic. I was in the century-old Yangon General Hospital, in a country with one of the world's lowest standards of medical care and waiting for a doctor to come along and put six stitches in my head. As far as crappy work days go, this one took the cake.

I was feeling so fragile that I actually wept a little when Sherpa arrived. Maisy from human resources was right behind him, as one of the kind nurses had phoned the newspaper to tell them where I was. I was discharged with iodine on my wounds and my head wrapped in a bandage. I also had a fat lip and a black eye, which made me look as if I'd been in a brawl. Nothing appeared to be wrong with me though – I think I literally had a sugar crash after downing three cans of energy drink in a misguided attempt to compensate for a bad night's sleep.

The three of us went back to the office to collect my bags, with Sherpa holding my hand as I wobbled my way up the steps. As I walked into the newsroom, the reporters stared at me, their mouths forming O-shapes.

'I wondered where you were,' said Tom, holding a pen aloft. 'You've been gone three hours.'

'I fell on my head and got stitches,' I blurted out.

'Take off the rest of the week and call me when you feel better,' he replied, still looking at me a little aghast.

I LAY on the bed and stared at the ceiling of MGM Hotel, where we had moved a few days earlier because it was cheaper. I felt wretched. Not only had I failed to redeem myself, but I was already draining the newspaper's limited resources by going on sick leave. Nor was I helping my colleagues to sub-edit the mountains of stories that came our way. My chances of passing the trial were surely shrinking by the day, I thought miserably.

WHEN I RETURNED to work the following Monday, it came as a complete surprise to discover that there was an upside to my accident. For one, Douglas showed real concern about how I was doing. We discovered that we had quite a few things in common, including our favourite authors, and before I knew it, he was a firm friend. He lent me books about Myanmar and made me laugh. He also taught me to pronounce Aung San Suu Kyi's name correctly.

'Mudditt, you are saying it wrong,' he informed me one day. 'Don't worry: it's a common mistake among newcomers. It isn't Aung San Suu "Key" – it's Aung San Suu "Chi". Think of it as Aung San "Sushi"'.

Geoffrey had a gruff exterior but could sometimes be generous and kind. He loved to meditate on the floor at lunchtime, with his long legs sticking out past his work area. I came to realise that he wasn't treating me differently from anyone else. Stuart could also be grouchy, and was quick to tell me when my work wasn't up to scratch or if something I did annoyed him – like when I overzealously attacked his proofing pages with a red pen late one Friday night. But at least I knew where I stood and he told me one day that my work was improving. Tom invited me out for tea a couple of times with the rest of the expat editors, though for some reason I never did feel at ease around him. But as someone who needs frequent doses of solitude, I became content to take breaks on my own anyway, or occasionally with a translator called Thiri, who took me under her wing after my fall.

THERE WERE ONLY a few days left of my trial when Tom invited me out to the tea shop – and only me. As I followed him out of the newsroom, my heart started thumping. I knew I was still much slower than the rest of the team in turning around sub-edited stories. But as soon as we sat down and ordered our drinks, Tom put me out of my misery by saying that Ross wanted to offer me a permanent job as a sub-editor. I grinned from ear to ear all day long.

What I didn't know was that getting the visa I needed to remain in Myanmar would be far more difficult than getting the job itself.

TROUBLE AT THE EMBASSY
AUGUST 2012

T his invitation letter isn't on a letterhead. I can't process your visa application if it doesn't have a letterhead,' said the man behind the counter, pointing a stubby finger at one of the documents I'd presented him with from *The Myanmar Times*. The visa officer walked away, leaving me standing there open-mouthed.

It was true that the letter didn't look very official. It consisted of a couple of deferential sentences asking for me to be given a seventy-day business visa, with Ross' huge 'R' signature scrawled at the end. I'd been so excited about being offered the job that it didn't occur to me to double-check anything before jumping on the next flight out to Bangkok. Unfortunately, the Burmese embassy was flagging the problem for me.

I shot a harried look back at Sherpa, who was sitting behind me in the waiting area. We'd spent an hour sweating in a queue that had snaked along the footpath while waiting for the embassy to open, and then another forty-five minutes once it did. Myanmar was swiftly becoming Asia's hottest new travel destination, which meant that embassy staff were overwhelmed and lines were getting longer and longer. When we fronted up at 7.30 a.m., there were at least twenty eager beavers ahead of us.

The visa officer returned with a mug of tea and gave me a cold stare when he saw me still standing there. His navy-blue uniform was exceedingly tight over his trim torso and his cropped black hair glistened with coconut oil. Although a brass nameplate identified him as Aung Myint, I knew better than to address him by it, lest he think me too familiar.

'But, uh, the thing is,' I said, craning my head down into the small gap of the barred counter window, 'if I come back tomorrow there may not be enough time left to process the visa before my flight leaves on Thursday.'

He shrugged in a not-my-problem kind of way. 'Ticket twenty-eight,' he boomed, staring past my shoulder.

Sherpa and I took a taxi back to the guesthouse in glum silence. Once there, I headed straight for the internet café in the foyer. I put thirty baht into the coin slot and shot Tom, Ross and Maisy an email explaining what had happened. I was cross to have been given sloppy paperwork, but I tried not to let it show. By that afternoon, I had a new letter. Maisy told me to print it out and ask for the express service so that I wouldn't miss my flight. I couldn't shake a bad feeling that I would. If there was one thing I had already learnt about Myanmar, it was that it operated on its own watch.

AFTER A FITFUL SLEEP, the alarm went off at 5 a.m. and we trundled back to the embassy, getting ourselves a marginally better spot in the line. Sherpa was waiting until I had my visa sorted out before submitting his tourist visa application, so there was no real reason for him to be there, but he came along anyway – and I loved him for it. He tended to see life as a series of obstacles and injustices to be borne or overcome, whereas I'd get indignant at the first sign of difficulty.

I leant back with a sigh against the huge concrete fence that wrapped around the embassy compound and hid everything but its roof. Despite the embassy's location in a smart diplomatic neighbourhood in glitzy Bangkok, the fence looked as though it had been transplanted straight out of Yangon, covered as it was in that city's trademark patches of black grime. My teeth felt furry and I regretted not having showered to conserve a few extra minutes of sleep.

I usually enjoyed visiting an embassy. As I was someone who loved nothing more than travelling to new places – the more unfamiliar the better – an embassy provided the first tantalising glimpse of a new culture and people. However, listening to the happy chatter of prospective tourists as they killed time in the line was irritating me in my stressed state. I groaned inwardly at the two guys ahead of us, who were trying to one-up each other as to how intrepid they were. I was feeling territorial about Myanmar, even though I'd lived there only a month. The fact that they were both Aussies intensified the feeling, although I couldn't put my finger on why. As they chatted with a confected nonchalance about a country they'd never visited, I wanted them to ask *me* for advice. If they did, I thought grumpily, the first thing I would suggest to one of them was to show less skin. His threadbare singlet wouldn't fly in Myanmar.

'I created a Gmail account last night to get around the ban on Yahoo,' said the tanned twenty-something with unruly bleached hair and an eyebrow piercing. His shorts had so many pockets that I'd been idly counting them to pass the time.

'Hasn't the military already lifted the ban on email providers?' replied the one in the singlet.

Yes it did! I was shouting inside my head.

'Hmm. Maybe it has. But I haven't heard that.' He took a long drag from a hand-rolled cigarette. 'It's probably good to have a backup email account though, just in case.'

I wondered whether he quietly hoped that he'd have to use the backup email account – his friends and family would regard him a daring traveller. But I couldn't blame him if he did; I was guilty of similar pretensions. In fact, Sherpa and I had a conversation much like theirs before we arrived in Myanmar.

'I know things are definitely still really strict with money. I heard of a guy who took in US dollars that were creased and he couldn't use them because Myanmar has weird rules about that. He had to cut his stay short because the money changers wouldn't take his creased notes and he ran out of cash.'

'Oh man. He must have been so disappointed. I still can't believe there aren't any ATMs. It's just so old school.'

'People say going to Myanmar is like stepping back in time.'

I continued eavesdropping as they compared their respective itineraries, which at any rate were almost identical due to the strict controls the military kept on the parts of Myanmar that were accessible to tourists. Much of the country was sealed off. There were some obvious no-go zones, such as Kayin State, where the world's longest-running civil war blazed on. Then there were other areas that may have been banned simply as a precaution, perhaps to avoid Myanmar's persecuted ethnic minorities having a chance to interact with foreigners, lest they tell the world about what was happening to them.

When my ticket number flashed up in red lights on the screen, I approached the counter with my best, most polite smile.

It was a different visa officer from the day before. This guy looked positively menacing, with pockmarks and a scowl so deep he looked perpetually insulted. He flicked through my documents for all of five seconds before saying, 'The documents have to be printed in colour. We don't accept black-and-white copies.'

This seemed pretty strict. Why did it make a difference what colour ink was used when the words remained the same? Of course, I didn't ask the question aloud, but my face would have belied my exasperation.

'Can I go and print it out in colour and come back?'

'Sure,' he said. 'But you will need to line up again.'

I WISH I could say that it was a case of third time lucky for me at the embassy.

I handed over my colour-printed paperwork somewhat triumphantly about an hour later to the same visa officer. He began flicking through the pages. 'The certificate of incorporation has expired,' he said abruptly.

I glanced at the offending document, which was written in Burmese, save for a couple of dates stamped across the top.

Don't lose your cool, I said to myself. *It will only make things worse.*

'Does that affect my application?' I whispered.

'I can't process it,' he snapped, thrusting the papers back at me. 'Next.'

I crumpled and slunk away from the counter, knowing it would be pointless to protest. I shook my head sadly at Sherpa, who sat waiting for me with his body hunched forward in anticipation. If only the previous visa officers had looked at my application in its entirety so that I could have fixed everything in one go. I'd wasted precious time and would miss my flight. I was beginning to wonder if they were throwing up all manner of obstacles to prevent me from working at the newspaper. Despite the quasi-civilian government proclaiming that Myanmar was opening up to the world and relaxing its ironclad grip on the media, I wasn't fool enough to think that these changes stretched far enough to include welcoming foreign journalists. I had inferred as much from the fact that my invitation letter described me not as a sub-editor, but as a 'technical consultant' who was going to teach English to the Burmese staff. Perhaps the visa officers saw straight through the lie and were responding with a checkmate move.

I CRIED as I read an email from Maisy saying that there was nothing she could do about this latest problem. *The Myanmar Times* had been waiting two years for an updated certificate of incorporation from the Ministry of Information. She told me it had never been a problem for other expat staff, and thought perhaps I should try again. I knew in my heart it wouldn't work, and Sherpa agreed. My dream of working at *The Myanmar Times*, something I considered the opportunity of a lifetime, was starting to fade before my eyes.

I also started panicking because I didn't know where in the world Sherpa and I could go. We had no prospects, very little money and were encumbered with a cat, who was being dragged back and forth between Myanmar and Thailand. Added to those difficulties was the fact that Sherpa, with his Bangladeshi passport, had problems getting a visa for virtually any country, other than Fiji or Nepal. He had started working at a small marketing firm in Yangon but they couldn't – or wouldn't – sponsor him for a business visa, so he was looking for a job at a company that would. We were both completely committed to living in Myanmar, and we were so tantalisingly close to achieving our goal. Losing out now would be so sad.

I decided it was time to take matters into my own hands. I

wanted to work at *The Myanmar Times* more than they needed me there. If I couldn't get the visa, the newspaper would simply hire another expat in my place. I'd already spent my first month in Myanmar working on a tourist visa because Ross wasn't willing to sponsor me for a business visa during the trial period. I thought I'd try a different strategy by giving my passport to a Burmese-owned travel agency in Bangkok. They had secured our first visas after our applications were rejected in Bangladesh. I was thrilled when the woman at Vega Travel told me that her personal relationships at the embassy would help. She gave me a date and time to collect my passport and visa from the embassy.

When I turned up to the embassy that fourth time, I was confident that things were going to be okay. I thought I'd beaten Burmese bureaucracy at its own game by leveraging personal relationships – something so central to Burmese society. I strolled up to the counter and when they handed my passport over I flipped through it. And, sure enough, inside was a visa. But instead of being a business visa, it was another tourist visa. I assumed there had been a mistake.

'This is a tourist visa. I applied for a business visa. Can this be fixed?' I asked the scary, scowling visa officer.

'We cannot give you a business visa because you can't provide a certificate of incorporation,' he began curtly. My heart started thumping. 'So we are giving you a tourist visa. You are lucky to have it. If you are caught working in Myanmar on this tourist visa, you will be blacklisted and you will never be able to return. Do you understand?'

I sure did. The mere mention of Myanmar's infamous black-list was enough to make me quiver. Although being blacklisted meant joining an illustrious list of human rights campaigners, democracy activists and foreign journalists (and randomly,

Cher's late ex-husband, Sonny Bono), it would be game over for my future in Myanmar.

'I understand. Thank you very much for the visa,' I said sadly.

I was in a tight spot. It certainly wasn't inconceivable that my movements in Yangon would be tracked. Burmese law required hotel managers to notify police as soon as a foreigner checked in, as a way of keeping tabs on us. Following me from the hotel to see whether I turned up for work at *The Myanmar Times* would be a piece of cake. But I'd already spent so much time away from my desk and was loath to take any more because the newspaper was painfully short-staffed. My only option, I decided, was to work remotely. Looking back, I'm surprised Tom ever agreed to the idea. He knew far better than I that working remotely was about as realistic as trying to work from the moon.

3

THE SPIES ARE EVERYWHERE
MID-AUGUST 2012

On my first morning back in Yangon, I hopped in a taxi and asked the driver to take me to 50th Street Bar and Café, which was the only place I knew that had Wi-Fi, other than the city's two posh hotels. 50th Street, as it was affectionately known, was a Yangon institution for foreigners as it was the only expat-oriented pub. It had steak nights, imported beer and an espresso machine. I'd been there before to see two amazing Burmese indie bands, Side Effect and Bloodsugar Politik.

But when I turned up 50th Street was closed; it wasn't due to open for another hour. What to do? The closest hotel was a fifteen-minute drive away, whereas directly opposite me was a busy, open-air tea stall. I figured it was the best spot to get some work done.

The tea stall occupied the edge of an empty plot of land that was overgrown with thick, lush foliage. At one end, near a collection of stacked blue buckets, was a monkey gnawing on a coconut shell. It had a chain around its neck and was tethered to a large slab of concrete. It looked miserable. I gave the monkey a wide berth and took a seat on a tiny plastic stool near a man pouring tea from a cast-iron kettle that sat atop a fire. For some reason, child-size chairs were part of the décor at Yangon's ubiquitous tea shops. Grown men sat with their knees up around their ears but seemed not to mind in the least. The seating was often also right on the edge of the footpath, so the cars almost grazed their elbows as they sped past. This too, left the tea drinkers unperturbed.

I ordered a *coffee kakka* – a strong, black coffee. But soon after I opened my laptop and a couple of heads swivelled in my direction, I realised I'd made a mistake. Working from a computer was a very suspect thing to do in Myanmar at that time: it screamed 'journalist' like nothing else could – well, other than speaking in front of a camera. As a foreigner, I already stuck out. I had to begin editing the stories, but if someone was keeping tabs on me, I was making it all too easy for them to bust me.

I lit a cigarette and looked around furtively. China clinked noisily and the mostly male patrons chatted away quietly to one another, seemingly absorbed in their conversations. The smell of cheroots wafted my way and a Premier League football match played on a boxy TV set that had been hitched onto a wall. I knew that anyone could potentially be a spy. Geoffrey had told me that Yangon was teeming with them. He said that he was often filmed by members of Military Intelligence while jogging with fellow members of the Hash House Harriers, though that had been some years back. The military government may have bungled the economy by nationalising virtually every part of it, but they were adept at spying. It was possibly their only talent. One of the regime's mottos, which it printed daily on the state-run newspaper and on random signboards around the country, was to 'Crush all internal and external destructive elements as the common enemy'. A lot of time and energy was put into doing that.

A man to my left, sitting alone at a table, was looking my way with interest. Uh-oh. That was unusual of itself because in general the Burmese do not stare openly – they are far too polite for that. But this balding man with spectacles was watching me and jotting something down in a notebook.

I wanted to get out of the tea shop as fast as I could, but I knew that suddenly fleeing might arouse his suspicions further.

Stay where you are. Take three sips of coffee. Then leave.

I was taking my second sip when two men in khaki-coloured uniforms strode in. The hairs on my neck stood up. They looked like members of the feared Military Intelligence. A quick search of my laptop would expose me as a journalist. My first thought was that the man taking notes had somehow alerted them to my presence, although I wasn't sure how because mobile phones were incredibly rare. (Inflating the cost of SIM cards to hundreds of dollars was another way the military prevented people from agitating against their rule.)

I shoved my laptop in my bag, left a crumpled 500-kyat note on the table and stumbled over a stool as I legged it. As I sped along the footpath past a huge construction site, a flock of pigeons startled me as they suddenly burst up into the air and jostled for a perch on a thick coil of powerlines. I turned a corner and almost collided with a woman carrying a couple of huge baskets. She hadn't seen me because her head was bowed determinedly. She was half my size, yet carried an enormous quantity of mangoes in baskets that hung off both ends of a plank of wood. No matter how tough things were or how heavy the rain, I admired how people went about their business without rushing or swearing. There was a quiet gracefulness to the Burmese that seemed all the more pronounced to me in my sweaty and breathless state. I apologised and kept on walking. By the time I had reached Sule Pagoda, I was feeling a little calmer. It was a smaller version of the city's incredible landmark, the golden, holiest of holy

Burmese Buddhist sites, the Shwedagon Pagoda. The Sule Pagoda was important in its own right: it marked the centre of the city and had served as a rallying point during past democracy uprisings.

I looked at my watch. Oh no. It was nearly ten o'clock and I hadn't so much as touched the news stories. I could imagine Tom tapping his watch while waiting for me to send him the first edited story. But thank goodness I hadn't been apprehended, and I could now get some work done at 50th Street.

I slunk past the tea stall as quickly as I could and slipped inside the café's heavy double doors. There was a pool table and vintage signs were dotted about the exposed brick walls, while a beautiful spiral staircase cut through the middle of the spacious room.

'You look like you've seen a ghost,' said a tall guy with a Kiwi accent who was drying glasses behind the bar. He had a shaved head and his arms were covered in tattoos, but he didn't look at all menacing because he was grinning at me.

I smiled back without saying anything, as I was unsure how to describe the experience I'd just had. He said, 'Grab a seat at a booth and I'll get someone to bring you over a menu.'

The menu made me swoon. After eating nothing but unfamiliar foods for weeks and having an unsettled stomach, the prospect of a ciabatta with smoked salmon was beyond tempting.

My sandwich was delicious, and when my latte arrived I discovered that it too was out of this world, so I ordered a second. I happily chain-smoked and ploughed through the stories in a bid to make up for lost time. But even there, I noticed with frustration, internet speeds were lousy. It took me ten minutes to upload a single Word document and multiple attempts to send it to Tom.

And then the barman brought me the bill.

I'd spent US$20, which meant that I'd just frittered away half my day's wage on a single meal. This was not sustainable.

Apparently, Tom agreed. A few days later, I poked my head in at the office. I'd only been there a few minutes when he took me aside and said, 'Jess – this isn't working. You need to be here to get work done. And you need to be able to ask the reporters questions if you don't understand what they've written. Stuart has said the same of the business stories you edit for him – you've left too many gaps saying you don't understand what they meant. I know it's difficult because you don't have a phone and neither do the reporters, but that is why we need you to work from the office.'

Stuart and Tom were right, of course. I went to see Maisy to ask her for advice. She listened sympathetically as I explained my predicament, nodding her head and saying what a surprise it had been to her when I encountered trouble at the embassy.

'You know what I think?' she said. 'I think it's worth trying for a business visa on arrival. I've heard that the visa officers on the desk at the airport are less fussy than those at the embassy. Some of those men at the embassy are really sour and unfriendly. They are not like most Myanmar people.'

The visa on arrival scheme Maisy was referring to had only just been introduced and the reformist government liked to point to it as proof that Myanmar was open for business.

That weekend, I flew back to Bangkok and waited four hours in the airport before boarding a Myanmar Airways flight back to Yangon. As the plane made a wobbly descent through a patchwork of undulating rice paddies, I hoped and prayed that I'd finally get the visa.

My prayers were answered. The same paperwork that had been rejected by the embassy in Bangkok was accepted at the airport. I didn't care that I'd flown 1600 kilometres – twice – to get a visa that would last me seventy days. I was in. Having a business visa meant that I could stop lurking in the shadows. I was a legitimate employee of *The Myanmar Times*.

It also had another huge advantage. I was now permitted by law to rent a property. Sherpa and I could move out of the seedy hotel and find ourselves a home.

It was time to be inducted into the weird world of renting in Yangon.

4

FINDING A HOME
SEPTEMBER 2012

*H*ey Mum and Dad
I hope that all is well and things back home are good.
I'm sorry to ask you if I can borrow some money. I
know I should have some savings at my age. But right now I don't
know what else to do. I'm really sorry but I need a loan ...

AND SO WENT my email to my kind and generous parents, asking
them to loan me several thousand dollars. The day before,
Sherpa and I had been taken to a township called Mayangon in
Yangon's north by a real estate broker called Nilar. She was very
pretty, with big brown eyes like a deer, and her speciality was
helping expats find a place to rent. Her husband was British,
she'd told me, and she knew what expats were looking for in a
home. I'd found Nilar on a Google Group called Yangon Expat
Connection, where the few hundred expats in Yangon could ask
each other practical questions, and would sometimes get a
response from a Burmese person who had some kind of business dealings with us, like Nilar. 'YEC', as it was known for short,
had been started the year before by a British 'trailing spouse'. It

quickly became something of a lifeline for expats: we were so collectively clueless about how to do the most basic things, and online information was so scarce, that the expat who had recently asked where she could buy spoons was only faintly ridiculed.

'Some houses in Yangon are strange,' Nilar had said after we'd squeezed into the back seat of her car and started trundling towards the northern end of the city. She was in the passenger seat next to the driver, and next to me in the back was Sherpa and Nilar's female assistant, who smiled a lot but hadn't said a word.

Nilar turned to face us in the back seat.

'Owners put in partitions to create extra rooms, but then the rooms are too small to even fit a bed. Or the bathrooms are no good, with squat toilets and no hot water. Or sometimes even no water. I'll only show you places that a foreigner would like.'

And sure enough, the second place Nilar showed us was The One. It was a single-level house on a corner block on Tharaphi Street, which Nilar said was also where a famous Burmese pop star lived. The house was white, with a small patio that had been painted lemon yellow, and it had maroon pillars, trimmings and roof. To the right of the front door was a bed of cactus, and to the right of that was a water tank perched on top of a timber frame. It had a sloping front yard that was mostly covered in cracked concrete. It was old, homey and inviting.

Nilar's assistant darted off to the side of the front fence, before reappearing in the yard of the house next door. She was with a Burmese woman who could have been in her early sixties and who opened the wire gate that connected the two properties. She looked very elegant as she slowly crossed the yard towards us. She wore a peppermint-coloured *longyi* and her grey hair was swept up into a bun. As she came closer I noticed that she still had killer cheekbones. She must have been a great beauty in her day.

'Mingalabar,' she said.

'Mingalabar.' At this point I had run out of Burmese words as pleasantries. 'Mingalabar,' I said again, but with more feeling. I really wanted her to warm to us. Nilar broke the silence that followed, telling us that this was Daw Kyi Kyi, the landlady. She then spent a minute or so introducing us as prospective tenants.

Daw Kyi Kyi's jade bangles clinked together noisily as she turned the key in the padlock to let us inside. I hadn't noticed the gates that were five inches from my face until then, having looked beyond them to the house itself. They looked like a shrunken replica of the gates at Buckingham Palace, with elaborate gold motifs and black wrought-iron bars. It was an odd choice for such a no-frills home. The gates were at least seven-feet tall and were reinforced at the top with rolls of razor wire that were tightly coiled and ready to slash the flesh of any intruder. All houses in Yangon came with razor wire – this was not so much protection from common criminals, as crime rates were very low, but protection from the military, who had a terrifying habit of coming for people in the night.

Inside, the house was completely bare, except for a brown settee. There was a bit of mould on the walls and the kitchen was incredibly basic, but it seemed enormous to Sherpa and me, who had grown used to living in a single room. This house was light and bright and everything our apartments in Bangladesh hadn't been. I shuddered as I remembered one apartment in particular that had no natural light, other than a spot in the kitchen where you could see the sky if you angled yourself properly. I was done with apartment living, and the feeling of being jammed on top of one another. I wanted a yard with a bit of dirt to muck about in, and some freshly picked flowers on the windowsill.

Sherpa and I grinned at each other. We walked ahead of the others into what we thought would be our bedroom.

'It reminds me of my family home in Chittagong before we moved to Dhaka,' he said.

This was high praise. Sherpa loved that place with its flower beds and pet duck. It was where his happiest memories were made, as it was where his family lived while his father taught at a university, until he died of a heart attack when he was only forty-three. As for me, just the idea of us having our own place again was wildly exciting.

We gathered on the settee. Nilar translated as Daw Kyi Kyi began to tell us about herself. She was a widow who lived next door with her adult son. The house we were in had been built for him, but a couple of years ago he suffered a stroke that left him paralysed down one side of his body. So Daw Kyi Kyi rented it out instead. I felt sorry for her.

I hadn't wanted to bargain after hearing that story, but Sherpa was insistent. And he was right to do so, because a bit of bargaining was customary in such a situation. Daw Kyi Kyi quickly agreed to shave off $100 a month, bringing the rent down to $600.

'Daw Kyi Kyi doesn't trust US dollars and wants to be paid in kyat,' Nilar said. I thought I detected a faint roll of her eyes but wasn't sure if I'd imagined it.

'Sure, sure – that's no problem,' I said, barely skipping a beat.

And then Nilar dropped the bombshell.

'You need to pay a year of rent in advance.'

'A year?!' I exclaimed, horrified.

'Actually, thirteen months,' Nilar corrected me. 'My broker fee is one month's rent.'

'We haven't got that kind of money,' I said. 'We'll have to find another place.'

I was indignant that Daw Kyi Kyi, smiling so serenely opposite me, would even ask such a thing.

'It's all the same. This is how things are done in Yangon,' Nilar said. 'I thought you knew that already.'

Sherpa and I were dumbfounded. It wasn't as though our salaries were paid a year in advance. Like everyone else, we were paid in arrears. Whatever savings Sherpa had from Bangladesh had been wiped out by the costs associated with moving countries. I had been living from month to month, as I always seemed to. It would take the two of us a year to save up enough to pay rent – but where would we live in the meantime?

We thanked Daw Kyi Kyi for showing us the house and left with everything up in the air.

'It's a shame you didn't get here a year ago when we were still living at the condo they rented out for us,' Stuart told me at work the next day as I was telling him about our troubles. I'd just sent Dad the email asking for a loan. 'Ross decided that things are easier now and that foreign staff can fend for themselves. But you'll still get some of the furniture that's left over from when we moved out. Ask if you can take a look in Ross' garage – I think there's a fridge and a couch,' he added cheerily.

'I might need to park them on the street,' I joked glumly.

Douglas, Stuart and Tom were all married to Burmese women and Geoffrey lived with Sonny's family, so it made sense that they didn't need help with rental arrangements. I, on the other hand, seemed to need a great deal of it.

Dad replied to my email within hours. He and Mum were willing to loan me the money. He didn't even berate me for being so hopeless as to not have any savings. That made me feel even worse. I had to grow up.

But before I even had time to let the relief wash over me, another problem arose. I told Nilar that we wanted to move in, and asked her not to show the place to anyone else. She asked when we wanted to sign the lease and hand over the money, and then it hit me that we had another problem: accessing the money. Due to international sanctions in place against Myanmar because of human rights abuses, there weren't any international banking facilities. It was a purely cash economy and there wasn't a single ATM. This meant that the money from my parents that was sitting in my account was completely out of reach. It could have been locked in an underground safe in Gibraltar, for all the good it did us. I told Nilar to set up a meeting with Daw Kyi Kyi a week later to buy us some time.

'THERE HAS to be a way around this,' Sherpa said as we sat on the bed and tucked into a box of fried rice from the Chinese restaurant around the corner. 'Surely people don't fly out to Bangkok every time they need more money.'

'Maybe they do,' I said. 'But it isn't an option for us, even if we could afford it. I can't risk losing my business visa after all the hassles I went through to get it, and you can't risk applying for another tourist visa so soon after getting the first one. We need a way to get the money without leaving Myanmar.'

'There must be some kind of hundi service,' Sherpa said as he crunched on a prawn tail.

A hundi is an informal remittance transfer channel – it's like a one-person Western Union. Hundis pop up wherever formal banking services are undeveloped and are especially popular in places like Bangladesh, which has millions of overseas migrant workers who want to send money back to their families. Hundis often charge a lot in commissions, but they get the job done – though it was still a mystery to me as to how.

'Let's talk to Day Day tomorrow,' Sherpa said. 'If he can't help us, he might know someone who can.'

Day Day was the son of the owner of MGM Hotel. He always stopped for a chat with us and I got the sense that he was a wheeler and dealer. Yet even so, I wasn't especially confident.

But once again I was proved wrong, and Sherpa's nous was an asset. Day Day wasn't a hundi, but he could channel in the money through his secret bank account in Singapore. The military government had made it illegal for Burmese citizens to have a foreign bank account, so the account was in the name of his Singaporean business associate. But Day Day used it as his own, and once he received the money from my father, he could access it from inside Myanmar. He didn't tell us how and we didn't ask.

'It's no problem,' he assured us. 'But I take a three per cent commission.'

Now all we had to do was trust him. He seemed like a nice guy – but of course we hardly knew him. Putting Dad's money into Day Day's account made me nervous. It wasn't as though we could go to the police if he disappeared on us. I imagined my dad, so cautious and sensible in all his business dealings, being absolutely horrified by the arrangement. I tried telling myself that Day Day's family probably made a lot of money from the hotel, which spanned six floors and included a karaoke lounge and a massive Chinese restaurant that kept a wide range of live seafood in buckets of water (a couple of times I'd seen massive eels leap out of their bucket, startling diners). Surely this amount of money would be chicken feed to Day Day's family. In any case, there was no alternative.

We transferred the money. An hour later, we headed downstairs to meet Day Day in the lobby as agreed. He wasn't there.

'I feel kind of sick,' I told Sherpa after twenty minutes had passed and Day Day still hadn't shown up. 'I can't believe how stupid we've been.'

'Be patient,' Sherpa said. 'He will come.'

But he didn't. We asked the two young men on the front desk to tell Day Day we were looking for him. When we came back an hour later, they told us they hadn't seen him. We came down again in the early evening and they said he had gone straight home.

We went back to our room and lay silently on the bed. If things turned out the way I feared, we were in big, life-changing trouble. Not only would we owe Dad thousands of dollars, but we couldn't ask for a second loan, so we'd never be able to rent a place in Yangon. Our time in Myanmar would be over, and we had nowhere else to go.

I went to work the next morning with a sick feeling in the pit of my stomach and played out worst-case scenarios in my head all day long. When five o'clock finally came, I rushed back to the hotel. I found Sherpa sitting cross-legged on the bed with his head buried in a Burmese dictionary.

He looked up with a smile on his face. 'Day Day came by earlier – he said he'll give us the money tomorrow. His wife is sick so he didn't have time to come by yesterday.'

I grinned, going over to the minibar fridge and cracking open a beer. I should never have doubted Day Day.

THE FIRST THING that struck me when I sat down in front of the ten million kyat was that it had a strong mildewy odour. This was because the kyat notes often got soaking wet during the rainy season and never really dried out due to the humidity. When there was so much money in one place, the smell was quite potent.

We were in Day Day's father's office, which was on the third floor. We walked past it every morning on the way to the room where our breakfast of oily fried eggs was served, and Day Day's dad was usually chain-smoking and bellowing into the landline phone in Mandarin.

It took an hour for Day Day and his father to count the money in front of us. They undid the elastic band at either end of each brick-sized chunk of money, and their fingers moved as quick as lightning as they flicked every green-and-purple 1000 kyat note, which was worth about seventy US cents. Sherpa counted it too, his eyebrows furrowed in concentration. I tried to help but kept losing track of where I was and had to start over. I gave up and watched, reflecting on Myanmar's strange relationship with money.

Most Burmese are devout Buddhists, and in their daily lives wealth comes a very distant second to spirituality. Early on in my time in Yangon I had noticed that people were refreshingly unmaterialistic – they simply didn't seem to pursue commerce with the same enthusiasm as citizens of other countries. In Bangladesh, people had often been trying to sell me things – perceived as I was as a wealthy foreigner – but the Burmese seemed uninterested in what I bought, and in several cases I had a hard time convincing someone to let me purchase something. I wondered whether it was also partly caused by what life was like in a dictatorship, where you never really got the chance to improve your lot.

In 1985, General Ne Win had suddenly decided to wipe out the existing currency and replace it with denominations that were divisible by his lucky number nine. Two years later, he did it again – but unlike the first time, there was no compensation. Overnight, millions of people's savings – which were kept at home under a mattress rather than at a bank – were wiped out.

It was a marvel that anyone ever bothered to save again, though I suppose they had no choice with the one-year-of-rent rule.

By the time British rule came to an end in 1948, resource-rich Myanmar was one of most prosperous nations in Asia. But it became one of the world's poorest under dictator General Ne Win, who nationalised and mismanaged the economy. In 2012, most people were surviving on the equivalent of US$50 a month. But I'd also heard stories about the excesses of high-level military men, who owned multiple Lamborghinis and threw their children birthday parties that cost hundreds of thousands of dollars.

Once our money had been counted and recounted, Sherpa and I divided it into two plastic bags and lugged it back to our room.

'They call me Money Bags,' I joked to Sherpa in a Russian accent as we stashed it in our luggage.

WE RETURNED to the house on Tharaphi Street for the lease signing with Nilar and Daw Kyi Kyi and I realised it was even lovelier than I'd remembered. We gravitated to the settee once more, which was in front of the glass-enclosed shrine room. The lease was on the table, ready for me to sign. The only thing that was comprehensible amid the swirly Burmese script was the cross where my signature was supposed to go.

'Is there no lease available in English?' I asked Nilar.

'I didn't prepare one. I thought you knew that you had to request that specifically. It costs extra.'

I looked at Sherpa for reassurance. His eyes held steady and he smiled weakly. He couldn't sign the lease because he was still on a tourist visa. I looked back at the money. My parents' money.

I gulped and signed my name, while wondering what legal conditions I'd just bound myself to.

It was another team effort to count and recount the money. I noticed that Daw Kyi Kyi counted it with ease – she was sharp. When that was done, we spent a few minutes making the kind of chitchat that takes place when one person has to translate back and forth between two parties. While dreamily thinking of being able to eat home-cooked food again, something that Nilar said made me click that the starting date of the lease was a Monday. For some reason I'd had it in my head that it was a Sunday.

'Next Monday is a big day for me at the office. We have an all-staff meeting first thing. Could we move in the day before instead?'

As Nilar translated, Daw Kyi Kyi's eyes narrowed and she shook her head. Next to her on the settee were two bags filled with the ten million kyat we'd just paid her, yet moving in one day early was out of the question. It was my first inkling that Daw Kyi Kyi was a tough negotiator. But to be honest, I wasn't much bothered. I was too excited about the fact that Sherpa and I would finally have a home again.

5

A STREET DOG NAMED RIPLEY

MID-SEPTEMBER 2012

A s I lit a cigarette on the footpath outside the office, I noticed that one of the two street puppies that frequented the area was missing. This was odd, as the pair were only about six weeks old and inseparable.

A few metres up from me was a street hawker sitting in her usual spot. We knew each other because I bought individual cigarettes from her makeshift stall, and we had exchanged a passing smile ever since she'd seen me fall on my head. She loved the puppies as I did, so I went and asked her where the second puppy was.

'A car hit her.' She pointed to the road and sadly shook her head. 'She is dead.'

I felt sick to think of the little puppy being crushed under the wheels of a car. I hoped she had died instantly. It was the prettier of the two pups that had been killed. With her large inquisitive eyes and creamy coat, she had reminded me of a Labrador pup. The remaining puppy that was lying listlessly by her mother's side had a long nose like a rat, a gummy smile and a dull, tan-coloured coat.

After leaving work that night, I went to the shop around the corner to buy some food for the puppy and her mother. I hoped that it wouldn't attract the male street dog who had started hanging about on the corner. Our head photographer, Kaung Htet, had warned me just the day before that the dog had bitten a shopkeeper and was particularly aggressive.

When I returned with the parcel of egg and rice, the hawker was packing up her stall. She carefully placed each item into a jute bag: four single packets of cigarettes, a pot of betel leaves, a tin of slaked lime that looked like wet plaster and chopped areca nuts.

'Where is the puppy?' I asked her.

She pointed to a sliver of a gap between the two buildings behind her. 'She won't come out.'

I could just make out two terrified eyes about a metre and a half away from me. I tried coaxing the puppy out by shaking the bag of food but she didn't budge. There was no way an adult could squeeze into such a narrow space but, by chance, one of the boys who worked at the nearby tea shop came walking past. The hawker explained what had happened. The boy set down his plastic bag of shopping and went in sideways, stepping over the cockroaches and decaying trash that squished underneath his flip-flops. He emerged grinning, holding the puppy by the scruff of its neck. She was wet and trembling. Her mother was nowhere to be seen.

I made a split-second decision to take the puppy home. I couldn't face the prospect of coming to work the next day and discovering that she too had been hit by a car, or mauled by one of Yangon's giant rats. The hawker smiled at me as she left with her bag of stock in one hand, and the plastic crate and wooden frame in the other.

Once in the taxi, I put the puppy on my lap. She nuzzled my hand, let out a big sigh and then fell asleep. When we got home, I put her in the kitchen sink and washed her filthy coat. I dried her off with a towel and put a bowl of sausages and rice out for her. She ate ravenously, then threw up all over the floor.

Just as I was wiping up the last of the vomit with a paper towel, Sherpa swung open the wire door.

'Hey babe, how was your day?' He stopped in his tracks. 'Who is this?'

'It's one of the two puppies I told you about that hang out the front of *The Myanmar Times*. Her sister was killed yesterday. I found her cowering between two buildings and her mum had disappeared, so I brought her home.'

Sherpa smiled. He loved animals too. We had rehomed several street dogs in Dhaka, and a couple of abandoned kittens.

'What shall we call her?' he said, scooping her up.

'I hadn't thought of a name. You choose.'

He held her up at eye level and studied her profile. 'Let's call her Ripley,' he said. 'Like *Ripley's Believe it or Not*.'

I was grateful that Sherpa didn't mind me adding a new addition to our household. I had already bought a couple of tortoises from a pet shop for the outdoor water tank.

Our maid, Sandar, was less enthusiastic. Her mouth set in a straight line whenever she saw her. I couldn't blame her. Ripley pooed in the house, nipped at the broom as Sandar was sweeping the floor and chewed everything in sight, including Sandar's cardigan. I bought her another one to replace it, but I suspected the one that was chewed was a favourite. Sandar and I saw different things in Ripley: I saw a vulnerable animal with delicious rolls of puppy fat, and Sandar saw a dirty creature of the street, who definitely did not belong in our home. She also seemed a little fearful of her.

∾

A COUPLE of months passed and Ripley shed her puppy fat, and with it went her roly-poly demeanour. During the frequent electrical storms, she would shake with fear under the kitchen table, her ears flattened back against her head and the whites of her eyes revealing her terror. On still nights, she would bay at the moon with the long, low howl of a sad and lonely wolf. When our cat crept stealthily up behind her in an attempt to start a game of chasey, Ripley would startle, and her first response was to snap. Thankfully, Butters was quick on her feet and Ripley's teeth only ever gnashed the air. She snapped at Sherpa and me a couple of times too but, again, she never actually bit us. I was careful not to surprise her.

I suspected that Ripley was traumatised from seeing her sister die, although I had no idea whether an animal could suffer from post-traumatic stress. Maybe she was just one of those dogs who was frightened of its own shadow. I hoped that she might be a bit less flighty after being desexed, although I wasn't sure if that was just a myth. A couple of expats recommended a vet called Dr Martin for the procedure, saying he was kind, competent and spoke good English. He also did house calls, which I figured would be less nerve-racking for Ripley.

Dr Martin arrived at our gate at two minutes to nine with a doctor's bag full of surgical implements and a gentle smile on his face. I held Ripley down as he injected her with anaesthetic, hoping that she wouldn't try to bite us. She went limp within seconds and I quietly breathed a sigh of relief. Together we lifted her onto the kitchen table, where I had laid out a couple of towels. I stroked her whiskers and rearranged her floppy tongue as Dr Martin shaved her groin. I turned my head the other way as he started to desex her.

'It's nice that you adopted a street dog. They have such a hard life on the streets,' Dr Martin said.

A metal implement clinked as it landed softly on another.

I agreed with him, saying how many street dogs I saw who were wounded, emaciated, and covered in mange or sores.

'Have you heard of Yangon Animal Shelter?' he asked me. 'It's just about to open. It will be run by an American teacher and a Burmese lady called Daw Roza, who is a friend of mine. She's asked me to treat the wounded dogs who are brought in, and to desex them, of course. I'll do the work for free, starting from next month.'

I said that the opening of the shelter might make a good story for *The Myanmar Times* and that I'd contact Daw Roza.

Dr Martin then started spitballing ideas for his next sermon at the local church, where he was a minister. I hadn't realised until then that being a vet was just his part-time gig, which I assumed helped pay the bills.

'All done,' he said, with evident satisfaction, after neatly tying up the last stitch. 'Now where's your cat?'

THE FOLLOWING TUESDAY MORNING, I caught a taxi to the International School Yangon in Golden Valley, an extremely wealthy, expat-centric part of Bahan Township, which lies between the downtown area and the north. I was looking forward to covering what I assumed would be a good-news story. Daw Roza had been excited to hear from me and said an article could help spread the word that the shelter needed donations and the dogs needed homes. The American teacher, Terryl, had offered to take me to the site where the shelter was being built so that I could see it for myself.

A winding road took me past neoclassical mansions with grand, pillared entrances, fountains and ten-foot-high gates. On a snaking driveway I saw a yellow Ferrari being washed by a young man in a singlet and *longyi*, who I could only assume was a houseboy. These were the homes of military high-ups, movie stars, ambassadors and senior UN staff.

I wandered inside the international school to look for Terryl's classroom. The campus reminded me of a resort in Fiji where I'd holidayed with my family when I was a kid. The grounds were beautifully maintained, with a lush oval, flower beds and an attractive colonial-era building with a long, covered walkway. It couldn't have been more different from the local Burmese schools, where utilitarian, boxy buildings housed as many as eighty students per class. Walking past those classrooms, I'd hear the students parroting their teacher in a sort of lacklustre chant, as Myanmar's education system was based almost entirely on rote learning.

Within minutes of me arriving, the bell rang for recess and gangly students in shirts and ties and tartan skirts spilled out onto the basketball court, racing past me to find their friends. I found Terryl in her classroom, where she was collecting bits of paper off the desks. One section of the back wall was covered with photos of street dogs and decorated with colourful cut-outs of love hearts and stars. Terryl appeared to be in her early forties and had a sun-kissed Californian look, with a long, bushy blonde ponytail, freckles and a trim physique. She greeted me with a big smile.

Already waiting for us in the minibus was a young volunteer called Emma, who was helping to get the shelter up and running during her gap year. As we headed out of Yangon with a refreshingly law-abiding driver at the wheel, Emma told me that trying to save Yangon's street dogs had become a personal mission after tragically losing her own dogs.

'There's never a good time to be a street dog in Yangon, but now is especially dangerous,' she said, as her plastic spider-web earrings swished to and fro.

That was because Southeast Asia's version of the Olympics,

the SEA Games, were about to be held in Yangon for the first time in nearly sixty years. Hosting the games was a really big deal and marked Myanmar's return to the global stage. Authorities from the city's administrative body, the Yangon City Development Committee (YCDC) were in a frenzy to beautify the streets. Slums that were inconveniently located near sporting facilities were being razed, with the inhabitants simply left to find somewhere else to live, and street dogs were being culled left, right and centre.

A couple of weeks ago, Emma had set off on her morning walk with her two dogs.

'Roxy and Pepper were sniffing something in the long grass by the side of the road. I didn't think anything of it until I saw Roxy start to choke. It was kind of like a cough but she was gasping for air. Then Pepper started choking too. It all happened so fast and there was nothing I could do. My dogs ate poisoned meat and died on the end of my leash,' Emma said. She looked stricken.

I said how sorry I was for her, and how upsetting it must have been to see her dogs in such pain.

'What disgusts me,' she added, wiping away a tear, 'is that the authorities claim this doesn't violate Buddhist principles. They say they simply lay out the poisoned meat and if a dog happens to come along and eat it, that it's not their fault. That it's not murder.'

'That's a very strange way of looking at it,' I said. 'I wonder how those YCDC workers sleep at night.'

'You ought to be careful that they don't throw poisoned meat into your yard when they see that you have a street dog on your property,' said Terryl gravely.

'But Ripley's not wandering the streets,' I replied, alarmed.

'That's true. But from their point of view, it would still be one less street dog in Yangon.'

Poor Ripley. Even after being rescued, she still wasn't out of danger.

~

THE WAY I SEE IT, there are three types of people in this world. There are those who spend their lives cleaning up other people's messes and mistakes, those who make a mess, and those who don't make a mess and don't clean anything up. That is to say, this last group contributes very little to the world around them, either good or bad.

There was no doubt that Terryl was the type of person who cleaned up other people's messes. She already had seven rescue dogs of her own, plus two cats that she'd rescued while living in Bolivia. She had been teaching in Myanmar for nearly a decade and even before starting the shelter project, her reputation as an animal lover was well known in Yangon. Now she was getting calls every other week, mostly from concerned expats who had seen a maimed street dog that urgently needed medical attention. A week earlier, someone had phoned her about a litter of tiny puppies whose mother was missing, and had presumably been hit by a car. Terryl was nursing them around the clock in her home. Whether her phone rang during the day or night, she would move mountains to get an animal rescued. As she told me about one particular dog whose life she couldn't save, even after personally funding its chemotherapy treatment, her eyes started to well up. It was clear that Terryl's heart bled for every single dog in Yangon that was suffering.

I told her how Sherpa and I used to rescue street dogs in Dhaka, but that it became sad and overwhelming when we couldn't find homes for them. We had eventually given up.

'It's getting easier for me to find homes now that there are more foreigners in Myanmar,' Terryl said. 'It used to be almost impossible. No self-respecting Burmese person would adopt a street dog. That would be like walking around with a cockroach on the end of a leash. It's pedigrees the Burmese want. The problem with that is the pet shops, who don't take care of the puppies.'

Terryl explained that a highly contagious disease called parvovirus runs rampant through Yangon's pet stores. She had heard stories of unvaccinated pups dying a couple of days after arriving in their new home. Their owners would be upset and furious, having paid a few hundred dollars for them.

I thought back to when I'd bought our tortoises from a pet shop at an open air market, and had seen a dead German shepherd puppy lying stiffly in its cage. I still found the memory of it upsetting to recall. I told Terryl about it and that I had assumed the dog had died of sunstroke.

'It was probably parvovirus,' Terryl said.

'How awful,' I said.

We settled into glum silence and half an hour later we arrived at the shelter in Mingaladon Township. It was a rural area, so I'd expected to see rolling paddocks, but the shelter was being constructed on a small suburban block. It was nowhere near enough space to house Yangon's convalescing dogs. According to government estimates, Yangon's total street dog population stood at 120,000.

Perhaps I gave away my surprise, because Terryl quickly said, 'This is Daw Roza's land. She donated it to the shelter. We are hoping to buy the block over there too, but we're having trouble finding out who owns it. For now, if we can't find a home for a dog, we'll take it back to where it was picked up. At least it will have recovered from any injuries and been vaccinated against things like parvovirus and rabies.'

According to the World Health Organization, Myanmar has one of the highest rates of rabies infections in the world, with more than 1000 people dying from it every year. Victims were usually bitten by a street dog, so it was understandable that YCDC wanted to do something about it. But culling was a cruel and ineffective practice. I knew from doing a story on rabies in Bangladesh that it was actually more likely to increase dog numbers, because it disrupted existing packs, which led to fresh fights over territory, more available food and the breeding that went with it. Spaying and neutering in conjunction with vaccines works best, but it tends to cost more than killing street dogs and dumping their bodies into landfill.

'Come over here and meet our first guests, whose mum wandered in last week,' said Terryl with a smile.

I followed her over to a half-built shed in the middle of the lot, where a litter of puppies lay with their mother in the shade. They were just a few days old and looked like fluffy jelly beans, with pink noses and tiny ears that were folded over like the flap of an envelope. Their eyes were still closed and their scrabbly, high-pitched whimpers made them sound more like mice than dogs. The mother licked each of her four pups with evident delight, then as they began suckling she sighed contentedly and closed her eyes. It was sad to think that despite all her devotion and care, a perilous future awaited them.

I looked at Terryl, who had wandered over to the edge of the lot and was fussing over a half-erected fence. I would never have said it out loud, but the task before her was so enormous that I had my doubts as to whether she could make a difference. I also wondered what psychological price she might pay while trying.

6

HIGH RISK OF NO RETURN

OCTOBER 2012

S herpa and I loved our new home. We bought a wide array of tropical plants and glazed pots to add some colour to the front yard, and I set about decorating the living room with local crafts, including parasols, puppets, a wooden carving of a Buddha and a set of papier-mâché owls. I didn't mind that the taxi drive to work was quite a long one, because every time I walked through our front door on my return, I felt overjoyed to have found such a spacious and light-filled home.

But one day our newfound happiness was shattered. Sherpa was told by the immigration department that he had to return to his home country to apply for his first business visa. We'd hoped he would be able to nip across to Thailand, but it wasn't alto-gether surprising to learn that there was a special rule for Bangladeshi visa applicants. Bangladesh's citizens were lumped together with those from a handful of other nations, most of them war-torn, who were regarded as being a high risk of no return. In other words, it was assumed that Sherpa wouldn't want to go back to Bangladesh if he were ever given the chance to leave, so there were more stringent rules in place. I just hoped that he would be allowed to return to our home in Myanmar.

SHERPA WAS MEANT to be away only a week, but his contact in Dhaka became delayed on a trip outside the capital. A couple of weeks passed, and he was no closer to getting the paperwork he needed for the visa. Maisy said she worried about me being all alone at night and gave me a mobile phone. It is difficult to over-state what a prized possession this was, and I wanted to hug her when she handed me the chunky, navy-blue Nokia. As Maisy wrote down her own phone number, telling me to call her anytime I needed help, I noticed that my new phone number was identical to hers except for one number at the end. This was because *The Myanmar Times* had procured six mobile phones for its key staff, and these were issued with one phone number after the next. It reminded me of when I'd learned that mobile phones were so rare in the early 2000s that phone numbers were only three digits long.

Thiri also noticed that I was a bit glum with Sherpa away, and to cheer me up she invited me to come with her to buy beef. I jumped at the chance to go to the wet market with her: it had been ages since I'd had red meat. I had never seen it in a super-market and assumed it was rare (pardon the pun) due to Buddhist sensibilities. Once our plans were made, I got a sudden craving for the flavour and juices of a well-cooked steak.

A soft rain had begun to fall as we set off from the office around 5.30 p.m. We took a right into Anawratha Road, where creaking buses were piled up one behind the other and the miserable faces of office workers were pressed against the glass. One bus was so crowded that two young men were hanging off its open doors.

It was almost dark by the time we reached the wet market, where the stall holders were lighting paraffin lamps. Thiri and I weaved our way through the crowds. We passed large buckets of smelly, spiky durian, as well as hairy lychees, yellow and green mangoes and cauliflower. Some produce was laid out neatly on a tarpaulin on the ground, while others were displayed from wide wicker baskets. There were crates stacked with eggs, enormous piles of green chillies and plastic buckets filled to the brim with white rice. There was a cacophony of sounds and smells and I couldn't identify a lot of what I saw. Most of the vendors were women, who sat on tiny stools or squatted, and would call out the name of what they were selling in low tones. Thiri stopped to buy some plump tomatoes and a long bunch of watercress from a cheerful woman with a booming voice, who threw in a couple extra with a wink and a smile.

We then came upon the seafood section, with dried prawns as small as my fingernail and translucent fresh ones as long as my hand. There was an incredible array of fish, either cut into chunks or whole, but never scaled. Next came poultry, with giblets and skinned chicken heads, with their eyes closed in repose and the occasional wet feather left on. There were also neat piles of chicken feet bound with twine – I bought some of those for Ripley, which I would boil up at home. A group of live chickens clucked nervously from under a wicker basket. The smell of blood hung heavily in the air.

We stepped over some puddles and came to a stall that consisted of two wooden benches and a set of cast-iron scales. Half a cow's carcass was strung up behind the vendor, who wore a skullcap known as a *topi*. A stained off-white singlet was stretched taut over his big belly. He grinned at Thiri, who was a regular customer. With a bloodied machete, he skilfully chopped up a hunk of the dark meat, then tossed it into two plastic bags. We each passed over 600 kyat and as we began walking away I was struck by a joke.

'I can't believe it, Thiri: my husband's away and I'm at a meat market.'

She looked at me quizzically. I thought about explaining it but I knew it would get lost in translation.

'Never mind,' I said with a smile, feeling lonesome again.

As I TOSSED the beef into the electric frypan and it met the garlic with a sizzle, my stomach growled. I was chopping up a handful of shitake mushrooms when the kitchen was suddenly plunged into complete darkness. No, no, no! What rotten timing for a power cut. I had no way of knowing how long it would last – sometimes the power was restored after half an hour, and occasionally it wasn't until the morning. At least in Bangladesh the power cuts were relatively predictable, and tended to last exactly one hour.

I flicked my lighter so that I could find a candle, then I dipped a spoon into the saucepan of rice. The water had only just started to boil, so it had the texture of crushed pebbles. Damn it. I swore again as I banged my shin on the coffee table on my way out to the patio. A light breeze made it cooler outside than in, and the glow of the moon cast a silvery light across the yard. I lit a cigarette and stared at the silhouettes of the palm trees. I wondered whether I was in Sherpa's thoughts at that moment. I sat there peacefully for a while, thinking how, despite the challenges, life in Yangon was incredibly interesting and varied. Then I heard a mosquito buzzing around my neck. I slapped it away, then felt tiny pricks on my ankles. I was being eaten alive. I wasn't worried about getting malaria as the risk in

Yangon was low, but the bites themselves were unpleasant enough for me to head straight back inside.

Back in the kitchen, I could hear the cockroaches scuttling across the sink. They were like tiny bulls, the way they charged about the place with their heads down and antennae wavering. Cockroaches were a nuisance, but I wasn't fearful of them – they didn't bite or anything. I'd learnt in Bangladesh that keeping them out was a losing battle. I'd tried every product I possibly could, from chalk to noxious spray, and it never seemed to make a dent in the size of the population. It was easier not to stress over them.

I went to have a shower. Out sputtered a quick burst of water, and then nothing. We had run out of water. Sherpa usually took care of keeping the tank full, though it was mostly a guessing game. Even if I had been keen to venture out in the night and wait an hour to refill the tank, the pump required electricity to work.

I figured that the beef had been sitting too long in the warm air for me to eat it without risking food poisoning. I threw it in the bin and ate another handful of prawn crackers.

If Sherpa was here, we'd have lit a candle, cracked open a couple of beers and played Scrabble. It would have been fun – romantic, even.

What a lousy night.

It was another two days before he returned – thankfully with a visa. He had been away a full month and I was so relieved and happy to see him. It also made me feel safer, as I had found Daw Kyi Kyi's son in our yard a couple of times. He never spoke, so I wasn't sure why he was there. It had creeped me out a bit.

On the evening Sherpa returned, we walked to our favourite neighbourhood beer station on U Wisara Road to celebrate, but just after ordering our food, my new mobile phone rang. It was

Sandar, our maid, and she was hysterical. It took a few moments for her to get any words out.

'My brother is in the police station. He was drinking with his friends all day long. The police came and took them away. Now he's locked up. I'm so scared for him.'

'Which police station? Sherpa and I will come and meet you there. Maybe we can pay his bail and they will let him out.'

Sandar's fear was completely justified: her brother was in a really serious situation. Myanmar's criminal justice system was notorious for handing down extremely long prison terms for even a trifling misdemeanour.

We asked the guy behind the counter to change our order to takeaway. Just as a taxi pulled over to the kerb for us, Sandar rang again.

'My friend says don't come to the police station. It isn't safe for you. Maybe they will lock you up too. My friend says that no one leaves a Myanmar police station after they go in.'

I heard her sobbing and then the line went dead.

Sherpa and I thought about returning for another round of beers, but decided to go home instead. We felt too flat to stay out.

When I saw Sandar the following week, she looked worn out. I noticed that her nails had been bitten to the quick.

'My brother got out from prison after three days,' she told me. 'But nothing changed. All day he drinks. All night too. He has no work. It is a big problem for my family.'

Sandar was devout and carried a little wooden cross and a picture of Jesus in her pastel pink handbag. It was hard to imagine her having an alcoholic brother. He must have been causing her family immense shame. Sandar herself was a very hardworking person. She made everything sparkle despite having the most basic cleaning equipment, and she was always cheerful, even though she had a rotten job. Possibly the worst part of it – to me anyway – was having to empty the rubbish bins of used toilet paper, because it couldn't be put in the toilet without clogging the fragile sewerage system. She also had to wait around for our drinking water to arrive in large bottles, which she hauled into the kitchen, and to listen for the cry of the garbage collector, who passed by at random times of the day. She worked part-time and we paid her eighty dollars a month, which seemed very little to me but was actually the equivalent salary for a full-time worker.

Nothing ever seemed to be a hassle for Sandar, and one day she even offered to sew curtains to cover our bare windows. I was grateful, but had to stifle a laugh when she showed me the end result: the material she had gone with was hot pink and featured a disco-dancing Minnie Mouse. Nonetheless, I was touched by her kindness in going to all the trouble of making curtains for our home.

SANDAR DIDN'T MENTION her brother again, so I assumed the scare with the police had helped him turn a corner. But about a month later, Sandar turned up at the door with tears streaming down her face. Her brother was dead. He had been poisoned by counterfeit rum. Imported liquor had been banned decades ago, leaving upmarket hotels and bars to navigate a complex 'permit system' for acquiring it, and creating perfect conditions for a rampant fake alcohol market to flourish. I'd read news reports about young men suffering kidney failure or going blind after drinking fake booze. It was unknown how big a problem it was because a cause of death often went unrecorded in Myanmar, and grieving families were usually too ashamed to speak out.

I offered Sandar a week off with pay so that she could grieve, but she refused to stop working. Overnight, she turned into a zombie. Her movements were eerily mechanical and she didn't even notice Ripley being a pest anymore. The following Sunday, she dropped by our house after church. She had brought along a small stack of photos from her brother's funeral. She wept on the settee as she passed each photo to me, and I then passed them onto Sherpa, who sat in solemn silence. Several of the photos were of her dead brother in the coffin, where he lay with roses all around his head.

When I got home from work the following week, there was a note from Sandar saying that she'd quit. She didn't say why and she didn't ask to be paid for the two weeks of the month she had already worked. I had no way of contacting her and I never saw her again.

7

OBAMAMANIA

NOVEMBER 2012

After working as a sub-editor for a few months, I was wildly excited when Ross promoted me to features editor. Although I'd been warned that Ross was a tough customer, he and I got on great. He was demanding and often unreasonable, yes, but also charming, funny and irreverent. He also lavished praise on me, even once saying that I was his best journalist. The new job he gave me involved putting together special reports every fortnight. Each focused on a sector such as health, property or travel. The topics were deliberately broad and were chosen by Ross according to the likelihood of attracting a ton of advertising. Although they were published as 'special reports', Ross saw them as advertising supplements and cared less about the content than ad revenue. I treated them as special reports: my reasoning was that quality content would attract more readers and, in turn, more advertisers. My new role was a terrific step up from being a sub-editor, which required little creativity and could sometimes be monotonous. I also moved to a bigger workstation, which was in front of Douglas and had a beautiful view of St Mary's Cathedral.

As I was working away one day, an email from Ross popped into my inbox. It was a forwarded email exchange between two of his business associates, who had subsequently forwarded it to him.

TO: Jessica Mudditt

FROM: Ross Dunkley

SUBJECT: FW: heads up

DATE: November 5, 2012

Hi Chris,

I have a pretty good source who reports the very strong chance that Obama is making SE Asian tour of Myanmar, Thailand and Cambodia. His dates for Cambo are supposedly 19–21st of November – I'm unsure of the rest.

Maybe an ad special around it?

Regards,

Kevin

To me, Ross had simply written: 'Come and see me about this.'

I was in his office faster than you could say 'Air Force One'. I was a die-hard President Obama fan and the idea of him coming to Myanmar made me giddy.

'Hey Missy,' Ross said, looking up from his screen. 'That was fast. So, if what Kevin says is correct, I want you to create an ad supplement for Obama's visit. We'll publish it the day he touches down in Yangon – so what's that ...' Ross began thumbing through his desk calendar. 'That's two weeks from now. Make it twenty or twenty-four pages – your call.'

'Sure thing, Ross. I can't wait to get started. I wonder if Obama will see it,' I replied dreamily.

'I'm sure it will be part of his daily briefing documents,' Ross said with a satisfied chuckle. 'I'm also going to write to the US Embassy and ask them if they can put in a request for Sonny to be released. It's best to make the most of all this goodwill – don't you agree?'

WITH BARACK OBAMA'S visit confirmed and little time left until it began, I went into overdrive putting the special report together. Ross gave it the title 'Sanctions to Success' because he felt certain that Obama was going to lift the last remaining sanctions against Myanmar during his visit.

Even though it was a tight deadline, getting enough content was a cinch. Everyone wanted to be involved, including a few of the expat editors, who didn't usually contribute to my special reports. I wrote to three commentators on Southeast Asian politics and all agreed to send me analysis pieces. Our talented cartoonist, Thein Tun Oo, drew a picture of a grinning President Obama suited and booted in front of Shwedagon Pagoda, with a bevy of monks behind him. I assigned a reporter, Naw Say, the job of hitting the streets to ask the public what they thought of the US president's visit for a vox pop (while most people were really excited, some didn't know he was coming and didn't care when she told them). I went with Naw Say for the first hour as I needed her help finding out which term was preferred: Burma or Myanmar. The military had abruptly changed the country's name from Burma to Myanmar in 1989 after killing thousands of people the year before during an uprising against its despotic rule. Many Western nations, including the USA and Australia, had refused to adopt the military's new name for the country. However, 'Myanmar' had always been widely used in Myanmar, as it was what the Burmese had always called their country when speaking Burmese – that was even true of Aung San Suu Kyi, a staunch 'Burmist'.' I'd decided to write an article speculating about whether the United States would officially swap 'Burma' and 'Rangoon' for 'Myanmar' and 'Yangon'. When Hillary Clinton had visited Myanmar a year earlier, she had dodged the issue by saying neither Burma nor Myanmar, but instead referred to it as 'the country'. I couldn't imagine Obama prevaricating like that.

I quickly realised just how hard being a reporter was in Myanmar. Very few people were willing to talk to a journalist. Most looked dumbfounded when Naw Say explained that we wanted to know their views. One man eyed us suspiciously and backed away, as though we were doing something unseemly like trying to sell him drugs.

'People aren't very keen to talk to us, are they?' I said to Naw Say.

'They never are,' she said. 'Voicing an opinion has been a dangerous thing to do in Myanmar. Have you heard the joke by the Moustache Brothers about the dentist?'

'No I haven't,' I said, though I had heard of the comedy troupe who were based in Mandalay. 'How does it go?'

'A Burmese man goes to see a dentist in Thailand. And the dentist says to him, "Don't you have dentists in Myanmar?" The patient says, "Sure we do. But no one opens their mouth in Myanmar."'

I laughed, but it made me sad.

Eventually we found an elderly man who told us he was a retired government officer. This is what he said: 'I like the name Myanmar because I like the government. I had no problem with Burma being a British name, but whatever the government does, I like.'

Ten minutes later, we came across a former insurgent who spent ten years living in the jungle. He said, 'People inside the country have called it Myanmar for a very long time, so when the name was changed it wasn't a big deal. It was more about the army trying to control everything. I didn't like it when the government told people like Daw Aung San Suu Kyi not to say Burma.'

Until then, I hadn't actually realised that the word 'Burma' had been prohibited in news reports until recently.

The man also pointed out that Daw Aung San Suu Kyi says 'Myanmar' when speaking in Burmese, but uses 'Burma' when speaking in English.

But apart from the two men we simply couldn't find anyone else willing to talk and with the morning in danger of slipping by, I left Naw Say and headed back to the office. I asked a few colleagues for their views, and then started weaving the quotes into my article.

I wanted to make it clear from the outset that both names are problematic. 'Burma' was a colonial name, and an Anglo corruption of the term 'Bamar', which is the majority ethnic group. The people I spoke to didn't actually know that choosing between Myanmar and Burma was such a political hot potato in the West. Nonetheless, if the United States did switch to saying 'Myanmar' and 'Yangon' instead of 'Burma' and 'Rangoon', it would be a diplomatic sign that legitimised Myanmar's government. Other Western countries would be likely to follow suit.

We usually worked a half day on Saturdays, but on the weekend before Obama's visit, I stayed back until 9 p.m. I'd become obsessed with my special report. I'd shown Ross a mock-up halfway through the day and he'd loved it, but I kept combing every line for typos and fiddling around with captions. By the time I went home that night, I'd never felt prouder of a piece of work in my life.

WITH THE SPECIAL report done and dusted, I took Monday morning off and went to the airport in a taxi with Sherpa in the hope of catching a glimpse of President Obama. Several of the main streets along our route were lined with stony-faced policemen and barricades. The authorities had pulled out all the stops for the visit. The roads had been swept clear of litter and the waxy purple plants that carpeted the verges were neatly trimmed, with not so much as a leaf out of place.

The taxi had to drop us off several hundred metres away from the airport's main entrance because the road was closed for security reasons. Sherpa set off at such a brisk pace that at one point I had to break into a jog to keep up. I was puffing and sweating as Sherpa merrily hypothesised about what he thought our chances were of actually seeing Obama in the flesh. Just as I was about to plead that he slow down, we came around a bend and realised we wouldn't get any closer to the airport: there was a crowd ahead of us that looked to be at least 5000 strong. A wall lined one side of the road, which fortunately had staggered ledges that afforded everyone an excellent view. Sherpa and I found ourselves elbow to elbow with a group of young monks holding huge American and Burmese flags.

We seemed to be the only ones who hadn't thought to bring something with us to wave. The young and the old held an assortment of English-language placards with messages that included, 'Release the political prisoners' and 'Please help us in developing our economy'. Dozens of people were wearing white t-shirts with the US president's face stencilled on them and a plea in red: 'Please Obama – save Myanmar'. Others held large banners that had juxtaposed Aung San Suu Kyi and Barack Obama next to each other, waving. Some posters showed Aung San Suu Kyi holding a big bouquet.

I saw only one poster that featured President Thein Sein (pronounced 'Tane Sane'), and on it he was sandwiched between Obama and Aung San Suu Kyi. While they were smiling, the president's expression was stern. It must have been a recent photo, because he was wearing a parliamentary hat, and Myanmar's parliament had been set up only the year before. These unforgettable hats were pastel-coloured silk caps with an extra length of material that sprouted out of one side and had a kink. At any rate, it didn't surprise me that Myanmar's president hardly registered among those who had turned out to welcome Obama. He was a man of few words and little outward emotion, and many assumed he had been hand-picked by military high-ups as a pliable puppet. The excitement concerning the visit centred around President Obama meeting Aung San Suu Kyi, who just about everyone considered the country's rightful leader.

A Singaporean TV news crew approached the monks next to us and began interviewing them. I noticed a handful of Westerners mixed in among the crowd, although I didn't see anyone I recognised. Public gatherings were incredibly rare, largely because they were in fact illegal. Since the crushed uprising of 1988 there had been a ban of gatherings of more than five people. As the political situation began changing, people had begun to openly flout the rule, which would soon be repealed anyway.

We'd been milling about under the hot morning sun for about forty-five minutes when Air Force One rolled into view from behind one of the terminals. Somehow, it had landed outside our line of sight. The plane had a steel-blue nose and an underbelly of sky blue, with 'UNITED STATES OF AMERICA' stencilled along its body. It taxied to a stop a few hundred metres from us. Excited murmurings rippled through the crowd. I strained to make out any moving shapes in the windows, but they were as small as matchboxes from where I stood. All the same, a shiver went down my spine as I thought of Obama looking out at us.

About twenty minutes later, the crowd roared as a sleek black limousine pulled out onto the road in front of us. Kids cheered as they waved tiny Burmese flags, the type that sometimes appear on international food platters. A father hoisted his son onto his shoulders for a better view. People clapped and stomped their feet.

'Mrs Hillary!' shouted the man on my left. 'Mrs Hillary! Mrs Hillary!'

The car's tinted windows made it impossible to know who was inside, but soon others were repeating his welcome to the US Secretary of State. The vehicle drove past us at a parade-like pace.

'Do you think that was Hillary?' I asked Sherpa breathlessly.

'No idea,' he said. 'Wouldn't they both be inside together? Or maybe they— oh look!'

An identical black car swung out onto the road and headed towards us. The crowd went ballistic, with people shaking their signs, waving and calling out Obama's name. Those who had brought along handheld cameras, including myself, were snapping away furiously. Once again, the limousine's tinted windows were closed and we were none the wiser about who we were waving at.

In a matter of seconds, both cars were out of sight and the moment was over. Barack Obama had seen us, but we hadn't seen him. It was a bit of an anti-climax, though I was still glad to have witnessed his arrival.

'Well that was exciting,' I said to Sherpa. 'I guess it's time to head back to the office.'

'I think I might follow them,' said Sherpa. He had a faraway look in his eyes. I hadn't seen him this starstruck since we'd met the Australian cricket team in Dhaka a year ago.

'What do you mean by "follow them"?'

'I'll take a taxi to Aung San Suu Kyi's house, as I might be able to see Obama there, or maybe at the University of Yangon afterwards. I really want to see him in person. Do you want to come with me?'

'Nah, I better head to the office. I told Tom I'd be there before lunchtime.'

'Okay then. I'll see you at home tonight. Wish me luck.' Sherpa smiled, squeezed my hand and disappeared into the crowd.

BACK AT THE OFFICE, the air of anticipation was almost as strong as it had been at the airport. Thiri and a couple of other colleagues came to my desk to congratulate me on the special report, and to speculate about what Obama might say during his press conference with Aung San Suu Kyi. We all kept repeating how incredible it was that the military had given her permission to meet him, although I suspected it would have been a deal-breaker for the visit if permission had been denied.

Meanwhile, reports had started to trickle in about President

Obama's hour-long meeting with President Thein Sein, which had just finished up.

'Obama said "Myanmar" instead of "Burma"!' exclaimed a reporter called Zaw Win Than. He grinned as he waved a press release. 'He said it in his public comments after their meeting. I just got the transcript from the White House.'

'Amazing. Just amazing,' I said.

It was all so exciting that I was having difficulty concentrating on the article I was supposed to be writing. I kept checking the news wires for updates on Obama. I was still working on the same sentence when our senior editor Sann Oo came out of his office holding a remote control. He switched on the small TV that was suspended from an iron pillar near the printers. 'Hey, guys. It's time for Obama and Daw Suu to make a speech at her house.'

We got up from our desks and gathered around the TV. A hushed silence fell. At long last, two of the world's great political leaders were about to meet; a new era in US–Myanmar relations was about to begin. We knew that the words which came out of their mouths would make history.

Aung San Suu Kyi spoke first. She looked radiant in a pale-apricot satin blouse and green sash. She thanked the US for supporting the democracy movement in Burma, and acknowledged the difficult years that still lay ahead. She'd spoken for less than a minute when she wound up by saying that her allocated three minutes were up. I was a little surprised by her brevity.

Then it was President Obama's turn to take the microphone. He began with flattery, saying that he couldn't hope to be as eloquent as she was. He glanced across at her and smiled warmly. 'I'm proud to be the first American president to visit this spectacular country and meet an icon of democracy. She has inspired so many people not just in this country, but all around the world.'

Obama paused and looked over at Aung San Suu Kyi again. He had that same starry-eyed look that I'd observed in Sherpa earlier. 'It is here where she showed that human freedom and human dignity cannot be denied.' Aung San Suu Kyi smiled demurely as Obama spoke. She was wearing flip-flop wedges, but was still a head shorter than him.

Barack Obama then took aim at those who complained that it was too soon for him to 'reward' Myanmar with such a high-level visit. He reeled off a list of reforms by the new government during the past two years. These included holding the first elections since 1990, releasing Aung San Suu Kyi from house arrest, freeing 200 political prisoners and passing a law to legalise peaceful protests. During this part of his speech, he referred to the country as 'Burma'. This didn't altogether surprise me, as it was Aung San Suu Kyi's preferred term. From this point onwards, the US would use both names.

'So again, I want to thank you, Daw Aung San Suu Kyi, for your extraordinary hospitality and grace; and the power of your example, which has been an inspiration to people all around the world, including myself.'

There was enthusiastic applause and a thousand camera flashes. I sighed contentedly. It was a beautiful speech and exactly what I expected from one of the world's greatest orators.

But what on earth was Obama doing now? He leant over and held Aung San Suu Kyi close, before kissing her on the cheek. It wasn't an air kiss either: his lips brushed her cheek, and would have probably stayed there longer had she not visibly shrunk from his touch. An awkward smile was plastered across her face. The cameras continued to flash until the pair had left her verandah and then vanished behind a curtain, with Obama's arm still draped across her shoulder. It was as if they were a pair of royal newlyweds retreating from the balcony after the wedding ceremony. I was stunned that the president hadn't been briefed properly. Public displays of affection between men and women were a big no-no in Myanmar.

When our photographer, Boothee, returned to the news-room from the press conference, a few of us stood around his computer as he began scrolling through every frozen frame of awkwardness. In one shot, Obama's lips grazed Aung San Suu Kyi's neck. In another, it looked as though they were about to lock lips. We fell around laughing. Sann Oo had tears in his eyes and it was a full minute before he could speak without choking. But I knew that not everyone would find it funny. Some people, especially older people, would consider Obama's misstep highly offensive.

SHERPA WAS ALREADY at home when I got back from work that evening. He leapt up from the couch and a torrent of words spilled out of his mouth before I even had a chance to say hello.

'I saw Obama. I saw Hillary too,' he said, beaming. 'I went to Aung San Suu Kyi's house but the only media allowed in had been pre-approved by the White House. So I walked for ages and got a taxi to the University of Yangon. I waited for two hours for Obama to appear after giving his big speech. He came out on the steps to say hi to the cameras and stuff. Obama saw me waving like crazy and smiled. Like, he smiled *at me*. It felt like a bolt of electricity passed through me.'

'That's incredible, babe!' I said. 'I wish I'd been there with you.'

'Me too, babe,' he said. 'It was unbelievable. I couldn't believe I was so close to him. He was only about a hundred metres away.'

We talked all night about how Barack Obama's visit to Myanmar made us feel as though the country's political transition was the focus of the entire world, even if only for a brief moment. It also made me hugely optimistic about Myanmar's future, as it seemed to confirm that it had shed its image as an isolated pariah state. If the upcoming general elections of 2015 were held peacefully, and the results respected, the transition would surely be complete.

8

STEPPING BACK IN TIME

DECEMBER 2012

I decided to make use of the office being closed for a week over Christmas to take my first trip outside Yangon. Sherpa couldn't join me because he'd just locked in an interview for an amazing job as the editor-in-chief of a new weekly newspaper called *Myanmar Business Today*. But he came along with me to an all-staff Christmas party at Ross' house, where we had kegs of beer, a 'lucky draw' present ceremony (which was basically a raffle with free tickets) and swam in his pool, complete with diving board. On Christmas Day, Sherpa and I went for a buffet at Inya Lake Hotel, where I ate my weight in prawns and oysters. Still feeling full the next morning, I wished Sherpa luck for his job interview and gave him an enormous hug as I set off in a taxi for the regional bus station.

There were more obvious destinations for my first sojourn in Myanmar, such as the ancient temples of Bagan or the floating gardens of Inle Lake. However, the capital of Mon State, Mawlamyine, appealed because it was closer and two people I was fond of had close ties to it: Thiri and George Orwell. Mawlamyine was Thiri's home town, and she had offered to show me around. The opportunity to see a place through the eyes of someone who lived there was too good to miss. Hanging out with the ghost of George Orwell, who had been stationed in the former capital of British Burma as a member of the Imperial Indian Police force in the 1920s, would require a bit of imagination, but I was willing to try.

I SLID into a window seat a few rows back from the bus driver, and the empty seat next to me was quickly filled by a wafer-thin teen in a flannel shirt with waist-length hair and a thin coat of dried yellow *thanaka* across her cheeks. Her mother and a little girl took the seats in front, and were both dressed in colourful cotton pyjamas. The little girl, who I assumed was her sister, kept stealing glances at us from between the gap in the middle of the seats. The teenager offered me some of her shucked sunflower seeds, and as I chewed them I told her, in my patchy Burmese, that I was from Australia and working at *The Myanmar Times*. She nodded and smiled, but still didn't say anything. I wondered why she was going to Mawlamyine, but lacked the necessary language skills to ask her.

The air-conditioning made my teeth chatter so I put on a cardigan, though it didn't help much. I'd never been so cold in Myanmar and wondered if the AC was stuck on the maximum setting. A boxy TV set above the driver's head played a slapstick Burmese movie through tinny speakers. Within half an hour, the girl had fallen asleep with her head resting gently on my shoulder, her mouth open like a fish.

I'd been up early for the bus but I didn't want to sleep, even if the loud TV volume and the cold air hadn't ruled it out. I was overjoyed to be on the road again, and to have left behind the stress of Sherpa trying to get a visa. I was completely carefree. I put my earphones in and stared out the window, happily soaking up the beautiful scenery. Frangipani and wax plants lined the road's edge, and limestone outcrops dotted gentle hills. Every now and again we passed herds of water buffalo happily half-submerged in muddy ponds, slowly munching their cud.

I loved observing village life, which felt so remote from my world. Most homes were thatched bamboo huts elevated on stilts. Pigs and goats were tethered underneath some of them, while chickens roamed freely, coming dangerously close to the road's edge. At one village, a barefoot boy looked over his shoulder and shrieked while being chased by two bigger boys. Another child was perched on the trunk of a sideways-leaning palm, languidly observing the commotion below.

A few minutes later, the bus trundled past a group of muscular men playing the national sport of *chinlone*, with a volleyball net strung across the middle of a level bit of dirt. The sport is similar to hacky sack, although the ball is much larger and made of wicker. With the players' *longyis* tucked up out of the way into their buttocks, they reminded me of ancient Romans in loin cloths.

The soil became more fertile as we travelled further south, and we passed acre upon acre of electric-green rice paddies. Harvesting season was in full swing, so there were scores of workers, mostly women, doubled over to do the back-breaking work of hand-plucking the stalks.

As we neared Mawlamyine, we passed over the enormous Thanlwin bridge. Its sloping iron pillars seemed to stretch on forever, while the eponymous river below was the colour of chocolate milk.

No sooner had I stepped off the bus than a short, wiry man appeared and propositioned me, his face inches from mine.

'Are you staying at Cinderella Hotel?' he asked.

I told him I was, and assumed that the rave write-up it got from *Lonely Planet* had made it a favourite among travellers.

'I'll take you there. Two thousand kyat only. Let me take your bag.'

'One thousand,' I countered.

'Fifteen hundred.'

'Okay.'

To my surprise, the man led me not to a taxi, but to a pony attached to a bright-green cart. He hoisted my backpack into the tray of the cart, which had two benches facing one another, and held an outstretched arm to steady me. I held onto a handrail as he cracked his whip and we lurched forwards, setting off at a brisk clip-clop. As we overtook a pony and cart carrying an enormous load of onions and tomatoes, I realised that this wasn't some kind of tourist gimmick, but an actual mode of transport. This quaint town was delighting me already.

Cinderella Hotel was sparkling clean and my room was nicer than any guesthouse I'd seen in Yangon. The large bed had a shiny satin quilt, and there was a cupboard to hang my clothes in, plus a dresser and chair that I could use as a writing space. Outside was a little porch with a wicker table and a lovely view of the town's sweeping hill. I had an early dinner at the family-run restaurant at the back and then read a book in bed.

After a long, restful sleep, I continued the fairy-tale theme by taking a ferry to Ogre Island the following morning. Centuries earlier, the inhabitants of the island were supposedly fierce and existed on a diet of raw meat. This was enough for them to be declared ogres, and the name alone was reason for me to want to go there. On the way we passed another place with a strange name: Shampoo Island. Legend went that the water from one of its springs was so pristine that during the fourteenth century it was used for an annual royal hair-washing ceremony.

It was clear from the moment the ferry pulled up with a shudder at the crumbling jetty that modernity hadn't arrived on Ogre Island. It was about the same size as Singapore, but that was all the two places had in common. It wasn't connected to the national grid, so there was no electricity. One of the first things I noticed was children pumping water by hand from a well, and then lugging it heaven knows how far to their homes.

I hadn't walked more than a dozen steps when I was again propositioned by a man with a pony and cart. He offered to show me around, so I took a seat next to him up front. However, it soon became clear that beyond quoting the fare, my tour guide didn't speak English. He pointed to a small, white-washed monastery where a few mangy dogs were curled up in the shade and said, 'Monastery.'

'When was it built?' I asked.

'Yes,' he said, nodding. 'Good.'

I was becoming increasingly frustrated with my lack of progress in learning Burmese. My efforts were all the more pitiful because for the past three months I had been taking lessons, which *The Myanmar Times* were paying for. I couldn't seem to wrap my head around the sounds, let alone the circular script, and nothing I was taught ever seemed to stick. I found my teacher a bit confusing, but the truth was that I wasn't putting any effort into practising. I looked forward to my weekly Burmese lesson, but that was only because I took lessons with an American called Nathalie, who was the flatmate of Phil Blackwood, the manager of 50th Street Bar, where we usually ended up for beers after our lesson ended. When I was in Dhaka, I tried really hard to learn Bangla, and life was easier and more satisfying as a result. Starting from zero with a new language made me feel weary. Sherpa, by contrast, loved learning languages. He was teaching himself Burmese and was already miles ahead of me. He often studied the Burmese dictionary I'd given him and he could even read a few words of script: street signs were beginning to make sense to him. Sherpa was on his way to becoming my translator for a second time, because I was totally hopeless. I was especially annoyed with myself in moments like these on Ogre Island. Unless I applied myself I would forever remain a mute in Myanmar, and so I told myself that I'd start learning in earnest when I got back to Yangon.

For the time being, though, I didn't know where I was going or what I was looking at. It was clear, however, that Ogre Island was a poor but pretty place. Its sandy paths were lined with palms and there were small collections of thatched huts that looked as though they might blow away in the breeze. Many had gaping holes in their roofs, which would need to be repaired by the time the rainy season came in June or families would be sleeping in soggy beds. We slowed down to navigate past a couple of humped white cows, who stared at us vacantly from the middle of the path. We stopped for lunch at a tea shop, which had half a dozen plastic tables and chairs that were extremely low to the ground, just as they are in Yangon. The tea shop was next to a small field where a group of boys were kicking a football around. Most Burmese kids are skinny, but these ones were nothing but bones, their clothes hanging off them. I noticed a group of women sitting cross-legged on a porch opposite the tea stall. They were sorting enormous piles of rubber bands, which looked disconcertingly like a mass of red hair. I later learnt that making rubber bands was one of the islanders' main sources of income.

I saw a couple of motorbikes, but the rattling buses I'd read about in my *Lonely Planet*, that supposedly connected the island's sixty-eight villages were nowhere to be seen. And there was not a single car on Ogre Island, because cars were banned. I never could find out why. Lots of things were banned in Myanmar, and often the public was in the dark as to the reason. I suppose that's the essence of an authoritarian state – to just do as you're told. For example, motorbikes were banned in Yangon, but the reason was a mystery. Most of the rumours had a common theme of a motorcycle gang being involved, such as a general's son being killed in a fight with a rival gang. Another rumour I heard was that a motorcyclist had dropped pro-democracy leaflets into a general's car window, or had stuck their middle finger up at the general while driving past. Whatever the reason, it was a mean rule, because it denied so many families their own means of transport, as cars were prohibitively expensive for the overwhelming majority.

I wondered how many places without cars were left in the world. As I stared at island life out past the pony's protruding ribs, Yangon suddenly seemed like a bustling, modern metropolis and not the time warp it sometimes felt like. Our home in Yangon may not have had a TV, phone, internet connection, air-conditioning or reliable electricity, but here on Ogre Island, when night came, the only source of light was from a candle, and food was cooked on primitive fireplaces using cow dung as fuel. If Yangon was indeed a relic of days gone by, Ogre Island was stuck in another century.

And yet despite its seeming remoteness from even Mawlamyine, the island had a liberal smattering of portraits of Aung San Suu Kyi, and red posters with a star and a peacock signifying her party, the National League for Democracy. Perhaps it was hoped that Aung San Suu Kyi could bring change to the island and its 200,000 inhabitants. And to an extent, she did. Electricity arrived in 2016, and in 2017, five years after my fleeting visit, a bridge between Mawlamyine and Ogre Island was built. Foreign tourists could also take well-organised tours of the island with an English-speaking guide if they wished.

One thing remains the same though: it is illegal for foreigners to remain on Ogre Island by nightfall (again, I did not know why). As I hadn't been able to make sense of the ferry timetable, I didn't linger after lunch.

WHEN I GOT BACK to the guesthouse, there was an email from Sherpa saying that he'd met with *Myanmar Business Today's* Thai managing director and had been offered the job as the newspaper's editor-in-chief. The paper would launch in a few weeks' time and his salary would be US$3000 a month. This seemed an enormous amount, as it was double what I made at *The Myanmar Times*. I was ecstatic and wrote an excited reply in capital letters saying how clever he was. Once again, it felt that the decision to come to Myanmar had been the right one. We had both received major career boosts, just a few years into our journalism careers. And every day, life was incredibly interesting.

I went out for a walk along the boulevard, but the sleepy streets were at odds with my jubilant mood. Many of the shops were shuttered, and none but a tea shop seemed to be doing a brisk trade. There were certainly some esoteric offerings: one shop sold Greek Orthodox knick-knacks, while another was a jumble of tyres and wires. There was no doubt that Mawlamyine had faded since it was the prosperous capital of British Burma. Even by the time Orwell arrived in 1926, the plundering of its forests by its British colonial administrators had caused the timber supply to run dry and the city's fortunes to dwindle. Due to its proximity to Thailand, Mawlamyine had a brief burst of economic activity in the late 1960s and 1970s when it became a major port for black market goods due to shortages of everyday supplies under the military regime. But it never regained what it had lost.

I wondered whether Orwell also came to Myanmar hoping to benefit from opportunities that didn't exist or were harder to achieve in England. It seemed to me that all expats left home with that hope, or to at least escape the monotony of the daily grind. I certainly had. Orwell did write about his elevated position in Burma, though it came with some significant downsides. His 1936 essay 'Shooting an Elephant', which is set in Mawlamyine (formerly spelt 'Moulmein'), starts like this: 'In Moulmein, in Lower Burma, I was hated by large numbers of people – the only time in my life that I have been important enough for this to happen to me.'

As a colonial officer, Orwell realised he was on the wrong side of history. But although his sympathies increasingly lay with the Burmese, the locals despised him and the imperialism he represented.

I knew all of this because I had recently gobbled up a beautiful book called *Finding George Orwell in Burma*, by Emma Larkin. She explains that even though Orwell's experience was ultimately a negative one, his five years in Burma provided him with a rich source of material. His disgust with the colonial system is portrayed in his searing novel *Burmese Days*, and his hatred of imperialism and authority led to his greatest works, *1984* and *Animal Farm*.

I imagined Orwell grumpily stomping around the streets of Mawlamyine, a cigarette in his mouth and a frown on his lips, his brain working overtime in tracing the roots of man's obsession with imperialism. I wondered what he would make of Myanmar now, a country many would describe as Orwellian.

By then I'd been walking for over an hour and my legs were starting to feel heavy, so when I came to a beer station that overlooked the river, I pulled up a chair near a few men with a large bottle of whisky on their table. They were eating fried watercress with chopsticks and laughing uproariously – my guess was they'd been there some time. I ordered a large bottle of Myanmar Beer and made a silent toast to Sherpa's new job and life in a smaller pond.

THE NEXT MORNING I walked over to Thiri's place. Thiri showed me her bedroom, which was a cross between an attic and a shelf. I climbed gingerly up the ladder and realised the roof was so low that I couldn't sit up without banging my head. I lay there quietly while Thiri prayed next to an open Koran for a few minutes.

I met Thiri's parents, younger brother and her cats, all of whom she clearly adored. Thiri and her brother had the same deep-set eyes and wavy hair. She described him as a hopeless romantic as he had recently sent her an email threatening to jump off a waterfall because of an unrequited love. It terrified her, especially as she had been in Yangon at the time and could do nothing to help him. We also went next door to meet a woman Thiri described as her 'spinster aunt'. She was elderly and lived in a beautiful traditional home – every inch of it appeared to be made from teak. The sun shone through the rafters and a couple of cats slept on cushions by her feet. Her balcony was crowded with pots of cacti.

Then we set off for the world's biggest reclining Buddha. While it may seem strange that, as a Muslim, Thiri wanted to show me a Buddhist site, it's less so when you consider there wasn't really an alternative. Myanmar isn't big on secular tourism.

It was a fifty-kilometre round trip, so Thiri's brother had borrowed a friend's three-wheel diesel cart, which was basically a modified motorbike with a covered trailer attached that had bench seats for passengers. Thiri and I sat opposite each other and grinned as we sped along the highway, the wind whipping our hair. We stopped off at some eerie limestone caves along the way; even they had large Buddhas tucked implausibly inside.

After a bowl of *mohinga* fish broth at a roadside stall that cost us thirty cents apiece and which Thiri insisted on paying for, we pressed on until we reached a gravel driveway that was lined with hundreds of identical Buddhas dressed in maroon robes, holding alms bowls.

Thiri's brother slowed down and pointed up ahead – we'd rounded a bend and the enormous Buddha, known as Win Sein Taw Ya, was in full view on the side of the mountain.

'Whoa,' I exclaimed. 'That is one big Buddha.'

At thirty metres high and 180 metres long, the Buddha is triple the height of the Hollywood sign, and almost double its length. We parked in a bit of shade and joined the families who were making their way up the hundred-odd stairs towards the Buddha's head. As we got closer, I noted that a single eyelash was taller than me. Each was fashioned out of a curved steel bar. Part of the Buddha's face was still under construction, and the steel wiring made him look as though he had fish hooks painfully implanted in his lips.

For someone who wasn't a Buddhist, Thiri knew a lot about the big Buddha. She had absorbed information on Buddhism in the same way I had picked up information about cricket in Australia, a sport that was an obsession for many. Even though I had no interest in cricket, I could reel off a dozen names of national players because there was just no avoiding it.

Thiri told me to note the emphasis on it being the world's tallest *reclining* Buddha. There are different record categories for what Buddha is doing: standing, sitting or reclining. There are also categories for the type of material the Buddha is made from, such as gold, bronze or stone.

'So you could have the world's biggest standing bronze Buddha, the world's biggest reclining gold Buddha, and the world's biggest sitting stone Buddha?' I asked.

'Something like that,' she said. 'That's what they taught us at school, anyway. And that Myanmar has a lot of the world's biggest Buddhas.'

We walked inside a tunnel that began as a small opening in the Buddha's skull. It was dark and pleasantly cool, and smelt pretty musty. Thiri held my hand, warning me that there were holes in the floor. We came to a dimly lit room that felt more like a cave. My eyes settled on a flickering lightbulb that crackled from the end of a suspended bit of wire. And then I looked at the walls, and saw an incredibly violent mural. Nubile women with torture devices attached to them writhed in agony. It quite took my breath away.

We entered another room: this one was filled with dioramas. A woman was being boiled alive in a cauldron, while another had her hands tied behind her back and was about to clubbed by her bare-chested male captor, as her husband watched on in horror. Black monsters with horns (which looked awfully like the devil) dwarfed the humans they were about to decapitate, and for some reason all the female victims had their breasts exposed. There were methods of torture I hoped I would be able to forget.

'This is purgatory,' Thiri whispered.

I inwardly agreed.

If this was what it was like to be inside the mind of the Buddha, it was a violent mind indeed. I couldn't reconcile what I'd seen with what I thought I knew about Buddhism – that it was a religion espousing peace and loving kindness. I'd thought that killing anything, even an insect, was forbidden – let alone gut-spilling, cold-blooded murder. Though it wasn't all gore and violence, I was nonetheless relieved when we came to the end.

'I wasn't expecting that,' I said to Thiri as my eyes adjusted to the daylight. 'It was really violent.'

Thiri shrugged, seemingly saying, 'Not my religion'.

We walked on towards the diesel cart and stopped for a cool

drink from a kiosk. Her brother and his friend were smoking and kicking pebbles up ahead.

Thiri turned and looked at me, and then she said quietly, 'People at work tease me because I'm Muslim. They ask me if I've got a bomb in my backpack. And sometimes when we're in the lunchroom, they try to put their pork curries under my nose and ask me if I want some. They know I can't eat pork.'

For a second time that afternoon, I was shocked. The reporters seemed so innocent and sweet. I had no idea they were capable of such bigotry.

'Who says these things to you?' I asked, trying to keep my voice level.

'A few of them,' she replied. She avoided my gaze by pretending to be absorbed by the straw inside her empty bottle of lemonade. I could tell she wouldn't be drawn further as to who the culprits were.

'Have you told Tom?' I asked.

'I don't think there's any point. The girls would only deny it and make me look stupid.'

I felt awful for Thiri. It was disturbing that this was happening at a newspaper, of all places, where I would have expected people to be fairly open-minded. Was this a case of a few nasty individuals, or a more broadly held attitude towards Muslims? I didn't know how to ask Thiri without appearing to trivialise what was happening to her. So I told her how sorry I was, and left it at that.

9

THE RELEASE

APRIL 2013

A few months after my visit to Mawlamyine, I was working away on an article one morning when I heard a loud gasp come from Maisy's office. I pricked up my ears. All went quiet. Being the nosy journalist that I was, I got up from my desk and went to see what was going on. Maisy was hugging her loyal assistant, Phyu Phyu, and the third member of their team, Khine Mar Nay, was on the phone. A couple of Burmese staff wandered in behind me. Something big was happening.

'What's going on?' I asked.

'We've just been told that Sonny is going to be released from prison tomorrow,' said Maisy. Her hand was interlocked with Phyu Phyu's, who stood there looking shell-shocked. 'He's been included in the latest amnesty and his plane from Lashio gets in tomorrow at 11 a.m. We'll all go to the airport to meet him.'

Myanmar's quasi-civilian government had announced a few amnesties since taking office in 2011, but no one I knew had been hopeful that our newspaper's co-founder would be among them. Sonny Swe's arrest had been too political in the first place. His father, Thein Swe, was a high-ranking member of Military

Intelligence, and after a power struggle in 2003 between the head of Military Intelligence and the then-dictator General Than Shwe, it was declared illegal and purged. Under a deal cut by Sonny's father, *The Myanmar Times* had been censored by Military Intelligence rather than the usual censorship board, and so it was retrospectively accused of publishing uncensored content. This was ironic, given that at least a quarter of all stories had been cut every week by Military Intelligence. In an added touch of cruelty, Sonny and his father had been separated and kept in remote prisons the entire time, so as to prevent them being a source of comfort to each other and to make it more difficult for family members to visit them. Sonny's father was still serving his 146-year sentence and was not included in the amnesty.

I lay in bed that night wondering how Nicky must be feeling. His dad had been in prison almost half his life and now he had just one more sleep until he got to see him.

I turned up to work the next morning feeling almost jittery with excitement. I ducked into Maisy's office to ask what time we'd be leaving for the airport.

'Be ready to go at 10 a.m.,' she said, beaming.

Back at my desk, the minutes crawled by. If this is what it was like for me, how must Sonny have been feeling? Surely those last hours of confinement were passing excruciatingly slowly.

Finally it was time to switch off my computer.

'Are you guys ready to go?' I asked Tom, Tim and Douglas.

'I've got too much on to come to the airport,' said Tom.

'Ah okay,' I said. 'Douglas, Tim – shall we head downstairs?'

'I'm waiting on a call back from the US Embassy this morning so I better stay put,' said Tim. 'I'm hoping they'll give me a quote for a story I'm working on.'

'I can't come either. I've got far too many stories to edit,' chimed in Douglas.

'Righto,' I said. 'Just me then. Tom, I was thinking of filing a news story on Sonny's release. Is that okay?'

'Sounds good,' he said.

I can't believe they aren't coming, I thought while having a quick smoke out the front of the office. Sonny lost eight years of his life for our newspaper, and spent two and a half of those years in solitary confinement, and yet they weren't bothering to show up to meet him. Ross and I would be the only non-Burmese staff members there – a poor showing. I hadn't seen Ross at the office that morning, but he lived uptown so it made sense for him to head straight to the airport from his place. He had a driver and a sleek white sedan.

I stubbed out the cigarette butt and then hopped up into the truck that was parked out front. It was the same truck that was used as a shuttle service for our Burmese staff to and from work. Employers in Yangon tended to provide their staff with a lift to work on a truck, as the public transport system was woeful and few people owned cars. I myself had never had a ride in the shuttle truck because, like the other expat journalists, I was able to afford taxis. I slid along the hot vinyl bench seat, taking the empty spot next to Thandar, our head of marketing. She had a mischievous sense of humour and was well travelled, having been a flight attendant. She was beautiful in a regal way, and we'd often have a smoke and a laugh together while discussing the advertising for the special reports. Ross chewed her ear off most days.

We were soon joined by other staff members and hit the road. I sat quietly as one of the reporters held court, and the group of ten or so around me laughed at the punchline of his story. Our senior designer smacked his thigh in delight. Everyone was in high spirits and didn't seem to mind that we were making very slow progress past Kandawgyi Lake. I wondered if a car ahead of us had broken down. It was a pretty place to be stopped, at least. I gazed out at Karaweik Palace, which was my favourite landmark in all of Yangon. It was a replica of a royal barge, with two gold geese-like creatures at its bow. At this time of day, its shimmering reflection took on a green tinge, while at sunset the colours became even more dramatic and beautiful. A couple of drivers behind us honked impatiently and, about a minute later, we finally began moving again. There was no doubt that Yangon's streets were getting busier and noisier. It was a tangible sign that Myanmar was becoming less of an isolated pariah state. So too was the fact that its prisons were being emptied of the innocent.

THERE WERE ABOUT thirty of us milling around the poorly lit arrivals lounge. Around half of those were newspaper staff, and the rest were Sonny's family and friends – though it was said he treated everyone like his family. In a way, I felt like I already knew him a little, because my colleagues spoke of him all the time. In a country where job switching was common, their loyalty over the years spoke volumes. Ross talked about Sonny a lot too, although his focus was usually on 'the bastards who locked him up' or 'the bastards who replaced him'.

Ross hated Sonny's replacement, a man called Tin Tun Oo, who had been forcibly installed as CEO by the government after Sonny went to prison. Ross and TTO, as we called him, were constantly fighting, and a month earlier Ross and TTO's son-in-law had a big fight in the middle of the newsroom. We were left gobsmacked when Ross punched him and grabbed TTO's wife by the wrist. I'd never seen anyone get physical in Myanmar until that day. They'd been arguing about *The Myanmar Times* becoming a daily newspaper, which Ross was in favour of but the Burmese partners didn't want to do. Ross desperately wanted to go daily, in part because of the much greater ad revenue it would bring. But he was now facing assault charges in court. If he were found guilty, he would be returning to prison for a second time. In 2011, he had spent a month in prison after being convicted of assaulting and drugging a sex worker. He claimed the charges were false and politically motivated. Ross would be absolutely delighted to have his old business partner back and to get rid of TTO for good.

I looked at my watch again. Where on earth was Ross? He was in danger of missing the moment when Sonny reappeared after all these years.

But Ross did miss it, because all of a sudden there was Sonny, walking alone towards us. His face lit up and he broke into a jog when he saw us. He was clean-shaven and wore a light-blue shirt, and was thin but not emaciated. People yelled out his name and his sister, Marlar, who was in her early thirties, started sobbing. She and three other people, including Nicky, swept him into their arms. They stood in a circle with their heads touching and arms around each other. For a minute or so, they just stood there like that, quietly weeping. Nicky then looked on with a dazed smile as his dad greeted every long-lost person with a smile and embrace. A translator in his sixties wrapped an arm around Sonny as though he were his son, and waved that week's copy of *The Myanmar Times* in the air. They said something in Burmese and everyone laughed. I wiped away a tear – it was so moving. I couldn't believe that Ross wasn't there.

I took a few notes for my article as Boothee snapped away on his camera. I chose not to interrupt the teary group by asking Sonny for a quote. Maybe a better journalist would have made a different decision. Instead I hung back, taking it all in.

I was still hovering in the background in the carpark twenty minutes later as Sonny and his family started the journey home in their 4WD. The car stopped in front of me and Sonny wound down his window from the backseat.

'You're Jessica, right?' he asked.

I stepped forward, saying that I was.

'Nicky says that you and he are friends. That's nice. I look forward to getting to know you.'

I stammered a reply and Sonny smiled and wound the window back up. Considering the momentous day he was having and the intense emotions he must have been going through, I was so surprised that he had thought to speak to me. But it was typical of Sonny to think of others, I'd soon understand.

10

NEW FACES

MAY 2013

Things started happening quickly at *The Myanmar Times* after Sonny's release. Ross saw it as a sign that Myanmar was open for business and his preparations for becoming a daily newspaper went into full swing. We still had no official permission from the government, but Ross wanted to be ready to go the moment we had it. He asked me to put together a media kit, which would be shown to prospective advertisers. I had no idea what that would involve, but I agreed nonetheless.

Ross also hired several expat journalists. They were Australians, Americans and Canadians who were mostly in their mid to late twenties, and a few had done stints in Cambodia on *The Phnom Penh Post*, which Ross also owned. There was Wade, Fiona, Justin, Vincent, Jeremy, Jesse, Peter, Kayleigh, Manny, and a couple called Bridget and Phil. An older American woman called Wendy arrived to help oversee the transition to becoming daily, as well as a few interns from universities in Australia and Denmark. Each time a new face arrived, I invited them out for coffee on their first day, along with everyone else who was new or just wanted to come along. I didn't want others to have a crappy first day as I had.

Ross invested considerable sums in the newspaper. Along with an increased editorial head count, he hired designers to give the newspaper a crisp new layout. Ross had our building painted so that it would look impressive when we had an all-staff photo taken out the front of it, which would be part of the media kit and which I helped him organise. Every journalist had a head shot taken, which appeared next to our articles as though we were well-known columnists. By then I was used to my name being known around town for my by-lines in *The Myanmar Times*, but once my photo was printed alongside my stories, I began to get recognised too. I introduced myself to a diplomat's wife at a Russian embassy event that I'd gone to as Sherpa's plus one and she exclaimed, 'Oh, yes, you're Jessica Mudditt. I know you. I've read your articles and your blog. You're famous in Yangon.'

I was completely over the moon, but I tried not to let it go to my head ('tried' being the operative word). Apart from the state-run rag, *The Myanmar Times* was the country's main English-language newspaper and it had a lot of status. I was 'famous' by virtue of appearing in its pages, as all its journalists were. My expat-oriented blog was popular, in large part because very few expats in Myanmar kept blogs, and information about daily life was hard to find. I wrote about how I arranged to bring our cat into the country and where to find the best coffee or a steak. Even so, I was pinching myself. Just three years earlier, I'd been an intern at a local London newspaper making cups of tea for the reporters.

It also seemed like much longer than a year ago that I'd joined *The Myanmar Times* and was begrudgingly welcomed into the tiny team of male expat editors. I started going for beers after work with some of my new colleagues, and things got a whole lot more fun. Vincent would entertain me with stories about his on-again off-again Burmese boyfriend and gave short shrift to certain expat colleagues who he deemed 'try-hards'. He had lived in Southeast Asia for a very long time, and seemed incapable of being shocked by anything, though some of the things he told me I found jaw-dropping – an effect I am sure he enjoyed. I also loved Queensland-born Bridget, who gave Burmese women a run for their money with her waist-length, dark brown hair. She was one of the sweetest and funniest women I ever met. We spent hours together at Gekko Bar, knocking back wines and falling about laughing. Justin was another great pal, at work and outside of it. He had previously worked as a business reporter at *The Bangkok Post* and within what felt like a matter of days of him arriving in the newsroom, he'd become another of my closest work friends. He was from Boston and was a confident, good-looking gay man. He and I often had lunch together and we had message chats at work. We also went out drinking with Vincent, dancing at GTR nightclub and sang karaoke at one of the many 'KTV bars'. Sherpa and Justin sometimes sang drunken duets that left me in stitches.

But within the newsroom itself, the truth was that there were a lot of egos jostling for prominence. I suppose the tendency among journalists towards one-upmanship is only natural, and probably a good thing for readers. Penning a front-page story was seen as a mark of status and how good our sources were. I was just as competitive as the rest of them, but I was not a breaking-news reporter, and preferred to write features for my special reports, or the odd article that sat outside of those topics, which I generally filed to Douglas for the arts and culture section.

There was also rivalry among expat journalists at *The Myanmar Times* and the publications that had recently returned from exile, including *The Irrawaddy*, *Democratic Voice of Burma* and *Mizzima*. Because *The Myanmar Times* had always operated from inside Myanmar, and because Sonny's father was a senior member of Military Intelligence, we were seen as being cosy with the junta. I didn't think that was fair, and felt some of the journalists at these other publications were a bit self-righteous. Regardless of who was right or wrong, it was a shame there was so much standoffishness among expat journalists. We were such a small group and had so much in common – I figured it would be a lot more fun if we were friends. I made up my mind to try to break the ice.

'Do you think I should start a Foreign Correspondents Club?' I asked Sherpa and Justin one Friday night after work. We were sipping Mandalay rum sours on leather armchairs at the Strand. It was happy hour at the iconic 100-year-old hotel, which oozed with colonial-era opulence and included George Orwell among its list of famous past guests. The lights were low and its décor was heavy on teak, with buttercream walls, and fans that whirred slowly overhead. That night, the Strand's public bar was packed with Westerners, who had been arriving in Yangon in droves after Obama's visit, encouraged as they were by the president's endorsement of the path Myanmar was taking.

'That's a fantastic idea,' Justin said. 'Do it. There are a lot of new faces in Yangon, and more and more journalists will be flying in to do quick stories in the lead-up to the elections.'

'You're not worried about the association laws?' asked Sherpa. He was stretched out languidly on his armchair, his slightly rumpled shirt now untucked. The warm glow from the table lamp next to him made his features even more beguiling. His eyes had such depth and sincerity, and he looked at me intently, with some concern.

Sherpa was referring to the Unlawful Associations Act, which dated back to colonial times and was used by the British to suppress dissent. Rather than being repealed, it was subsequently used by Myanmar's military regime to quell agitation against its despotic rule, most often targeting a member of a minority ethnic group. It was a very broad law, and it meant that without express permission from the government, my new club would be illegal.

'I think the Ministry of Information would be alarmed if I said I was going to start a club for foreign journalists,' I said. 'They would probably say no, or make me provide a list of names of attendees, and that could cause those people visa hassles. I think I'll keep it low-key and not ask for permission. It would just be a group of journalists meeting up for a few beers once a month, not an official club with rules and voting and all that.'

Sherpa didn't look entirely convinced.

'Justin, do you think I could get in trouble?'

At that moment, a waiter in a starched white shirt and black vest arrived with our next round of drinks. His name badge said 'Tony' but I suspected that it was a Westernised work name and not his real one, which happened at upmarket places like the Strand – I guess it is a way of trying to make life as easy as possible for guests. We paused as the waiter wiped away the condensation left by our empty glasses and set out a fresh bowl of peanuts. He gave a half bow and whispered almost inaudibly, 'Thank you, sirs' before gliding back across the marble floor to the bar.

'It's hard to say whether you'd get in trouble,' said Justin thoughtfully, reaching for a handful of peanuts. 'You never really know in Myanmar. But the government isn't out to be heavy-handed right now. They want to be seen as supporting democracy, and journalists are a big part of that.'

'Sherpa, do you think it's a bad idea?'

'No. I love the idea. Just be a bit careful. Don't include any photos of the meet-ups in the social pages of *The Myanmar*

Times. If the government doesn't know there is a foreign corre-spondents club, it should be fine.'

So with that, I decided to go ahead and do it.

THE FIRST MEET-UP of the Myanmar Foreign Correspondents Club took place midway through 2013 and was attended by just five people, and that included Sherpa and me. The second and third meet-ups were also pretty tiny. It wasn't until I set up a Facebook group that our numbers started to swell. I had been a little reluctant to post anything about it online in case it got me into hot water, but I realised that it was the only way to get the FCC off the ground.

On the first Tuesday of every month, I would rush to China-town after work to reserve a few tables at Kaung Myat beer station, which was the local term for a pub. It was an atmos-pheric, open-air establishment on 19th Street, which was nick-named 'Beer Street' because the entire lower block of the pedestrian-only thoroughfare was made up of beer and barbecue joints. Once the group had a presence on Facebook with details listed for each event, the monthly meetups began attracting a wide array of journalists – happily, several of whom were from Yangon-based publications. They were friendly and none struck me as aloof, although there were a few who never showed up (nor did any of the old hands at *The Myanmar Times*, except for Douglas).

At our sixth meet-up, we had foreign correspondents from *The New York Times, Reuters, The South China Morning Post* and a couple of other places. One of them seemed to me the quin-tessential foreign correspondent: a grizzly hard-drinker with incredible stories from covering wars in Afghanistan and Iraq. He told his high-stakes anecdotes with cool detachment, which suggested that he had plenty more up his sleeve. Equally fascinating was veteran journalist Paul Mooney, who I met for the first time that night. He told me that he had recently been expelled from China after being based there since the eighties. In contrast to Myanmar, China's regime seemed bent on kicking out its expat community, and especially those who were involved in anything other than business.

Sherpa arrived with a few of his Burmese colleagues, including Zarni and his incredibly clever and helpful translator Aye Chan Wynn (he was so good at his job that he had been nicknamed 'Agent').

I was starving, so as the guys settled in with their first round of beers, I left the table and headed for the cart of food. I grabbed a set of tongs and heaped skewers of raw squid, liver, lotus root and quail eggs into a plastic tray. My food was then taken out the back and barbecued in a marinade so delicious that even Anthony Bourdain had given it the thumbs-up when he filmed an episode of his travel show, *Parts Unknown*, in Myanmar.

Back at the table, Sherpa ordered a whole fish to share, and when it arrived, he and his Burmese colleagues began tucking into it with their chopsticks, peeling away the crisp scales and swallowing all but the biggest of bones. When the soft white flesh was gone, they flipped the fish and began on the other side. Polite negotiations began over who got to eat the eyeballs, which were considered a delicacy. I was glad that Sherpa always came and brought a few people with him. Even though the group I'd created was called the Foreign Correspondents Club, I had never intended it to be an expats-only social group. My own identity as a 'foreigner' in Myanmar was well and truly cemented – locally, this term was used instead of 'expat' (by locals and foreigners alike). I had come to use it myself without skipping a beat.

'Sherpa!' I exclaimed as a waitress from Ko San Bar next door appeared with a second round of mojitos for the table. At eighty cents a pop, it wouldn't break the bank, but knowing Sherpa, there could be a third or even fourth round coming soon enough. He loved the FCC as much as I did, though I suspected in his case it was at least partly because for him the novelty of it being legal to drink in a public place wasn't close to wearing off.

The conversation turned to the upcoming elections of 2015, as it did every month. Although still eighteen months away, they had long been a topic of intense speculation.

'Who thinks the election results will be honoured this time around?' asked Alex, a British journalist with the *Democratic Voice of Burma*. He had a quirky, provocative sense of humour and I'd taken an immediate liking to him.

'I don't,' said Bridget, who had swept her hair into a loose side ponytail that cascaded down to her waist. 'Because I don't think the military realises that they will lose again. When they do, they'll be furious with the "ungrateful" public.'

'I totally agree,' said Justin. 'They might have swapped their military gear for parliamentary uniforms, but underneath they're still the same power-tripping egomaniacs they always were. "Same wine, different bottle" – as people say. When they lose, they will ignore the result and roll out the tanks. Just as they have done twice before.'

The table went silent for a moment, so I ventured a counter view.

'I think they have so much more to lose this time around if they don't honour the results. All this international goodwill and lifting of sanctions has been conditional on completing the transition to democracy.'

'There's always China and North Korea left to do business with,' said Alex.

'Or perhaps the USDP will win,' said Jaiden, referring to the current, quasi-civilian government. The Union Solidarity and Development Party had been in charge since it was created in 2011, and was merely a change of name for the military's former 'State Peace and Development Council', which had ruled since 1990 after overturning Aung San Suu Kyi's electoral landslide victory.

'If Aung San Suu Kyi can't be president, why would anyone vote for her party?' added Jaiden.

'Because the people love her unconditionally, and will support her in any capacity in government. And because Aung San Suu Kyi *is* the NLD,' said my Australian friend Bronwyn, who was making a documentary film about Aung San Suu Kyi and had spent part of her childhood in Myanmar.

Aung San Suu Kyi was barred from being president because her late husband and estranged sons were British. In a provision of the 2008 constitution written especially for her, anyone with a 'foreign allegiance' was deemed ineligible.

'I agree with Bronwyn. And I really believe that Aung San Suu Kyi is going to lead Myanmar into a new era,' I said.

'Not a chance,' said Alex. 'The military would never allow her to become president.'

'But the military have already made so many changes. Why won't they make this one? They must be aware that the whole nation wants her to be their leader. It seems pretty cynical not to give the military government the benefit of the doubt about this,' I said.

'Cynical or realistic?' asked Oliver, Sherpa's new deputy editor.

'Cynical,' I insisted.

A British magazine writer who had been visiting Myanmar longer than most expats I knew leant over to me and said, 'But haven't you heard? The military can't stand Aung San Suu Kyi, but not just because she's pro-democracy. She's more Margaret Thatcher or Indira Gandhi than Mahatma Gandhi. That is to say: she's a bitch to deal with. They'll never give her the satisfaction of becoming president.'

For once, I was rendered speechless. I'd never even heard Aung San Suu Kyi criticised before, let alone in such personal terms.

My mind was still reeling when a long-legged photographer called Julian called to us from the street. He waved his camera and said, 'Hey, you guys! Let's get a group shot.' We turned our chairs to face him and he took a few shots with us holding our beer mugs in the air. Julian always uploaded a few of his pictures onto our Facebook page in the days after the meet-up. After copious mojitos and jugs of beer, his photos were often my best means of remembering who had come along each month.

As the others slowly filed off into the night, Sherpa and I gave the waiters a large tip. They were as quick as lightning and always gracious, even when we remained after the other beer stations had closed up, as we had that night. Sherpa and I staggered up the alleyway with our arms around each other as the rats noisily rummaged about for the scraps of food. My hangover would be monumental, but I always considered the pain the next day worth it.

ORGANISING the FCC came with some serious perks. I got an email from the incoming BBC correspondent, Jonah Fisher, who was about to set up a bureau in Yangon. He wanted to come along to the next FCC drinks to get the lowdown on life in the city, and suggested we meet first for a chat.

Then a *Lonely Planet* author called Simon Richmond got in touch: he too wanted to meet up. I was wildly excited. To me, a

Lonely Planet author was some sort of travel god, with the best job in the world. In 2006 I had spent a year travelling overland from Cambodia to Pakistan and my dog-eared *Lonely Planets* had been my travel bibles. In Yangon, I'd followed the guidebook's every suggestion until I'd exhausted them.

Simon met me at *The Myanmar Times* office and I gave him a tour of the newsroom with my chest puffed out like a peacock. I then introduced him to a few colleagues who I'd excitedly told of his visit. After exchanging a few pleasantries with Douglas the arts editor, Simon turned to me and said quietly, 'I don't need to meet every single person.'

'Oh righto,' I said. 'Let's head straight out for lunch then.'

So you're a little bit of a grumpy god, I thought to myself. I also realised that his job was less glamorous than I'd imagined it to be. For one, it involved a heck of a lot of legwork. Simon had to physically check that every hotel and eatery listed in the guidebook was still open and half decent. Then he had to track down any new ones (which was where I came in, as I gave Simon a few suggestions).

Myanmar had changed substantially since his last visit a couple of years earlier. Less of the country was off-limits to tourists, a growing number of people had mobile phones and access to the internet, and pre-publication censorship had been abolished shortly after I had joined *The Myanmar Times*. Most sanctions had been lifted, and Coca-Cola was finally back after a sixty-year absence. Yangon had gone from having one expat pub to at least a dozen, plus a handful of new restaurants and bars. Simon told me he'd have to entirely rewrite the introductory chapters.

Lonely Planet had never bowed to pressure to exclude Myanmar from its guidebook series – not even in 2000 when there were calls to boycott every title for its insistence on encouraging travellers to visit a country with such grave human rights abuses. Now that Myanmar was making positive political reforms, it had become the new travel darling of Asia and an updated guide was going to fly off the shelves.

AMONG ALL THESE NEW FACES, there was one I wasn't seeing as much as I expected: Sonny's. In the first couple of weeks after his release, he'd been in the office every day. He'd often be found standing at someone's desk animatedly discussing a story. Nine times out of ten, a circle of reporters would form around him. Sometimes when I was talking to him, I had to remind myself that he had only recently walked free from a prison cell and ended eight years of hell. His disposition reflected his name: sunny.

But then he started coming in less frequently and his face looked pinched and drawn. One morning I'd popped out the front of the building for a smoke when I saw Sonny coming towards me on the footpath. I smiled and called out a hello, but he walked straight past me as though I wasn't there. I figured there would probably be days when he was so consumed by traumatic memories that he wasn't fully present.

WHEN I RETURNED from lunch with Justin one afternoon, a mere few weeks after Sonny had been freed, we saw a couple of reporters reading a piece of paper that had been sticky-taped onto the glass wall next to reception. It was a note from Sonny, explaining that he was leaving *The Myanmar Times*.

'I am sad to go and it was a difficult decision, but it is the right decision,' the typed notice said.

I was stunned. Back at my desk, I began hearing rumours

about Ross freezing him out of the company he'd co-founded and done hard time for. Many of my Burmese colleagues were furious, though they still appeared outwardly calm. If what people were saying was true, I couldn't fathom why Ross would treat Sonny that way. Everyone adored him, and relationships meant everything in Myanmar.

The exodus of Burmese staff began the very next day. By the end of the week, we'd lost six senior editors and reporters. When Maisy resigned the following Monday, another four people went with her. We were haemorrhaging our best staff, right as we were expecting to get permission to become a daily newspaper. And we were losing them to our rival, the weekly current affairs magazine, *Mizzima*.

That was because Sonny was going to run it.

11

A MODEL MONK

JUNE 2013

I was too happy in my role as features editor to contemplate jumping ship to *Mizzima*. Ross allowed me to do plenty of travelling, so I spent a week working from our Mandalay bureau and another week in the Thai border town of Mae Sot, where I met Burmese people who had lost limbs to landmines laid by their own government.

I was also building up a solid network of contributors, and I loved getting to know the writers of Yangon. One of my favourites was the columnist and author Ma Thanegi. She had contributed an excellent opinion piece on gender relations in Myanmar for a special report called 'The Modern Woman' and after filing the piece, she invited me to her apartment for a cup of tea. I was frankly honoured to go.

Ma Thanegi opened the door with a mischievous smile on her painted red lips. She was short and slight and full of energy, with cropped hair and oversized spectacles that gave her an owlish look. Her apartment was halfway up an ugly block of flats on the edge of bustling Chinatown, but as soon as I stepped inside I discovered she had created her own world: it was light and breezy and full of bookshelves, pot plants, rattan furniture and antiques. A serene-looking Buddha made of marble sat on a mantelpiece above a court jester carved out of teak and dipped in gold leaf. She told me who some of the people were in the sepia photographs on her display cabinet, and showed me one of herself as a young intellectual. For a time she had worked as a volunteer assistant to Aung San Suu Kyi; not only was the job unpaid, it also came at a high price. She was arrested after the mass student protests of 1988, known as the 8888 Uprising, and spent the next three years in Insein Prison (which is pronounced 'insane' and rightly so, from all the accounts I've heard of it). She subsequently fell out with her former boss over sanctions – Ma Thanegi believed that they only hurt ordinary people and didn't stop the military from behaving appallingly. Aung San Suu Kyi and her party disagreed.

I told Ma Thanegi once again how much I enjoyed her essay, and she grinned and said that most Westerners fail to understand gender relations in Myanmar.

'Things aren't how they appear on the surface. Outsiders assume that because Myanmar is a poor country, its women are oppressed and that there is nothing more to say. And of course we do have these sexist sayings, like: "Treat your husbands like a god and your son like a master." But it's an illusion. Burmese women have far more power than they let on. This is what allows them to keep it.'

She stared at me intently, giving me time to think over what she'd said.

'I don't know of any other country but Myanmar where it's customary for the husband to hand over his entire salary to his wife every month,' I ventured. 'That certainly doesn't happen in the West. It would be unthinkable, actually. To me, it shows that Burmese women make some important decisions at home about the family's finances.'

'People sometimes gloss over the fact that women control

the purse strings,' Ma Thanegi replied. 'It's one of those inconvenient truths. Fancy another biscuit?' She handed me the plate and wandered off towards the kitchen, saying the kettle had boiled. Ma Thanegi had never married, and thus had always been in charge of her destiny: I couldn't imagine it any other way.

When she returned, I asked her how long it had taken her to write her memoir. She'd given me a copy of *Nor Iron Bars a Cage* when we first met at the office, and I'd found it so interesting. She maintained that prison wasn't entirely bad, and described how the motley collection of female inmates banded together to keep up morale, such as by caring for the mice that became like pets to them. One of my favourite lines from the book is this: 'We were supposed to be miserable and were damned if we'd oblige.'

'Was prison actually tolerable?' I asked, amazed by her strength of character.

'It was okay – really,' she told me. 'It certainly didn't defeat us. Us women got through it together, and we came out as strong as ever.'

I encountered a similarly indominable spirit as Ma Thanegi's when I later interviewed a stand-up comedian called Zarganar. He went to prison four times, for a total of eleven years, for telling jokes that offended the military (needless to say, he just kept on telling jokes, and had been released only a year earlier in a pardon). Zarganar had also been tortured. He told me that one time he was buried up to his neck in sand. A jeep was driven at full throttle towards him and the driver shouted that he was going to crush his skull. The vehicle swerved to miss Zarganar at the very last moment. This particular torturer found himself in prison following a purge of Military Intelligence, and Zarganar took it upon himself to visit him and send him food parcels every month. It made the once cruel man weep.

ALONG WITH GETTING to know contributors and collaborating on story ideas, another aspect of my job that I loved was creating the cover image for the special reports. For the 'Modern Woman' report, I put some of my budget towards photographing a model called Khin Thazin. She had only recently been discovered, but she already had an enormous social media following, with hundreds of thousands of online fans. She was lovely, with huge eyes, dewy skin and an incredible figure. I picked her up in a taxi on the way to a photography studio on the perimeter of Aung San Stadium, along with our photographer Boothee and the make-up artist, a tall transgender woman with frizzy, copper-coloured hair.

As neither Khin Thazin nor the make-up artist spoke English, Boothee explained my vision for the cover, which was to highlight the opposing forces of tradition and modernity on Burmese women. We would 'split' Khin Thazin in half, with one side representing modernity, and the other, tradition.

As Myanmar had started opening up to the world, young people in particular were being exposed to outside influences, such as the wildly popular Korean soap operas, and overseas fashions were beginning to creep in. Although the vast majority of women still wore ankle-length *longyis* and blouses with high necklines and sleeves, a few women in cities like Yangon and Mandalay had started wearing trousers and shorter skirts. A colleague at work had told me that short skirts were out of the question for her as an office worker – but this was for purely practical reasons. Like most people, she rode to work each day in a pick-up truck. 'How could I step up into the back of the truck in a short skirt?' she explained.

Although tastes were changing a little, society was still so conservative that when Aung San Suu Kyi was photographed wearing jeans during a recent visit to Mongolia, she had been lambasted on a couple of Burmese-language news websites. Even the country's democracy icon could find her clothing choices criticised.

As soon as we were inside the studio, the make-up artist got to work, dipping into her large make-up case to retrieve sponges and tiny brushes. With deft strokes and flourishes, she made half of Khin Thazin's face natural-looking, with the yellow bark paste *thanaka* smeared across her cheek. Her other side looked like she was headed for a nightclub, with a smoky eye and dark cherry lips. Boothee then photographed Khin Thazin in two different outfits. She wore traditional dress for the first one, and for the second, she was dressed in somewhat more revealing clothes: it was the type of outfit that would alarm some Burmese parents if their daughters wore it. All the clothes belonged to Khin Thazin, and she seemed to have equal affection for both looks. She showed genuine pride about the beauty and elegance of Myanmar's traditional dress.

Later, our graphic designer Ko Phyo melded Khin Thazin's two looks together and superimposed a zipper that ran down the middle of her face and body. The headline I chose was: 'The Modern Woman: Who is She Today?' We had an article on why modesty should not preclude women from getting a vaccine for cervical cancer, another on housewives sharing their frustrations and dreams (all under an alias), another on changing fashion trends, and a profile of a female taxi driver – an incredible rarity in Yangon. We also included the names and professions of 50 outstanding Burmese women, alongside their photos. My contribution was an interview with an extraordinary woman called Susannah Hla Hla Soe. She had been lobbying the government to properly respect the UN's convention on eliminating discrimination against women, and to update a divorce law from 1947 stipulating that a former husband must pay a woman the equivalent of just ten cents a month in child support. As a member of the Karen ethnic minority group, she was also lobbying the president to include women in the ongoing peace process with Myanmar's ethnic minority groups.

I was thrilled with the final product, and got major props from Ross. The feedback from our readers was so good that I decided to take everyone involved out for lunch to a nearby Chinese restaurant. Ross was more than happy to foot the bill.

ANOTHER COVER SHOOT that went really well was for a special report on Myanmar's automotive industry. My idea was to make it look like a James Dean movie poster. Myanmar scarcely had any new cars, but it had some beautiful old ones, and I'd arranged to borrow a 1969 Holden Premier that was owned by a friend of the newspaper's head designer. Our cover model was Pyi Phyo, who worked in the marketing department with Thandar and did some modelling on the side. He had a fresh-faced, boy-band look, with gorgeous, toffee-coloured tresses and a smile that could advertise toothpaste.

We met up for the shoot at a vacant lot and the car appeared bang on time, its engine emitting a deep rumble as it reversed in next to an old rusty shed. It was a burnt copper colour, with a long bonnet and bucket seats. Pyi Phyo wore a fitted black t-shirt with his sleeves rolled up, a pair of jeans, banged-up leather boots and shades. His hair was gelled to the nape of his neck. First Pyi Phyo sat on the bonnet, with one foot up on the fender and a smouldering, disaffected expression on his face. Then he sat in front of the car on the ground, with a knee raised and a nonchalant expression. In between each sitting, he checked his appearance in the side mirror, and would smooth down a stray hair or two. He wanted to be pictured smoking, just as James Dean often was, but I thought we'd better not encourage smoking among our readers – even though Ross wouldn't have minded (in fact, at the time, Ross told me he was contemplating putting the newspaper's logo on oversized lighters as free, branded merchandise).

We wrapped up the shoot at eleven, and by then it had become incredibly hot. The guy holding the shade reflector had drops of sweat rolling off his chin and Pyi Phyo's t-shirt was drenched. He was still as animated as ever though, and he laughed and joked in between shots.

Although I wasn't especially interested in cars, when it came to putting the content for the report together, I found it just as interesting as the one on women. I was discovering that even a mundane topic was turned on its head in Myanmar. That was because the country had been overseen by General Ne Win from 1962 to 1988 and then by General Than Shwe until 2010, and both dictators were probably clinically insane. Decisions were based on a combination of astrology and paranoia, and the consequences for the people were often devastating. By the time I had arrived in 2012, U Thein Sein had taken over the reins. He didn't have a personality disorder, though some claimed he was a puppet for General Than Shwe. Some people believed that the general wanted to avoid going to prison for the various war crimes he'd committed against his people, so he began launching reforms through his yes-man, Thein Sein.

Myanmar's automotive industry was a perfect illustration of how bizarre everyday life could become. One of our articles explained that as Myanmar was a former British colony, cars drove on the left side of the road. But in 1970, General Ne Win decided that everyone should drive on the right. He didn't give an explanation, although one popular theory is that he believed the country was moving too far to the left economically. His plan also had a tragic flaw. The vast majority of cars in Myanmar are second-hand, right-hand drives imported from Japan. These vehicles were of course designed to be driven on the left side of the road. With most drivers' line of sight badly impaired under the new rules, 5000 people died on Myanmar's roads every year, according to figures from Myanmar's traffic police force. As part of our coverage on the auto industry, we called on the authorities to do something to stop those preventable tragedies.

A COUPLE of days after the special report was published, I was heading for a meeting with Thandar upstairs when I almost collided with a young man as I came around the corner.

'I'm so sorry,' I began to say, before I realised it was our cover model Pyi Phyo. I almost hadn't recognised him because he was completely bald. Even his eyebrows were missing, which made his forehead look enormous.

'What happened to you?' I asked, my mouth agape.

'I just came out of the monastery,' he replied with his beautiful smile. 'I spent a week there as a novice monk. My family are very proud of me and made a lot of blessings.'

I knew that most young men in Myanmar had one or two spells in a monastery, but Pyi Phyo was the last person I could imagine living a spartan existence, rising in the dark, reciting Buddhist scripture, fasting until noon, not smoking and surrendering all his worldly possessions. Not to mention having his beautiful locks shaved off. And yet he looked positively delighted about it. I realised at that moment that it wasn't just young Burmese women who were being exposed to two diametrically opposed worlds. On an almost daily basis, Myanmar's youth were having to choose between an ancient set of customs and beliefs and the pleasures that were associated with becoming part of a globalised world. If Pyi Phyo and Khin Thazin were anything to go by, the young people of Myanmar would do just fine at this balancing act.

Jessica and Sherpa at the Shwedagon Pagoda

The Myanmar Times building in Yangon.

Moh Moh Thaw, Ross Dunkley, Tom Kean and Jessica Mudditt at the Christmas party of 2012 at Ross' house.

A trishaw driver in Yangon.

Our first home in Yangon was here in Mayangon township.

Sein Thein with a king cobra at Yangon Zoo.

A wet market in Chinatown in Yangon.

A fisherman in Labutta township in Ayeyarwady region.

Ogre Island in Mon State in 2012.

Children on Ogre Island (Bilu Kyun Island)

Win Sein Taw Ya reclining Buddha in Mon State.

Sherpa enjoying Myanmar Beer in Chinatown in 2012.

The cover of the special report titled, 'The Modern Woman.' Model - Khin Thazin. Photo - Boothee

The cover of the Wheels special report. Model - Pyi Phyo. Photo - Ko Taik

Monks wait for US President Obama to arrive at Yangon Airport in 2012.

With everyone who contributed to the special report on women by The Myanmar Times. That's Thiri to my left.

Sonny after his release from prison in April 2013.

Yangon Animal Shelter. Photo - Terryl Just

12

GONE

SEPTEMBER 2013

I had been the editor of the special reports for nearly a year when things at work began to change for the worse. One day I found myself stretching out yet another lunchbreak when I realised that my happiness in the office had been replaced with an actual loathing for it. My change in sentiment had coincided with the arrival of an American called Wendy. She was a friend of Ross' and he had hired her to help the newspaper transition from being a weekly to a daily. She made my life miserable.

The problem was the delay in getting the green light from the government to go daily. Several Burmese-language newspapers had received it, which maddened Ross, because he'd been certain that we would be the first cab off the rank. In the meantime, Wendy had turned her attention to what she called 'improving' various parts of *The Myanmar Times*, including my special reports. After an argy-bargy over introducing story quotas for reporters, which I opposed, fearing it would erode the quality of our reporting and my colleagues' willingness to pen features rather than quick news reports, Wendy had begun singling me out for criticism during meetings. I'd made a few attempts at calmly holding my corner, but when that proved futile I'd started to respond as Ripley would – by snapping back at her. I resisted every attempt to turn the special report articles into actual advertorials, but she was like a dog with a bone. Like a rottweiler, to be precise. Justin, Vincent and I were united in our dislike for her, and we sometimes fantasised about her downfall.

I was exasperated by her latest request, which was to audit my section to justify its existence. I'd dragged my heels, and when I eventually asked Thandar in marketing for some figures, I'd made a discovery that filled me with disgust. Ross was heavily inflating our readership numbers to advertisers, who were paying big sums. Ross also bartered advertising in exchange for free flights for expats on visa runs to Bangkok, as well as a number of other things. It seemed particularly low for a newspaper to be dishonest.

Gone was the overly enthusiastic, hard-working employee I once was. I had transformed into a snarky, sniping staffer and had even started pulling sickies for the first time in my life. I was tired of working six days a week, especially as Ross was batting away my requests for a raise from US$1500 a month.

I didn't like the person I had become, but what I felt worst about was bringing my frustrations home with me. In the evenings I'd have too much to drink and would start arguing with Sherpa. I could tell that he was getting fed up with me.

But even though I knew that things were bad at work, I didn't expect what came next. When I came into work one morning and saw an email from Ross that he'd sent the night before, I had to read it twice. As I did, stinging tears came to my eyes. I was being sacked.

Unsurprisingly, Ross cited my inability to get along with Wendy as the main reason for letting me go. But he also said that he had a problem with my husband working for a rival newspaper, and that I was 'badmouthing' the company. I didn't understand what he was referring to, as I thought I'd managed to keep my opinions to myself, other than confiding in Justin and Vincent. Ross tried to soften the blow by giving me two months' notice and even offered to give me a reference letter, provided I agreed to resign.

I had never been asked to leave a company before, and I felt winded by the rejection. Another part of me was enraged that Ross hadn't bothered to ask for my side of the story before siding with Wendy, even though they did have a longstanding friendship. Once the flavour of the month, I now felt like a discarded scrap.

I couldn't think straight, so I went outside for a cigarette. I took one deep drag after another and when I finished that cigarette, I immediately lit another.

Ugh, damn Wendy. Up until she came along, I had my dream job. Now I have no job.

By the time I'd stubbed out my second cigarette on the footpath, I knew what I was going to do. I had no legal obligations, as I'd never been given any paperwork to sign (which was yet another bugbear of mine). I wasn't going to work for another two months at an organisation that wanted me to leave. That would be humiliating. This would be my last day at *The Myanmar Times*.

I spent the day trying to tie up loose ends and at 4 p.m. I sent an email to my colleagues explaining that I was leaving and why. I'd also emailed Ross, but he'd not replied and hadn't been in the office that day. I'd preferred it that way, and maybe he had too. I got my belongings from my desk and drawers and put them into a cardboard box, and stuffed my backpack full of past issues of the special reports.

I met up with Justin at a beer station around the corner.

Justin had started working at *Mizzima* a couple of weeks earlier because he had been fed up with *The Myanmar Times*. He was the perfect drinking companion, and together we got blind drunk. Sherpa met us around 9 p.m. after working late, by which time I could scarcely string a sentence together. He had a couple of rounds with us and then helped me get my cardboard box into the back of a taxi.

Once home, I stumbled over the raised threshold in the doorway to our bedroom and fell flat on my face. My backpack landed on my head with a thud. I started sobbing, partly because my head hurt, but mostly from the pain of rejection.

Sherpa got down on all fours and rubbed my back.

'Everything is going to be okay,' he said. 'You weren't happy there and things had got pretty toxic. You loved freelancing in Bangladesh and now you can do it here.'

'I guess,' I said, and then hiccupped.

Sherpa wiped my wet cheeks with the back of his sleeve and smiled at me. 'Let's get you into bed,' he said gently.

WHEN I WOKE up the next morning, the reality of what I'd done began to sink in. I got up, but only to lie on the couch in an old t-shirt and boxer shorts, with my bottom lip sticking out. Sherpa had already left for work, so I switched on our TV and flicked through the channels on our new cable TV box. I realised with dismay that the TV and the couch belonged to Ross and that, at some point, I'd have to give them both back. The fridge too.

I started to feel scared. By being hot-headed and throwing Ross' offer to stay on for a couple of months back in his face, I was now jobless in a foreign country. There was no safety net of unemployment benefits – not even Burmese people had those.

After collecting my pay the following week, I'd have precisely $1500 to live off.

Wallowing in self-pity was a luxury I couldn't afford. I had to start finding freelance story ideas, and work out who to pitch them to. I switched off the TV and never turned it back on.

13

AUNG SAN SUU KYI AND ME

OCTOBER 2013

Cameras started flashing the moment Aung San Suu Kyi's diminutive frame appeared out of a doorway at the hotel where she was about to give a speech. People shrieked: 'Daw Suu! Daw Suu! Daw Suu!' Bony elbows jabbed my sides and I winced as someone trod on my toe. There was a strong scent of sweat and nicotine. As she took a right towards the podium in the ballroom, the media scrum surged after her as though trying to escape a burning building. She had no obvious security detail in sight and the photographers closest to her were motioning for others to back off and give her some space. Despite the fact that everyone else was hyperventilating, she seemed completely calm. She walked slowly towards the front of the room, a small smile playing on her lips.

Every journalist in Yangon had turned out to see the democracy icon in the flesh. I was there for the Sunday pages of *The Bangkok Post*. Behind the media were a couple of hundred others who had got wind of the event. Aung San Suu Kyi's public appearances were still quite rare, and she had been released from house arrest only three years earlier, in 2010. She had come to the Inya Lake Hotel that day to launch a book by an American photographer called Richard K. Diran. At first, I thought it was odd for someone of her stature to head up a book launch, but I soon realised that it was no ordinary book. I also think she genuinely loved books. She had recently become the patron of Myanmar's first literary festival, and no doubt reading had been a great comfort to her during the years of house arrest.

I had interviewed Richard the day before. He had been doing back-to-back interviews at the coffee shop in the hotel but in no way did I get the sense that he was trotting out the same lines to reporters. He told me with dreamy eyes how Aung San Suu Kyi had agreed to be the guest of honour at the event for his book, which had first been launched by the UN in London in 1997, but had never been available in Myanmar under military rule.

'Aung San Suu Kyi was under house arrest in 1998 when I first sent her a copy of *Vanishing Tribes*,' he said. 'I couldn't believe it when I got a thank-you note back from her. She said she hoped we'd meet one day. It's taken fifteen years, but that day is tomorrow.'

Richard had begun visiting Myanmar in 1980, before I was even born. He originally came looking for rubies and sapphires but got distracted when he noticed the incredible traditional dress of various tribes, the likes of which he'd never seen before. Tourist visas were only a week long back then, but he was a determined man and made countless flying visits from his home in Thailand over the next seventeen years. Getting in and out of these remote areas quickly was an impressive feat in itself, let alone capturing stunning images of forty different ethnic groups. Most of the places he went to were off-limits to foreigners, but a chance encounter with the son-in-law of Myanmar's dictator General Ne Win allowed him to get the travel permissions he needed. The last time anyone had undertaken a similar project was a century earlier, when a Scottish journalist and colonial administrator by the name of Sir George Scott compiled information on Myanmar's ethnic groups. Scott later published a book called *The Burman* under a Burmese pseudonym. Richard referred to the classic text as his 'tribal bible'. No one had ever created such a comprehensive visual collection, which was why Richard's photos were about to be exhibited, first at the Inya Lake Hotel for a month, and then permanently at the National Museum in Yangon. It was yet another sign of the changing times.

To me, Richard's stories were as incredible as his photos, and I listened to him, enraptured.

'A couple of girls from the Lakha tribe told me that there was just one month a year when marriages were permitted to take place,' he said as he stirred a teaspoon of sugar into his second black coffee. 'Who a person could marry was determined by throwing chicken bones into the air and seeing which way they landed.'

'What if they weren't happy with the result?' I asked.

'They were allowed to repeat the process. But just the once. And if that still didn't work out, and if they'd had "improper relations" with someone else, they were given a length of rope and a hole was dug. They were expected to hang themselves from a bamboo pole.'

'That's so terrifying,' I said.

'Well, by the time I got there, the practice had ended. It was recorded by Scott in 1900. Another extinct practice I learnt about was the putting to death of twins. The Akha tribe believed that only animals had multiple births and that it was impossible to tell the "good" twin from the "bad".'

'Gosh, that is really full on. Tell me, Richard, of all the tribes you photographed, which was your favourite?'

Without missing a beat, he replied, 'It has to be the Naga people. These guys were real warriors, and had muscles like mountain goats. Their faces were stone cold, with glazed eyes. They wore tiger-claw necklaces. And I knew that they them-selves, or certainly their fathers, had taken heads. What I found interesting was that the head-taking was a symbolic ritual of manhood and not an act of violence or revenge.'

Richard was clearly in his element, and leant forward in his seat.

'The Wa tribe were more indiscriminate. They would take any head. I once met the formidable king of the Wa, who told me that the season for tribal killings is April and May. He said the most prized heads were either Indians, Manipuris or Bengalis, because they had long beards that were good for fertil-ising crops. In one Wa village, a whole pathway was lined with lanterns containing human skulls. Mind you, I didn't see that. By the time I got there, the Communist Party had smashed all the skulls.'

Myanmar is one of the world's most ethnically diverse nations, but its ethnic minorities are among the most perse-cuted. The military government tended to treat them as terror-ists or savages, or both. At best, they were ignored – and at worst, they were stripped of their citizenship and herded into camps with no schools or doctors, such as the Rohingya. The majority Burman race was considered racially superior in an old-school eugenics kind of way, and this type of thinking had grown worse under the military regime. Many ethnic minorities were having to abandon ancient cultural practices as a means of self-preser-vation. So the fact that Richard had taken the time to photo-graph Myanmar's ethnic minorities had impressed Aung San Suu Kyi, and launching his book was an act of defiance against a xenophobic government.

As we wrapped up the interview, Richard invited me and Sherpa out that night for a drink with him and his wife, Junko. Delighted, I agreed, and we met up a few hours later at a beer station. Richard's wife reminded me of Yoko Ono, both in her looks and the fact that she seemed a powerful muse for her husband. She'd dreamt that Aung San Suu Kyi launched Richard's book – that's how the idea for it came about. She flicked a strand of her long, straight, jet-black hair as she told me they had a pet bald eagle and a baby cheetah at their apartment in Bangkok.

'Don't they fight?' I asked.

'Oh no, our apartment is huge. They don't even notice each other,' she said with a quixotic smile. 'All our animals get along just fine.' I figured Richard must have made a mint on those Burmese rubies.

As we downed more beers and snacked on skewered prawns, lotus flower and liver, we became increasingly sentimental about Aung San Suu Kyi.

'I adore her,' I declared. 'She's a big reason for me being here. I wouldn't have come to live in Myanmar if it were simply under military rule and without any hope of democracy being restored. It would be too depressing – like working in North Korea.'

'Yes,' said Richard. 'Myanmar has definitely had its share of dark days.'

'More like dark decades,' said Junko.

'The question,' Richard said thoughtfully, 'is whether she will get the opportunity to lead the country. The military may have released her from house arrest, but it doesn't mean they will let her be president. Her father held so much promise but he was dead before he had the chance to govern. I often wonder where Myanmar would be today if he hadn't been murdered.'

I had never heard of Aung San before I arrived in Myanmar, so I was surprised to discover that he was far more famous than his daughter. Don't get me wrong: Aung San Suu Kyi was very famous, but her dad had almost reached deity status. He was the father of the nation and had fought for independence against the British, who had ruled the country since 1885. After World War II, he signed an agreement with Britain that guaranteed Myanmar independence within a year, by 1948. He also negotiated a deal guaranteeing autonomy to several of the country's ethnic minorities. But just months before independence became official, he and six members of his cabinet were shot dead by assassins in the middle of a meeting at the secretariat. At the time, Aung San Suu Kyi – his only daughter – was just two years old. The heinous crime was never solved.

Photos of Aung San were everywhere: in shops, living rooms and on the dash of the taxi I had taken to the hotel that morning. His face had been on the currency too, until the military decided to remove it. Aung San was one of the nation's most prominent student leaders and his refusal to bow down to authoritarian colonial rule continued to inspire young people in their fight against military rule. He had also founded the present-day military, but became an inconvenient icon for them because of the association with his democracy-loving daughter. It was almost always the same sepia photo of Aung San that was on public display: he wore a peaked military cap and a military-issue winter coat with huge lapels. He was an unusual-looking man and did not share his daughter's good looks. His eyes were as small as peanuts, and he had pointy ears and extremely broad cheeks that made him look a bit emaciated.

By contrast, until recently, people dared not even say Aung San Suu Kyi's name aloud: she was instead referred to in code as 'The Lady'. But this was changing, with street-front shops beginning to sell posters both of Aung San *and* Aung San Suu Kyi.

'I think one of the reasons why Aung San Suu Kyi has been able to play the long game so successfully is that she feels duty-bound to finish her father's work,' said Richard as he refilled our glasses from a frothy jug of Myanmar Beer. 'I am certain that the persecution of Myanmar's ethnic minorities will end if Aung San Suu Kyi leads the country. They have lived in the shadows for too long.'

'I couldn't agree more,' I said. 'If only the world had more leaders like her.'

We held up our glasses and made a toast to better times ahead for Myanmar's ethnic minorities. What fools we were.

DURING THE INTRODUCTORY speech made by one of the event organisers, I snaked my way further to the front. I had watched a lot of bands over the years and used the same ploys I did at concerts to secure myself a better vantage point at press events. I tried to avoid getting dagger looks by mumbling an apology, smiling and making eye contact with the person I was side-stepping. But after doing that a few times, I realised it wouldn't be possible to get any closer. The crowd was simply too unyielding; reporters and photographers stood shoulder to shoulder, without so much as an inch between them. There was a kerfuffle just as Richard was wrapping up his speech, with one of the photo panels almost toppling over. As the crowd resettled and the organiser asked for quiet, I took in the portraits next to me. One featured a striking shot of a young Hkahku woman with a large amber cylinder in her earlobe. Next to it was a portrait of a fierce-looking Chin woman whose face was covered in intricate black tattoos.

The crowd roared as Aung San Suu Kyi approached the podium. She was about two and a half metres from me. She looked out at the crowd and our eyes met for a brief second – it felt surreal. Up close, I was even more impressed by her ageless-ness. She was sixty-five, yet her hair was still almost completely black, with a few wisps of grey around her temples. A string of yellow roses framed the base of her ponytail, which were the same colour as her shimmering satin *longyi*. To me, she looked like a lovely little mouse, with a perfectly straight nose that broadened ever so slightly at the end, inquisitive, soulful eyes and high cheekbones. Hers was a look of gentle femininity – it was hard to believe she'd defied one of the world's most ruthless armies and spent sixteen years under house arrest. And here I was, in the same room as her.

But when Aung San Suu Kyi opened her mouth and started talking, I did a double-take. Who was this person in front of me speaking in a posh British accent? I knew she'd spent a quarter of a century in the UK and had studied at Oxford University, but it was nevertheless surprising that there wasn't a trace of a Burmese inflection. She also seemed uncertain of where to place her emphasis and came off sounding stiff and remote. It was so unexpected and jarring. Had I really never listened to one of her speeches on YouTube? Now that I thought about it, I suppose very few were broadcast. She'd penned bestselling books, so I'd assumed she'd be a skilled orator. As she continued talking in a monotone about peace and national reconciliation, I hated myself for feeling disappointed. Just one sentence tickled me, and I later saw that every media outlet ran it as a quote: 'Thank you to Mr Diran for bringing beauty into my life when it was least expected.'

As I FILED out of the exhibition hall, I knew that I wouldn't tell anyone my feelings. I wouldn't dare, even if I knew how to articulate them. Criticising Aung San Suu Kyi for having a snobby-sounding accent wasn't even valid. Deep down it felt like more than the accent though – it hinted at an attitude I found troubling. But I knew that I would be the one to come off as an idiot

143

for criticising someone so iconic, and a Nobel Peace Prize winner. It was like saying, 'What do I think of Nelson Mandela? I don't really rate his live performances.'

But then I went home and Sherpa asked, 'So, how was she?'

'She was okay.'

'Just 'okay'? You were so excited.'

'Well, the thing is, I was actually a bit disappointed. She wasn't as I imagined her.' And then I blurted out how I felt. I should have known I'd tell Sherpa everything – I always do. When I finished, he said, 'Well, maybe she is a bit of a snob.'

I laughed at the sacrilege.

'Maybe,' I said. 'A much-loved snob though.'

14

TAKE ME TO THE TEMPLES

JANUARY 2014

After getting a few freelance stories under my belt for *Mizzima* and *The Bangkok Post*, I decided to take advantage of the freedom I'd gained when I lost my job. I longed to go travelling again, and it seemed remiss of Sherpa and me to have lived in Myanmar for so long without visiting the country's two most popular tourist destinations, Bagan and Inle Lake. I asked *Mizzima*'s commissioning editor, Julian, if he'd take a couple of travel stories and he agreed, so I figured I could make back some of the money I spent.

The truth was that I also wanted to lick my wounds outside Yangon. Every time I was anywhere in the vicinity of the *Myanmar Times* building it triggered painful memories of being terminated. My self-esteem had taken a hit and I found myself going back over events and asking whether I should have done things differently (most often, the answer was yes). My confidence as a journalist had also nosedived, and I'd started second-guessing my story ideas and even my choice of words in articles, which was maddening. I hoped that by bookending the *Myanmar Times* chapter of my life with a journey, I could begin a new one without constantly looking over my shoulder into the shadows of the past.

I usually had a hard time convincing Sherpa to take time off work, but not for this trip. It was plain to see that I was still a bit down and out, and he too wanted to visit Bagan's thousand-year-old temples and Myanmar's famed Inle Lake.

Unfortunately, our holiday began badly when we checked into our hotel room and I realised that I'd left one of my bags at the airport. It happened to be the bag containing all my clothes – the smaller one that I hadn't forgotten just had my toiletries, shoes and a couple of notebooks. I prided myself on being a savvy traveller, so I kicked myself for being so careless.

'I can't believe it,' I moaned to Sherpa. 'I don't want to waste our time here looking for undies.'

With most Burmese women being so petite and me being quite tall, I knew I'd struggle to find any underwear that would fit me – if I could even find any at all. I had given up on buying shoes in Myanmar long ago for the same reason. Plus, ladies' underwear tended not to be on display at street stalls for reasons of modesty, and Bagan was far too small to have a shopping mall. I grimaced as I imagined myself hand-washing my one pair of underpants in our bathroom sink at the end of each day.

We hailed a shabby-looking taxi from the main road in the riverside town of Nyaung-U for the return trip to the tiny airport, which was about twenty minutes away. As we pulled up at the entrance, I rushed inside ahead of Sherpa, leaving him to pay the driver.

I held my breath as I scanned the airport hall, where a few Japanese tourists were milling about. There on its lonesome in the middle of the room was my dusty black bag, ripe for the taking but untouched. Ecstatic, I grabbed it and started wheeling it outside, where Sherpa met me with a grin. I was relieved, although not altogether surprised. Myanmar may be a poor country, but theft was very rare. While the criminal penalties were severe, I believed that the Buddhist society's belief in karma and non-materialistic values were also at play. And it certainly wasn't the first time that I was immensely grateful for it.

FOR ME, the more I learn about a place, the more excited I get about visiting it. In the case of Bagan, I was hardly able to contain myself. I had written an article about its pending bid for UNESCO World Heritage status when I was at *The Myanmar Times*, talked to everyone I knew who had been there, and ogled countless photos of its beguiling terracotta temples ensconced by mist, with hot air balloons drifting dreamily overhead. This very scene graced the cover of my dog-eared *Lonely Planet* guide, and I read parts of it to Sherpa over our first breakfast at the hotel. We were filling ourselves up on a buffet of greasy fried eggs, white toast, chow mien, and fruit juice so sugary that it was more like a syrup.

'The temples were built between the eleventh and thirteenth centuries, as the region transformed from Hinduism and Mahayana Buddhism to Theravada Buddhism.'

'Which, as we know, is the most hardcore branch of Buddhism,' Sherpa noted, referencing the fact that this school considers itself the closest to maintaining the original teachings of Lord Buddha.

'Conservative, yep,' I agreed.

'The timing is interesting,' he added, before taking a sip of black coffee. 'It means that modern-day Myanmar became overwhelmingly Buddhist at around the same time Islam took over Bangladesh, with Hindus there also becoming a minority.'

Sherpa loved finding linguistical and cultural connections

between neighbouring Bangladesh and Myanmar. Just the night before, he'd been reading his Burmese dictionary in bed when he exclaimed delightedly, 'I've worked out the Sanskrit roots of the Burmese word for "moon"!' Many words in his native Bangla also had Sanskrit roots, and it excited him to discover that the two languages shared links to India's ancient language.

I found Sherpa's intelligence very attractive. His late father had been a professor of Islamic studies and it was clear that Sherpa had inherited his love of learning. I myself was totally lacking in linguistical aptitude and still could scarcely string a sentence together in Burmese, yet continued telling myself that I would mend my ways.

Mercifully, Sherpa was in charge of the map of the vast temple complex that the hotel had given us. It included 3000 temples, pagodas and monasteries in an area covering 100 square kilometres. I didn't fancy my chances of navigating us to the big-ticket temples.

We set off on electric bicycles that we hired from a rental place a short walk away. I zoomed along behind Sherpa with a huge grin on my face. I loved having the freedom of cycling combined with the bike's silent motor, which meant that my thighs wouldn't turn to jelly and I wouldn't be drenched in sweat. We overtook tourists lolling about in the back of horse-drawn carts who, by the looks of it, didn't mind that they weren't getting anywhere in a hurry.

'Do you want to take a look down there?' Sherpa asked as he pulled up beside a narrow track that led to three temples, each no bigger than a garden shed.

I agreed, and we began skidding along the sandy path towards the temples. Up close, I saw that one was in ruins, while the other two looked suspiciously perfect, as though they'd been built just the day before. I ran my hand over the reddish-brown bricks, which looked like any you'd find on a suburban home. I suspected the two temples had been overzealously restored by the military government – although it seemed strange that they hadn't touched the third. In my research for the article, I'd learnt that *National Geographic* magazine had accused the government of going on a careless restoration blitz in the 1990s after an earthquake in 1975 had damaged many of the monuments. The regime had apparently used cookie-cutter replacement bricks that detracted from the temples' authenticity, and added questionable new additions to the area. These included an eighteen-hole golf course (because many military high-ups are keen golfers) and a highway that cuts through the middle, which we'd been riding our bikes along. They also forcibly relocated the local residents of Old Bagan to a peanut field in what is now unimaginatively known as 'New Bagan'. This was part of the reason why Bagan's bid for UNESCO World Heritage status had not progressed for twenty years (happily, it got there in the end in 2019).

Nevertheless, as we poked around the base of the padlocked temples, I marvelled that there was not another single soul in sight. I'd loved Angkor Wat in Cambodia, but it was clear that this was going to be a very different experience. Due to Myanmar's reputation as a repressive pariah state, it got a fraction of the tourists Cambodia did, and Bagan had far more temples to explore. Another plus for Bagan was that it wasn't littered with landmines, so it was safe to wander off the beaten track.

We headed off again in the direction of Dhammayangyi Temple, which is Bagan's biggest. It really is enormous, with a pyramid-shaped roof and four grand wings that extend out in each direction. It is surrounded by a solid brick fence that is taller than a bus and yet only a fraction of the temple's height. Within its expansive grounds is a scattering of acacia trees, under which a few hawkers park their motorbikes in the shade. A small group of grey-haired Western tourists stood out the front of the temple's elegant arched entrance, swatting flies and listening to their Burmese travel guide explain its 800-year history.

King Narathu reportedly built the temple to atone for his sins, which included murdering his brother and father so that he could ascend the throne. He had also killed one of his wives, an Indian princess, because she'd continued to practise Hinduism instead of converting to Buddhism.

It's questionable how repentant the king was, though, because he had still behaved atrociously while the temple was built. He demanded that his workers make the bricks fit together so tightly that a pin couldn't pass between them. If they failed to achieve this ridiculous degree of perfection, he had their arm chopped off. The amputations took place inside one of the temple's entrances so that all the other workers could see and take note.

Unquestionably a man with many enemies, King Narathu was assassinated before the temple was completed. Its entrances are bricked up and the military government has never attempted to restore it, possibly because it festers with bad karma.

I didn't chop off anyone's arm, I mused as I padded my way along an outer corridor with enormously high ceilings. *And I didn't kill anyone either. I just didn't get along with Wendy and was probably quite annoying and lost my job as a result.*

I've always found history very calming, and an excellent antidote to being self-absorbed. Bagan was living proof of how empires rise and fall, and how kings and queens, no matter how vast their wealth, end up dying just like the rest of us. My dramas and foibles suddenly seemed microscopic, and acknowledging this made me more peaceful. I was pleased to already be gaining some much-needed perspective on the recent past.

We rode our bikes to a nondescript restaurant for lunch, where we were served by a young woman whose entire face and neck were smeared with dried yellow *thanaka*. Even her eyelashes had a dusty yellow hue. Her two children played on the floor near our table, while their grandma peeled garlic out the back.

With full bellies after a delicious lunch of Shan tomato salad and pork curry, washed down with avocado smoothies (a Burmese speciality), we wandered into the textile mill across the road. According to the sign out the front, it was operated by Padaung women, who were the real drawcard for tourists. The 'giraffe-necked' Padaung women are the most striking of all Myanmar's ethnic groups, if not the most striking in the entire world. They look as though they have been decapitated and their dismembered heads placed on top of a set of brass coils, which could be four or five times the length of the average human neck.

Even though I was expecting to see them, I still did a double-take at the sight of two Padaung women sitting on the bare floor. They had their legs straight out in front of them, which I noticed were also covered in brass rings from the ankle to the thigh. They wore chunky silver bangles and operated the handlooms a bit like an upside-down harp. It was unfathomable to me how they could wear so much metal while maintaining this position all day long – I can scarcely sit cross-legged for ten minutes without my back starting to ache. Their faces were lined with deep wrinkles, like the grooves in a silty creek bed, and they wore brightly coloured peasant-style head scarves, with a choppy fringe poking out underneath. The women smiled at us as we entered, and I tried not to gape.

One theory goes that the coils were originally a form of protection against tiger attacks, and that over time the custom came to be considered a mark of beauty. The process begins when a Padaung girl is as young as two, as her bones are small and supple. Longer coils are gradually added over the years. I'd assumed that a woman's neck would snap if the coils were removed, but apparently this is not so. That's because the coils only give the illusion of the neck being stretched; it's actually the collarbone that is pushed down by the weight of the brass to the point of collapse, with the rib cage also becoming compressed. However, although the coils chafe the skin, they are only removed every few years for a refit, and certainly not for a quotidian event like sleeping.

I tend not to wrap my own neck in anything, and especially not while living in a hot climate like Myanmar's. But I nevertheless chose a striped black and white scarf from the display table. I paid a third Padaung woman about ten dollars more than what I felt was the going rate, but I didn't try to bargain because I was paying both for the scarf and the photos I was about to take. I understood that it was an implicit part of the deal.

In northern Thailand, tourists can pay a few dollars to poke around a Padaung village, where they live as refugees. Curious tourists turn up by the busload and the tribe have become financially self-sufficient; however, some people have labelled it as an exploitative 'human zoo'. I suppose it was voyeuristic of me to take photos of the Padaung women, but I also thought it may be condescending to decide that they shouldn't earn a living in this way. But I do think it would have been wrong to take photos without paying them for the privilege.

NEXT WE HEADED for Ananda Temple, which some historians have dubbed the 'Westminster Abbey of Burma'. Unlike the other temples, its vast facade is covered with a faded whitewash, and its architectural influences are quite strongly Hindu. It too, has a violent backstory: the king who commissioned it had the architects murdered so that its beauty could never be replicated.

I was getting the sense that many of Bagan's kings were afflicted by megalomania.

We left our shoes by a sign instructing visitors to enter with bare feet and escaped into the temple's cool and cavernous interior. It was officially winter in Bagan, yet by midday it felt as if someone was directing a giant blow dryer at us from above. With heat like this in January, the month of May had to be close to uninhabitable.

We walked around a shadowy passage until we came to a room filled with candles that housed a towering Buddha covered in gold leaf. Unlike the big-bellied Buddhas often seen in China, this one was lean, and dressed in a long cloak. While the Padaung women appear to have elongated necks, many Buddhas in Southeast Asia have noticeably elongated earlobes. This is not some artist's fancy but a key part in the story of how a mere mortal came to be known as the Lord Buddha.

While Buddha was growing up as a young Indian prince known as Siddhartha Gautama, his earlobes were stretched by the weight of jewel-encrusted earrings. When he was twenty-nine, he removed the earrings and relinquished all his worldly possessions to wander the earth in search of the end of suffering. Six years later, he discovered enlightenment as a monk. His extra-long earlobes therefore signify a rejection of the material world in favour of spiritual wisdom.

Three men in *longyis* kneeled before the Buddha, their hands clasped together as they gently rocked to and fro on their heels. They emitted a low hum of prayer recitations. Unlike Cambodia's Angkor Wat, Bagan was a place of active spiritual worship, and this made its temples even more atmospheric.

We continued along the dark passageway and discovered another three Buddhas that were almost identical to the first, before emerging into the blindingly bright sunshine. A group of child hawkers rushed over to us with cold drinks, sand paintings and postcards. I chose a set of postcards from a barefooted boy who looked to be about eight. He was a beautiful kid, with a megawatt smile and huge, almond-shaped eyes. His t-shirt was ripped and his forearm had a weeping sore, which buzzed with a couple of flies.

'Where are you from, miss?' he asked me.

'Australia.'

'G'day mate,' he quipped. 'Home of the kangaroo and koala.'

I'd never met a child who spoke like this in Yangon – he had the confidence and posturing of a twenty-year-old. And I was pretty sure that if I'd said I was from Spain, the boy would have greeted me in Spanish. I'd been sad to read in my *Lonely Planet* that a lot of local kids were quitting school to get into the growing tourist trade. It was a far bigger earner than working on the family farm – and apparently school couldn't compete with either alternative.

Sherpa and I continued biking our way around the dusty plains, and revelled in having so many of the temples completely to ourselves. Then, as the sun began to dip and the shimmering heat waned, we raced towards the towering, tent-shaped Shwesandaw temple – only to infuriate ourselves by making three consecutive wrong turns. By the time we arrived, hordes of people had already fanned out on the temple's five terraces, which were topped by a bell-shaped stupa and a bejew-elled parasol. A few strands of Buddha's hair are supposedly enclosed in a vault inside the temple, which is how the temple got its name: 'Shwesandaw' means 'golden holy hair'. I was discovering that Buddha's body parts are strewn across Asia, and this inspires devotees to undertake pilgrimages of vast distances.

As we queued to climb a set of extremely steep, thousand-year-old steps that cut through the middle of the tiered monu-ment, a busload of Chinese tourists chatted noisily as they filed off an air-conditioned coach, which was parked directly behind two others. As the tallest pagoda in Bagan, Shwesandaw has the best vantage point to watch the sunset, so the tourists that were dispersed during the day had congregated by the end of it.

We were a few minutes into the climb when I made the mistake of looking up to see how much further we had left to go. All I could see were bottoms, and at the same time, the man ahead of me accidentally kicked a gravelly bit of temple into my eye. I motioned at Sherpa below that I needed to stop, and we found a spot on a terrace midway up as I continued blinking furiously while trying to dislodge it. I wondered how much damage the temple was sustaining with a few hundred people climbing over it every afternoon.

Shwesandaw temple has 360-degree views but, even so, tourists were jockeying for the best spots for a photo. I took a few photos of an Irish couple who grinned with their arms round each other, and who then returned the favour for us. A rugged-looking German traveller with a blond topknot apologised as he stepped past the four of us, and then proceeded to back so close to the crumbling edge of the eastern side of the temple with his selfie stick that I had to look away. I half expected to hear his screams as he fell.

The sun soon dipped lower and everyone turned to face the sunset. Quietness fell over the motley collection of tourists. Rising above the flat-topped trees of a savannah were temples as far as the eye could see, shrouded in haze and turning a deep shade of red. Beyond that was a ridge of undulating mountains. This magnificent sweeping vista had been savoured by humankind for at least a thousand years. I could think of no other word for it than perfect.

~

OVER DINNER at a restaurant run by a French expat the following night, I flicked through the remaining pages of our guidebook's chapter on Bagan. The section describing the temples seemed to go on and on.

'The past couple of days have been amazing, but I think I'm templed out,' I confessed to Sherpa. 'And we haven't even scratched the surface of what there is to see.'

'That's true – but we'd need to spend at least a couple of weeks here to say that we had,' he said as he stroked a cat that was swishing opportunistically around his ankles. 'Maybe tomorrow we could swim at that hotel pool you mentioned, and just explore the temples in the afternoon?'

'Sounds perfect,' I said, suddenly awash with relief. 'Let's do that.'

A FEW DAYS LATER, we stepped off a small plane in Shan State. I was surprised by how crisp the breeze was, considering it was all blue skies and sunshine. We'd left the hot central plains for the cooler north-easterly region, which has a higher altitude and a temperate climate that makes it the nation's food bowl, as well as a place of respite for tourists unaccustomed to Myanmar's heat.

We spent the next few days speeding across placid Inle Lake in a chartered longboat, drifting by floating gardens, visiting monasteries, markets and stupas, and photographing Intha tribe fishermen, whose unique fishing technique has become one of Myanmar's most iconic sights. They stand right on the tip of their wooden vessel with one leg wrapped around an oar as they manoeuvre a large cylindrical net. It is an incredible feat of balance that makes for a striking silhouette. Our Intha guide told us that we'd need to pay the fisherman a tip to get any closer, and added with a smile that posing for photos had become a lot more lucrative than fishing.

For centuries, the Intha tribe have lived their lives on the lake and the word 'Intha' itself translates to 'sons of the lake'. Even so, I was gobsmacked as we passed through floating villages and saw toddlers calmly observing us from the porches of their homes on stilts. They were seemingly mature enough and balanced enough not to plop off the rickety bamboo structures and into the deep waters below.

When Sherpa and I weren't exploring the sights on the lake, we walked everywhere or rode bicycles. In the evenings we drank cheap cocktails at the local town of Nyaung Shwe's assortment of expat-friendly venues, and lingered over dinners where I savoured long-lost Western comfort foods. The nights were cold, so we snuggled up, talked for hours and slept in. Our days were slow and easy, and the bustle of Yangon felt light years away.

We spent our last afternoon at Red Mountain Winery. I knew that Myanmar had wineries, but it was still a delightfully unexpected experience. We sat at a picnic table sampling cheeses and wines cultivated by a French winemaker, while gazing at the picturesque valley below, where the rolling fields were a patchwork of verdant greens and fertile browns. It was bliss.

'I feel like I'm in France,' I kept boozily exclaiming to Sherpa, who had once again attracted a couple of hungry cats.

Before the light faded, Sherpa took a photo of me grinning among the grapevines, and when I uploaded it to Facebook, the Australian editor of *Democratic Voice of Burma* asked me to write an article about Myanmar's nascent wine industry. For a brief, winning moment, it felt like all my commissions would be that simple to come by.

❦

LIKE ANY GOOD HOLIDAY, it seemed all too soon before we found ourselves boarding our homeward-bound flight. I was pleased when we took off without incident, as Heho airport is notoriously tricky for pilots, as it has a short runway and is surrounded by mountains. A fatal crash on Christmas Day 2012 had brought this to my attention, and I'd heard from fellow travellers that things could get a bit hairy.

I got out my book to distract myself and was absorbed in it when twenty minutes later the plane suddenly hit turbulence. My first thought was how ironic it was to have assumed the danger had passed after take-off. Much to my relief, after a few frightening jolts, things went calm again. Sherpa and I exchanged a bashful smile, and I felt embarrassed by how quickly I'd taken fright. I wiped the sweat off my palms onto my trousers and resumed reading.

But then the plane encountered more turbulence, and this time it was severe. Drinks spilled and people screamed. I heard myself screaming. The plane couldn't seem to right itself – it was like we were in some kind of demented clothes dryer. I clawed at Sherpa's hand, probably painfully. He was staring blankly at the seat rest in front of him, composed but clearly afraid. An American woman behind us was crying. Two female flight attendants had managed to strap themselves into the jump seats ordinarily used for take-offs and landings after the first bout of turbulence. Both looked stricken.

When the plane nosedived sharply, I believed that we were done for. I thought about the children I'd wanted to have with Sherpa, and how we may never get to meet them. I also regretted not having quit smoking. I felt sickened by the prospect of our pain and powerlessness. Then I closed my eyes and prayed for the first time in twenty years.

After what felt like an eternity, though it was probably only a couple of minutes, the bumps became less violent. Still, I braced myself for yet another nosedive and could feel my heart thumping wildly inside my chest. Finally, there was stillness and we remained in the sky. I allowed myself to hope that we were going to make it to Yangon. The plane continued flying for another twenty minutes without so much as a word from the captain.

When we landed in Yangon, a few of us became teary-eyed. I gripped the handrail as I made my way down the stairs to the tarmac, unsure of whether my knees would buckle. If I'd needed further proof that my past troubles at *The Myanmar Times* were insignificant, I had it now.

'I'm not doing that again,' I said to Sherpa that night, as we chugged beers at home and delighted in being back on solid ground. 'At least, not if I can help it. I don't ever want to get on a plane again.'

Sherpa didn't try to argue with me, or say I was overreacting. He'd been terrified too.

About a month before I had been fired, *The Myanmar Times* had got me a one-year visa. These were incredibly rare. Like virtually all expats in Myanmar, I'd previously been going on visa runs to Bangkok every seventy days. I looked forward to those trips because I craved the creature comforts of Bangkok, such as uninterrupted supplies of electricity, microwave meals from 7-Eleven and buying clothes that fit me.

A year was a long stretch to spend in Myanmar, but I made up my mind that night to stay put, and that was exactly what I did. Once an intrepid traveller, I'd developed a fear of flying so great that just hearing the roar of a plane overhead gave me the heebie-jeebies. I told myself that by the time a year was up and I had no choice but to fly again, I'd somehow have overcome my dread of air travel.

15

SNAKES ALIVE!

FEBRUARY 2014

Our holiday had the desired effect on me. Once back home in Yangon, I threw myself into my new life as a freelancer and stopped beating myself up over things that had gone wrong in the past. I even went to meet Thiri for lunch and although I didn't dare accept her invitation to set foot inside *The Myanmar Times* building, I was no longer rattled by being in close proximity to it. Instead of averting my eyes, I waved a friendly hello to Tom as he walked past our table. He looked surprised to see me, but not aghast or anything. Over the years, Ross had fired a number of journalists, and my friend Vincent had been given the boot shortly after me. I decided that Yangon was too small a place to let things feel weird with my former colleagues.

Thiri and I were chatting away when a woman walked past with hair so long that it brushed her thighs. I commented that she was the third person I'd seen that morning with incredibly long hair.

'You should do a story about Myanmar's human hair trade,' Thiri said.

'What human hair trade?' I'd asked her incredulously, leaning forward in my seat.

~

WITHIN DAYS of being tipped off by Thiri, I found myself in a damp room in Thaketa Township staring dumbfounded at a mass of human hair covering the floor. I was sitting on a plastic chair and in keeping with custom, I had left my shoes outside by the doorstep. Strands of hair kept brushing up against my bare feet, which quite literally made my toes curl. I kept tucking my legs further underneath me, but the floor was scarcely even visible under the bounty of lopped-off ponytails.

I was interviewing a wholesale hair trader called U San Hlaing for a feature for *The Bangkok Post*. He was a big shot in Myanmar's human hair trade.

'U San Hlaing says that we are looking at about 20 kilograms of hair and that it was collected in just two days,' said my translator Raj. 'When Myanmar women become Buddhist nuns they must shave off their hair, and U San Hlaing buys it from them. He has four workers who circle the big monasteries in Yangon while calling out, "Cash for hair."'

I scribbled this down and then asked two more questions: How much hair can U San Hlaing sell each month? And where does it end up?

'The most he has sold is 650 kilos in one month,' said Raj, after listening intently to U San Hlaing. 'It is taken to China, Korea, India and the United States, where it is turned into wigs. Burmese hair is very beautiful and healthy, because it hasn't been damaged by hair dryers and chemical dyes.'

I watched U San Hlaing's slender young wife as she examined a bunch of hair, tenderly smoothing over the strands as though she were stroking a cat. The ponytails were mostly black and dark shades of brown, although there were also a few brassy oranges and even the occasional clump of brittle grey, which Raj said fetched a much lower price. The longer and more lustrous a ponytail is, the higher its value.

For reasons that weren't clear to me, U San Hlaing's wife popped a wispy dark brown ponytail into a small cabinet. Its single drawer was already overflowing with hair and couldn't close properly. Even though I knew there was nothing sinister going on, there was something downright creepy about the sight of so much human hair.

I was still getting a handle on the basics of the trade when a scruffy-looking buyer arrived. He greeted U San Hlaing perfunctorily and began stuffing a hessian bag full of hair without so much as glancing at it.

When the bag was full, the man took it out to his car and returned with several thick wads of kyat notes. U San Hlaing and the buyer lit cigarettes, while U San Hlaing's wife set about counting the money. Her gold bracelets jangled as she deftly flicked each note.

While she was still tallying up the total, a third man entered the room. Grinning, he held up a single ponytail that was at least a metre long. Despite its obvious value, U San Hlaing sent him away with a dismissive wave. The man shrugged and left, presumably headed straight for another buyer's premises.

Raj later told me that U San Hlaing couldn't buy the ponytail in front of the first buyer, because there was bad blood between the two men.

Along with constant infighting, U San Hlaing also had to deal with the occasional cheat who tried to sell him animal hair or synthetic hair.

'If he suspects the hair is fake, he will test it by burning a strand. Only human hair will turn to ash,' Raj translated.

With my notebook filled with fascinating insights into this

most unusual trade, we thanked U San Hlaing and his wife for their time and took our leave. It was time to meet the women who sold their hair.

RAJ and I took a taxi across town to a market in Insein Township. After wandering about the stalls for ten minutes, we found one with a thick black plait strung up from a pole above a set of metal scales. I was relieved, as it was drizzling and the market's grounds had already turned soupy. A thickset woman with a large mole on her cheek got up from her chair as we approached. She said that business had been slow that day, and complained that the hair trade wasn't as lucrative as it used to be. That was because overseas fashion trends were beginning to creep in, which meant that women were starting to sport shorter hairstyles.

'Sometimes a woman will sell her hair if her family falls on hard times – for example, if they suddenly need to buy medicines. But some days I have no customers at all,' she sniffed.

I was wondering how long we might have to hang around to meet a customer when a woman who looked to be in her fifties approached. Her own hair was thinning, so I was surprised when she produced a small freezer bag full of hair. Frankly, the clump of hair looked pretty unappealing, but the woman with the mole didn't even bother weighing it before handing over a 500-kyat note, which was the equivalent of about 50 American cents.

On my behalf, Raj asked her whose hair it was.

'It's mine,' the woman replied in Burmese, beaming. 'I brush my hair every morning and night and gather the hairs that are left in my hairbrush. After six months I have enough hair to sell and I come here. I'll go straight to my local monastery to donate the money. I'm so happy that I can give something to the monks.'

The woman shuffled away in the rain with her 500-kyat note tucked safely in her purse. For once I was silent, too humbled to speak.

LIFE AS A FREELANCER agreed with me. I loved being my own boss and I was free to pursue the stories that intrigued me, as opposed to being assigned a pre-arranged topic for the special reports every month, and which I'd been bound to repeat in my second year in the job. I'd set myself up with a desk that looked out onto the dirt road outside our house, where a herd of black goats was shepherded past every afternoon. Ripley often slept at my feet as I typed, as did an old red hen that I somehow ended up with after visiting a poultry market while on assignment for the *Democratic Voice of Burma*.

But while the article on Myanmar's human hair trade was quirky, if not a tad creepy, some stories were heartbreaking. I'd taken up writing for IRIN, the United Nations news service, for whom I'd previously freelanced in Bangladesh. The problems I wrote about tended to be monumental, such as the dire shortage of anti-venom in a country where 12,000 people are bitten by snakes every year. This was the focus of the first story I filed from Myanmar.

I began by meeting a snake bite specialist called Professor Khin Thida Thwin at San Pya Hospital, which had one of the country's few specialist kidney departments. She was working with the World Health Organization to try to lessen the number of snake bite deaths, which in recent years had been as high as 1000 people per year. By comparison, of the 5000 people bitten in an average year in Australia, only two people tend to lose their lives.

The problem was that Myanmar could only afford to produce half the antivenom it needed. For decades, Myanmar's military regime had spent as little as 0.5 per cent of gross domestic product on healthcare, which was among the lowest rates in the world. Millions of people simply couldn't afford to pay for medical treatment and often went without it, meaning they died a preventable death or lived in terrible pain. The reformist government had started to spend more, but it was still totally inadequate for overcoming years of systemic neglect.

Khin Thida Thwin made us a cup of tea from a thermos that she kept under her desk. She shared an office with another female doctor, who had left as I knocked on the door.

'Antivenom is made by injecting a non-fatal amount of venom into the veins of a thoroughbred horse and then extracting the antibodies from its blood,' she explained. 'But in Myanmar we can't afford to buy the horses, so last year we started using sheep instead. But they produce a lot less antivenom than a horse. And we haven't been able to buy nearly enough sheep. The budget constraints are severe.'

She said that Myanmar was also importing antivenom from India and Thailand to make up the shortfall, but it was often ineffective. Antivenom must be made locally, because even within the same species, snakes develop their own strain of venom, in much the same way as unique regional accents develop over time.

Despite her busy caseload, after the interview Khin Thida Thwin insisted on giving me a tour of the hospital. We walked up the hallway and I followed her into what I thought was a broom closet, but when she switched on the light I found myself facing four shelves of preserved snake specimens in jars. The snakes' yellowed faces were frozen mid-bite and their bodies wrapped in messy coils. There was an assortment of smaller jars containing baby snakes. It was a terrifying sight.

I trotted after her up a set of stairs as she led me to a ward in the kidney department, as it is kidney function that a snake bite impairs. We hovered briefly over a listless young man, scrawny as a rake and with the darkest of circles around his eyes. A clear tube had been placed under his nose and another poked out of his bandaged torso, parts of which were stained brown. The dialysis machine was no doubt working overtime in an attempt to rid his blood of toxins.

'This patient was bitten by a krait snake while working in a rice paddy,' said Khin Thida Thwin. 'Luckily, other workers were nearby when it happened. Often the snake bite victim is found dead and their family assumes they died of a heart attack or a stroke.'

We then entered a large ward where there were about 30 snake bite patients and their immediate family members, who cared for them around the clock due to the hospital being short-staffed.

I followed Khin Thida Thwin over to a fourteen-year-old patient called Day Wi. She'd been walking barefoot through a palm forest in southern Mon State when she was bitten by a Russell's viper, which is one of the most dangerous snakes in Asia. She lay on a thin metal stretcher and opened one eye when she heard Khin Thida Thwin's gentle voice asking her how she was doing.

I looked down at Day Wi's foot and gulped. It was a ghastly mess. My eyes were first drawn to two angry sores that were the size of lemons. One was a luminous red and the other, a hideous purple. The skin around the wounds was so blackened that it appeared to be charred. Across her foot and up her ankle was a series of festering blisters. It was so dramatic that it looked as though it had been created with stage make-up.

Day Wi's anguished mother stood over her, trying to cool her with a palm-shaped handheld fan. There was of course no air conditioning and the heat in the room was so oppressive that drops of sweat had begun running off my forehead and landing onto my notebook, making a mess of the ink of my scribbled notes. On the concrete floor next to the stretcher was a rolled-up sleeping mat and a bag of belongings. The mother and daughter were hundreds of kilometres away from home.

I showed Day Wi's mother my camera and gestured that I would like to take some photos of the wound. She nodded and took a couple of steps back from Day Wi, who I noticed at that moment was very beautiful. She lay there with her eyes closed like a Burmese Snow White after eating the poisoned apple.

I know that there is no such thing as an evil animal, but the horror and pain inflicted by the viper's bite was appalling. Day Wi's life had hung in the balance since she was bitten three weeks ago – it was only in the past day or so that Khin Thida Thwin had started to hope that the teenager might survive, because her kidney function was showing early signs of normalising. I wondered how long it would be until she could walk again.

'Day Wi is one of the lucky ones,' Khin Thida Thwin said gravely as we walked away. 'She is being treated in hospital. Many Myanmar people prefer traditional medicines. Those treatments include spreading a chicken carcass over the snake bite, or getting another person to suck the blood out of the wound. If the snake can be caught, its tail is chopped off and the victim swallows it. We are trying to educate the public about how ineffective, or even dangerous, this all is, but eradicating such practices is difficult. It's how things have been done for years,' she said with a sad smile.

This last bit of information fascinated me, but my word limit for the article for IRIN only allowed me to skim over it. So I pitched another story to my editor at *The Bangkok Post*, along with the idea of focusing on the cobra, which I thought was the most magnificent and terrifying of all snakes. In the course of my research I had learnt that cobras were plentiful in Yangon and were often found inside people's homes. I couldn't think of anything worse.

My editor gave me the green light, so I went with Raj to meet the reptile keeper at Yangon Zoo. He was reportedly the man to call if a snake was discovered somewhere it shouldn't be. And if it turned out to be a cobra, all the better: cobras were Sein Thein's favourite animal.

No sooner had he told us this than he stepped inside the cobra enclosure and fastened the latch on the wire door behind him. The cage was a bit like a chicken coop but with assorted ledges for the snakes to sunbake on. In the centre was a hutch, where I presumed they slept. It was absolutely teeming with snakes. They slithered all over each other, making it almost impossible to work out where one snake ended and another began.

'I get two or three calls every month from people who have found cobras in their home,' said Sein Thein. 'Last month, a housewife found a cobra in the toilet. Other times they've come peeking up through the kitchen sink. I've lost count of how many times I've been called after someone found a cobra in their suitcase. I always tell people: zip up your bags when you're not using them. It's a nice spot to curl up in if you're a snake.'

I counted six cobras slithering across the thatched roof of the hut, which stood at eye level with Sein Thein. They seemed intent on getting closer to him, but he didn't seem fussed in the slightest. In fact, he turned and faced Raj and me through the wire, thereby turning his back on the approaching snakes.

'Once I got a call from a young couple who had just returned to Yangon after spending a month visiting family in Singapore.

When they got home they were tired, so they got straight into bed. There was a cobra under the sheets!' Sein Thein roared with laughter. 'It just slithered out. They were fine, but the woman said she wanted to move house.'

As Sein Thein began telling us another story, one of the cobras flexed its hood and lifted the upper part of its body off the ground. It swayed to and fro behind him, flicked its forked tongue and zoned in on the back of his head.

'Oh my god!' I exclaimed – just as Sein Thein took a single step sideways and missed being struck by a hair's width. I had no idea how he sensed to do this. He turned around and waggled a finger at the snake.

'You come here,' he said, grabbing its tail with one hand. 'Let's take a good look at you.'

He brought the snake out with him and laid it on the concrete at the zoo's entrance area. With one knee on the ground, he used both hands to manoeuvre the snake, cupping one hand under its hood and the other to drape its body along the ground. Its silver scales were interspersed with thick beige stripes and it was at least three metres long. When it hissed, it sounded like a growling dog.

'This is a king cobra,' Raj explained, while looking on in disbelief. 'They are the world's longest venomous snakes. They eat pythons and other snakes in the wild, but here in the zoo we give them chickens. Sein Thein caught this one two months ago.'

The man and the snake eyed each other off – in Sein Thein's eyes I saw almost tender fascination, and in the cobra's, pure hatred. Zoo visitors had no option but to walk through the turnstile at close range to the spectacle, but the ever-calm Burmese families scarcely raised an eyebrow, although I did see one mother grab her little girl's hand as they approached us.

'Of course cobras come into people's homes,' Sein Thein

said, without breaking eye contact with the snake. 'Other snakes do too. They are hungry. With all these new apartment buildings going up in Yangon, the snakes are losing their habitat. A Buddhist will never kill an animal, but Myanmar people do all sorts of things to prevent them coming inside. They stir gold jewellery in a pot of boiling water and then sprinkle the water on the ground around their yard. If they have no jewellery, they drizzle lemon juice. Of course, none of this works in the slightest and the cobras come right on in,' he said, laughing again.

As the cobra kept trying to strike at Sein Thein, I asked him whether he had ever been bitten during his years working at the zoo.

'So many times!' he said. 'Twelve times, to be exact. I got bitten on the head a couple of months ago. I went blind for about three minutes. I was drenched in sweat too. My boss sent me to hospital, but I was fine. I was back at work the next day. It's no problem for me if I get bitten, because I have special tattoos. You want to see them?'

'Yes please.'

To our relief, Sein Thein returned the king cobra to its enclosure, snapped the door shut and motioned for us to sit at a nearby picnic table. It was only then that I became aware of how fast my heart was beating. Sein Thein, still standing, peeled off his blue polo shirt. Spanning his shoulder blade was an intricately detailed cobra with a flexed hood. Across his chest were smaller snakes and squares filled with numbers, swirls and squiggles.

'The ink is mixed with cobra venom,' he said. 'That is what protects me when I'm bitten. I get the tattoos re-inked three times a year, on the nights of a full moon.'

Sein Thein's face was deeply lined with wrinkles and his hair and eyebrows were greying, but he had the body of a teenage boxer – he was as lean as the reptiles he wrangled all day. I later asked a doctor whether Sein Thein's tattoos could actually provide protection, and was told it was impossible. It was the repeated bites that protected him: quite incredibly, he must have developed a resistance to the venom.

'Are there other snake catchers in Yangon?' I asked Sein Thein.

'I am the most famous,' he said. 'But there are others who catch cobras and sell them to Chinese restaurants. It is a popular trade in poor rural areas. The restaurants pay a good price because the Chinese love to eat cobra. They believe it gives them virility – you know, sex power,' Raj translated with a blush. 'I can tell you where to go if you want to write about it in your story.'

Sein Thein then excused himself, saying it was time to feed the crocodiles.

I'D DRIVEN past this particular Chinese restaurant in Bahan Township a thousand times, though I never thought I'd wind up there to eat a snake. I brought an American friend, Nick, along so that I looked like a tourist rather than a journalist, and left my notebook in my bag.

Sein Thein had told me that cobra wasn't listed on the menu, but available on special request. And sure enough, when I pretended to scan the menu and then innocently asked the waiter if cobra might be available, he seemed delighted and asked me how I would like it – as a soup, fried skin or kidney wine? The soup sounded the most palatable. Suddenly feeling daring, I asked the waiter if I could see the kitchen. I held my breath as I watched his face. Had I gone too far and triggered suspicion?

'Of course,' he replied, still smiling. 'Please follow me.'

I picked up my camera and jogged after him, leaving Nick at the table with a wink.

It was a large restaurant, but even so I was surprised by how enormous the kitchen was. There was a long L-shaped prepping bench, where a column of steam rose up amid a strong smell of sautéed garlic and ginger. A chef in a bloodied apron diced a white lump of flesh with a cleaver, while a young kitchen-hand separated the leaves from the stalks of watercress. The tiles on the sides of the bench were splattered with all manner of juices, both animal and vegetable. Even though the floor was wet and had probably recently been hosed down, I noticed that chunks of food were stuck in the grates of a drain that ran parallel with the bench.

At the end of the room was another grey slab of a bench, but this one was topped with six or seven hot plates, next to which was an enormous gas cylinder. Adjacent to that workbench was a row of chest freezers. Two idle kitchen-hands stared at me as we approached – or rather, I thought they were staring at us until a waitress in a high-necked fuchsia blouse with a comb speared through her bun overtook us. In between her thumb and her forefinger was the scaly tail of a pangolin. It writhed upside down in distress, with its long snout making a futile attempt to decode its surroundings. I managed to discreetly snap a picture of the unusual creature just before the waitress turned a corner and went out of sight. I later learnt that the pangolin is the world's most trafficked animal. Its scales are used as a traditional medicine or turned into fashion accessories.

We walked to the end of the kitchen and entered a dimly lit backroom that smelt of death. There were cages jammed on top of each other containing rabbits, ducks and sick-looking bald chooks. Four turtles sat motionless in a shallow bucket of water on the floor. The waiter picked up an iron rod with a hook on the end and rapped on the lid of an oil drum.

'Inside are ten cobras and three vipers,' he said, waving the rod at the three drums. 'Would your friend like to try the viper perhaps?'

'We would both like cobra,' I said, feigning enthusiasm.

He removed the lid from the middle drum and retrieved a hissing, furious black snake. I took several steps backwards as the magnificent creature was whisked past me to the nearby kitchen, where its head was cut off and blood drained.

About fifteen minutes later, two bowls of clear soup with floating pieces of cobra arrived on our table. I smiled again, pretending to be delighted. The meat tasted a bit like chicken, though it was tougher and less flavoursome. There were lots of small bones to somehow avoid and I ended up ditching the chopsticks and nibbling at it like a corn cob. I was reminded of the frogs I'd once eaten in Vietnam, and which I hadn't much enjoyed. Of course, cobras are not eaten because they are a delicacy but for their supposedly functional effect. And boy were a lot of them being eaten. I later discovered that even though the Burmese police will arrest anyone caught smuggling cobras to restaurants, the snakes aren't covered by any wildlife laws. The lack of legal protection combined with habitat destruction had recently resulted in one species of Burmese cobra being internationally listed as vulnerable to extinction. Yet with people finding more and more of them in their homes, the snakes' perilous situation was likely the last thing on anyone's mind.

I FELT that I was learning more about Myanmar as a freelancer, because I was doing more on-the-ground reporting. One of my frustrations at *The Myanmar Times* was that expat editors were primarily expected to edit and only occasionally write, so there were no arrangements in place for us to hit the streets with a reporter or translator. With the exception of Tom and Douglas, who both spoke Burmese, the newspaper's expat journalists wrote stories that relied on English-speaking sources – and of course this considerably narrowed our options. On the few occasions when I asked a reporter to come with me to translate, I felt guilty about adding to their already busy workload. I had ended up feeling desk-bound.

With Raj as my translator, I could talk to anyone, within reason of course. He had been born in the arid central region of Magwe, but had come to Yangon to study and had recently developed an interest in journalism. He was about eight years younger than me but seemed mature for his years, and I trusted that what he translated was exactly what he had been told, rather than colouring the message with his personal lens. This had been the case with translators I'd used in the past, though I am obviously not referring to Sherpa here: he was the best I ever worked with.

Raj wasn't Buddhist and I got the impression that he viewed Myanmar as an outsider, partly because he was treated like one. He was descended from Gurkas, whose roots lie in Nepal. They had originally come to Myanmar during World War II to support the British effort, and later fought alongside Burmese freedom fighters to gain independence from the colonial rulers. Yet despite this, they often faced discrimination in their adopted home of Myanmar. Like all ethnic minorities, they were regularly denied citizenship and this led to all manner of problems, including their children being barred from attending school.

As Raj and I returned home in a cab from a story we'd done on the Yangon Circular Railway, I told him that I had married my translator in Bangladesh. His eyebrows shot up.

He then smiled when I told him that my husband had been nicknamed Sherpa by his father, who loved the Himalayas and the mountaineering Nepalese tribe, although he had never had the chance to travel to Nepal.

'How is your husband treated here in Myanmar?' Raj asked me.

'Really good,' I replied. 'Myanmar people are very kind and sweet.'

'That's great to hear,' said Raj. 'Sometimes people who look Indian face prejudice. That has been the case for me, but I'm glad that it hasn't been for Sherpa. Maybe it's because he is a foreigner, whereas I "claim" to be Burmese.'

As it turned out, I had spoken too soon. Myanmar was beginning to change, and entering a new period of religious fundamentalism. Some of these changes were downright frightening.

16

THE ANGRY MONK OF MANDALAY

APRIL 2014

When Sherpa came home from work a bit later than usual one Thursday night, I didn't need him to tell me that something was wrong. He seemed drained of energy and dumped his backpack on the floor as though it were a boulder. After mumbling a hello, he reached past me where I was cooking dinner to take a beer out of the fridge and started to head back towards the living room. I put down my wooden spoon and tapped him softly on the shoulder.

'Hey,' I said. 'What's up?'

'I just got thrown out of a taxi.'

'What? Why?'

'The driver asked me where I'm from and when I told him Bangladesh, he kicked me out.'

'That's crazy.' I switched off the electric cooker. 'I'm so sorry. What exactly did the driver say to you?'

In Sherpa's upset state, the words tumbled out of his mouth. 'After I said that I was from Bangladesh, he asked me if I was Muslim. I said that I wasn't, but he didn't believe me. He said that all Bangladeshis are Muslims. He asked me why I can speak

Burmese if I'm from Bangladesh. I said I've been living here a while, but he was acting all suspicious towards me.'

'He sounds horrible,' I said.

'Yeah, he was. He started ranting and wasn't making any sense. Then he pulled over just as we were about to cross Shwe-gondine overpass and told me to get out. The car behind us started honking, so I just leapt out and walked. After a while I was able to get another taxi home.'

'Oh, babe,' I said. 'That's really awful. What a nutter.'

'Well, you know, I am a *kalar*.'

'A what?'

'A *kalar*. A dark-skinned person. It's like calling someone a "nigger."'

'That's so racist and awful. And I don't understand it either, because you're not black.'

'In Myanmar I'm black, because my skin is darker than theirs. That's what they call me at work.'

'They're calling you a *kalar* at work?' I asked, horrified.

'Not to my face. I walked into the kitchen last week and over-heard Aung Moe Zaw and Ko Ko Naing talking about me. When they saw me they changed the subject and looked all guilty. But sometimes I think they forget that I can understand them when they speak Burmese, because it wasn't the first time I've over-heard the reporters calling me a *kalar*.'

'Oh, babe. Why didn't you say anything about this until now?'

Sherpa shrugged. We both took a gulp of beer. I gave him a hug and we stood there like that for a few seconds. As I pulled away, I rubbed his back and we exchanged a sad smile.

I returned to cooking our fried rice, but my mind was else-where. I felt so hurt and angry on Sherpa's behalf. I thought about what I'd say to that screw-loose taxi driver if ever I saw him, or if I'd been with Sherpa at the time. As for Sherpa's staff using a racial slur behind his back – that was deeply disturbing and hurtful. I had thought those guys were our friends. Although there was initially some resentment towards Sherpa because he was such a young boss – and in Myanmar, seniority and respect is very much accorded by age – he seemed to have won them over. Sherpa took his team out for beers every Friday after the weekly edition of the newspaper was finished and sometimes I came along too. I was proud of how well they gelled as a team – they were so animated in their conversations with one another (much of which, admittedly, I couldn't understand) and they'd all drunkenly hug goodbye at the end of the night, with Sherpa often footing the entire bill. I also recalled how they called him 'Boss' and 'U Sherpa' as a mark of respect. I was shocked that journalists were using such an offensive term. I expected more of them.

Sherpa and I ate dinner and talked of other things, but I kept going over the two bombshells in my mind. Sherpa too was preoccupied and picked at his meal. We didn't really speak of the incident with the taxi driver again after that night. I didn't want to bring it up in case I upset him more – I couldn't think of anything constructive to say about it. But I knew that he was wounded and I hated being so powerless in my ability to ease his pain.

One Saturday night a couple of weeks later, Sherpa and I caught a taxi to a new Mexican restaurant downtown. The driver asked us where we were from, as they sometimes did. I said that I was from Australia and Sherpa cut in and said, 'And I'm from Sri Lanka.'

The driver smiled and turned up the radio, which was belting out a Burmese cover of a Rod Stewart hit. I raised my eyebrows but said nothing until we got out of the car.

'Why did you say that you're from Sri Lanka?'

'I don't want any issues,' Sherpa said with a shrug. 'Sri Lanka is a Buddhist country and I could pass as a Sri Lankan, so this way no one will think I'm Muslim. But, actually, yesterday I had a driver who had been to Sri Lanka and he was asking me all these questions about Colombo, where I'd told him I was born. I couldn't wait to get out – I'm not sure he believed me.'

I was sad that Sherpa felt he had to lie about where he was from. But I agreed wholeheartedly that it wasn't worth the trouble of telling the truth. What if he came across a taxi driver who did something worse than kick him out? It wasn't inconceivable, considering that a radical religious movement was taking flight in Yangon.

The 969 Movement decried Islam's supposed expansion in Myanmar and part of its strategy involved boycotting Muslim-owned businesses and patrons. Stickers featuring the movement's strange logo started appearing on shopfronts and on the rear window of taxis. The logo featured thick stripes of pink, yellow, blue, red and white, and looked a bit like a television test signal. In the centre were three lions on a plinth surrounded by something akin to daisy petals. Across the top in Burmese script were the numbers '969', which had recently taken on a special significance among ultranationalist Buddhists, who saw it as countering the significance of the special number of 786 in Islam. I shuddered whenever I saw the logo. If I was alone when a taxi with a 969 sticker pulled up to give me a ride, I'd give its driver daggers and would motion for them to keep on driving.

Incredibly, this hateful movement was led by a monk. His name was Wirathu and he gave rambling sermons from his monastery in Mandalay. He uploaded videos to YouTube and Facebook that attracted tens of thousands of views. Both platforms had been taking off like wildfire since the state-owned telecommunications monopoly ended and mobile phones became affordable. Wirathu called Muslims mad dogs, parasites and *kalars*, and often used rape as a metaphor. He was known to say abhorrent things when referring to Muslims, such as saying that their supposedly increasing numbers in Myanmar was like 'being raped in every town'. The warnings he gave about Myanmar becoming a 'Muslim land' were dangerous and far-fetched: Myanmar is one of the most overwhelmingly Buddhist nations in the world, with almost ninety per cent of its population professing to be Theravada Buddhists. Muslims are a minority of less than five per cent and Burmese-Indians less than two per cent. I mention Burmese-Indians because there was a mistaken but widespread belief that a person who looked Indian was Muslim.

But the fact that what Wirathu was saying was patently false didn't stop people from dying as a result. His sermons had been inciting violence in pockets of the country for several years: it was just that comparatively cosmopolitan Yangon had been spared until 2013, when a spate of deadly attacks took place nationwide. In Wirathu's home of Mandalay, Muslim neighbourhoods were torched and scores of people died. In the central town of Meiktila, monks had burned down a Muslim family's home and mobs of Buddhist youths had killed at least thirty Muslims, many of whom went into hiding. In Yangon, thirteen children died when an Islamic school known as a madrassa burned down. Many claimed it was arson, although no arrests were made. Muslim-owned shops in Yangon had begun shuttering their doors at dusk and curfews were imposed in several other cities.

But it was the Muslim Rohingyas in Rakhine State who suffered the most. After sectarian violence erupted in 2012, they had been forced into camps for internally displaced people and were denied every human right imaginable by the government – from citizenship to education and medical attention.

As Wirathu's notoriety grew, he remained surprisingly amenable to interviews with international news outlets. In fact, he seemed to lap up the attention in the classic way trouble-makers do. But he was furious when he appeared on the cover of *Time* magazine in 2013 as 'The face of Buddhist terror'. The magazine issue was promptly banned in Myanmar and angry groups deriding the article formed on Facebook, and the American journalist who wrote the article, Hannah Beech, was subsequently denied a visa to return to Myanmar.

Even though Wirathu was one of the biggest international stories to come out of Myanmar and I could have almost certainly sold a story about him to my pick of outlets, I didn't go anywhere near him. He disgusted me, and I was also worried that there could somehow be repercussions for Sherpa and me if I wrote about him.

One Sunday morning in 2015, I was stuck in a taxi, cursing the exceptionally bad traffic for making me late to my yoga class, which I had taken up in a partially successful bid to help me quit smoking and lose a few kilos. As we came to a complete standstill out the front of Thuwanna football stadium, I saw an enormous 969 banner draped across the entryway and realised that what was holding us up was a radical Buddhist rally. A law had just been passed that required a Buddhist bride-to-be to inform authorities if she wanted to marry a non-Buddhist, and presumably convert to his religion. Public objection could then prevent the marriage from going ahead. Thousands of people were lined up out the front of the stadium, which had a seating capacity of 30,000. This wasn't merely a fringe movement.

It also wasn't necessary to be Muslim or 'look' Muslim to invoke the ire of the militant Buddhists, as my friend Phil Blackwood discovered. Phil was the outgoing Kiwi manager of 50th

Street Bar and Restaurant, where I'd hung out countless times after my Burmese lessons with his flatmate Nathalie. I had also written a profile of Phil for *The Myanmar Times*, which he later showed me was hung in a frame in his living room.

The last time I saw Phil was at 50th Street, towards the end of 2014. His face was flushed and his rugby jersey was grass-stained, as he'd come straight to the pub with his team mates after a rugby match. I congratulated him on recently becoming a father and he told me that he was on a health kick.

'Good for you,' I'd said.

'It doesn't include stopping beer completely,' he said, and we laughed and clinked our glasses.

A few weeks later, Phil was in a prison cell, after falling foul of the 969 brigade. He had left his job at 50th Street to start managing a newly opened bar. As a means of spreading the word about it, he created a Facebook post for a night of discounted drinks. The image he used was a serene-looking Buddha with headphones on and a psychedelic background. The objections began immediately, with people complaining that it was disrespectful to Buddhism. Phil quickly removed the image and apologised in a separate Facebook post. But it was too late. An angry Buddhist mob turned up at his house baying for his blood. Then the police came and took him away.

I found it really distressing to see photos in the news of a terrified-looking Phil in handcuffs as he turned up to court hearings, surrounded by dozens of police officers in helmets and scrums of reporters trying to take his photo. Phil was found guilty of insulting religion and was sentenced to two and a half years in prison. The bar manager and the bar's owner – both Burmese – received the same sentence, even though they weren't with Phil when he uploaded the image, and had no knowledge of it. That three young men were losing a combined seven years of their life over a deleted Facebook post was beyond comprehension to me.

By the time the three men were released in a presidential pardon thirteen months after their arrest, Phil had lost thirty kilograms. He told a New Zealand newspaper that 'sadistic' prison officers put stones in the inmates' rice.

ALL OF THIS WAS FRIGHTENING, although I knew that anti-Muslim and anti-Indian sentiment in Myanmar was nothing new. Before Sherpa and I had left Bangladesh, we had done some reading on the history of Myanmar and what we'd discovered had been worrying. Hostility towards Muslims and people of Indian descent seemed to have existed for as long as people from those backgrounds had lived in Myanmar – which was centuries. As far back as the eighteenth century, King Bodawpaya of Mandalay had executed four Muslim imams because they refused to eat pork. During the years that Burma was governed as part of British India, ethnic Indians formed the backbone of the economy. They were given the plum jobs and were successful entrepreneurs and, as a result, they were massively resented. The wave of immigration from India continued and by the time World War II broke out, half of Yangon's population was Indian. But in 1962, dictator General Ne Win expelled hundreds of thousands of Indians, including those who had been living in Myanmar for generations. Sherpa and I had read that discrimination continued to bubble away to the present day, which worried us both, but wasn't enough to deter us completely. We had been relieved to discover that Sherpa's 'Indian' appearance appeared to be a non-issue. We had taken it as a sign that Myanmar was undergoing some really positive changes as part of its journey towards democracy.

But that assumption had been shattered by 969. The religious intolerance it was cultivating was vociferous, virulent and unashamedly out in the open. And it was about to throw into question our shared belief that we had found a home in Myanmar.

17

OUR HOME IN MYANMAR
JUNE 2014

W e somehow slept through the monsoon storm that destroyed our front fence, but the sound of crashing bricks woke Sherpa, who was hopping around by the bedroom window as I began to stir one morning.

'Look outside! Look outside!' he said as I opened my eyes.

It looked as though someone had taken to our seven-foot fence with a wrecking ball. The entire left half had collapsed and lay in a mess of broken bricks and mud. The red and yellow hibiscus that we'd planted only the week before lay crushed underneath the mass of concrete and were swiftly being submerged by rising brown puddles. If the fence had fallen onto the road and not into our yard, it might have killed one of the trishaw drivers who regularly parked there while waiting for a passenger.

Sherpa and I left Ripley quivering under the kitchen table and dashed across in the pelting rain to our landlord Daw Kyi Kyi's place. In between claps of thunder I heard muffled shouts coming from inside, but all went quiet when Sherpa tapped on the door.

'Yikes,' I mouthed silently to Sherpa.

He'd told me that he'd heard Daw Kyi Kyi yelling at her son before, but I never had. We knew she rose daily at 5 a.m. for prayers, so I was pretty sure that the fallen fence wouldn't be news to her, but when she opened the door and we pointed it out, she looked all concerned and surprised. However, she was also clearly preoccupied and kept glancing behind her into the dark corridor, so we left. She'd never invited us in before anyhow.

A couple of hours later, I was finishing up an article in the study when I heard the soft clinks of broken brick pieces landing on one another. I went into our bedroom and peered out the window. Two girls, who looked no more than twelve years old, were gingerly picking up the bricks and tossing them into the back of a small white truck, whose driver was nowhere to be seen. They were shivering in the rain and at the rate they were going, they would be there for three weeks. I was appalled to think that if I wanted to document child labour in Myanmar, I needed to look no further than my own front yard.

I grabbed an umbrella and went back over to Daw Kyi Kyi's place to ask for more workers – and preferably, adult ones.

'You pay for extra workers,' she said. 'The cost is seven hundred dollars.'

'You are the owner – you pay,' I said in simple but unavoidably blunt English.

'Your new trees broke the fence,' she said, and gave me a stony, stubborn look. 'You pay.'

'The monsoon broke the fence,' I countered indignantly.

She shook her head as forcefully as a horse with flies in its eyes. I stomped back over to our place, already composing an indignant email to Sherpa in my head. She wants $700 for workers! Ridiculous. And laughable was the idea that our hibiscus broke the fence. I'd have had an easier time believing Daw Kyi Kyi if she'd blamed it on evil spirits.

Having a broken fence meant that Ripley had to be kept inside all day so that she didn't run away, and being cooped up was making her miserable and whiny. Later that afternoon I took her out to relieve herself after the girls had gone home, and found a couple of scraps of paper tucked neatly under our door-mat. It was so unusual for someone to come right up to the door of a home that I was unnerved. I stuffed the papers into my back pocket and cursed Daw Kyi Kyi and her money-scrimping ways. At the time, a minimum daily wage of 3600 kyat (US$2.50) hadn't been introduced. Daw Kyi Kyi was perhaps paying half that amount for the girls, who it was safe to assume would cost far less to hire than adult men.

In Australia, I'd grown up in a house without a fence. Very few people in our Melbourne suburb had one either, or else they had little knee-high ones that were more for decoration and to demarcate where their responsibility for mowing the lawn ended. But I realised I'd grown accustomed to having a high fence topped with rolls of razor wire, which was completely standard in Yangon. I knew it wasn't a crime-riddled city by any stretch, but I felt exposed without the usual home-security measures.

Another two days passed and the poor girls had scarcely made a dint in the pile of bricks. Fed up, I decided to upload some photos of the damage onto Facebook so that I could ask my Burmese friends and fellow expats for advice on how to speed things up. I was taking photos from the dirt road opposite when one of our neighbours, who looked to be in his sixties, approached with his fluffy white Maltese on the end of a leash. We'd never spoken before and I'd wrongly assumed that he didn't speak English.

As he came closer he shook his head at the scene and with a smile said, 'What a mess.'

I told him that Daw Kyi Kyi wouldn't pay for more workers and that we'd reached a stalemate.

'The foundations were no good,' he said. 'It was built cheaply and it is being repaired cheaply. It's not safe for you without a fence. I'll just put my dog back inside and then I'll take you up the road to the township authorities. Maybe they can help you get it fixed.'

I was touched that he had offered to help, but I did worry that we might be about to make the situation worse. Getting officials involved could easily backfire: some took bribes, their decisions were unpredictable and they were under no obligation to provide any justification or reasoning for their decisions. I remembered interviewing an expat who told me that she was driving through Yangon's poorly lit streets one night when her car fell into a ditch. An official from the local township office accused her of damaging the ditch and said she was lucky not to be fined.

I was a bit apprehensive as we stepped inside the tiny office, and the two men in white mandarin-collared shirts and navy-blue *longyis* certainly looked startled to see me. But over the clunking of a noisy desk fan, they listened to my neighbour explain the situation and shook their heads and clucked their tongues in sympathy.

'They will come and speak to your landlord,' my neighbour said after they'd spoken for a few minutes.

I beamed and said to the men, '*Cezu tin ba deh*', adding in a couple more thank-yous for good measure as we stepped out. I was so grateful to my neighbour that I wanted to hug him.

As we walked back along our road, he asked what had brought Sherpa and me to Myanmar, and he told me that he was a retired ship captain and had travelled all over the world. We then said goodbye and I thanked him profusely. He just smiled and stepped back inside his property's own enormous fence.

To my relief, the next afternoon the two girls were replaced by three men and a new fence was built in just over a week. But while Sherpa and I had won that battle against Daw Kyi Kyi, we soon realised that she would forever have the upper hand – and that she was intent on making back the money she'd spent on the fence.

Our lease came up for renewal a month later and she raised the rent and insisted on giving us another six-month lease. She had done this before and to our dismay we had realised that it allowed her to hike the rent twice a year instead of once. However, this time around it was an even bigger increase. And on top of that, she said that if we wanted to sign a new lease, we had to get the outside of the house painted.

'This is insane,' I fumed to Sherpa. 'Why doesn't she understand that it's the owner, not the renters, who pays for this stuff?'

'Why don't we just find out how much paint and a few workers would cost? It might be really cheap to get it done.'

'That isn't the point,' I replied. 'Daw Kyi Kyi is out of control. Our rent has gone up three times already, and it will go up again in another six months. She knows that we love this place and she's taking advantage of it. Plus I'm worried that the leaking ceiling in the bedroom might cave in on us during another storm. It drips on my forehead when it rains. I'm sad to say it, but I think we need to move.'

Sherpa reluctantly agreed to start looking for a new home. His lack of enthusiasm was completely justified – house-hunting turned out to be a major pain. For one, it was confusing and time-consuming. There were no signs to indicate which properties were available for rent and real estate agencies didn't have websites. I found one website that carried listings for multiple agencies, but I suspected the listings were merely for show, because we were never once able to view a property that we'd seen listed online.

We told agents that we wanted to live in a house, but were shown apartments. We said that our budget was US$650 a month and were then shown places that were wildly out of our price range. One place was within our budget but totally decrepit: it had a dead pigeon in the living room and a thick layer of bird poo covering the floor.

'Did the pigeon die from inhaling all the poop?' Sherpa jokingly whispered.

Rental prices were skyrocketing with the influx of expats to Yangon and a shortage of what some called 'international standard housing'. Incredibly, the median rent in some townships was on a par with New York City. One real estate agent boasted of having a property that cost US$25,000 a month to rent. Another apologised for a landlord who was demanding three years' rent upfront. Many landlords were simply pulling a number out of the sky when it came to rent – and clueless new arrivals who worked for companies that covered their rent were often amenable.

One agent took us to a property that we'd already seen – but the cost of renting it through his agency was fifty per cent higher. Another place looked promising from the outside and lifted our spirits as soon as we saw it – but the agent then told us that he didn't have the keys so we couldn't go in.

'This is a waste of time,' I muttered to Sherpa as we spent another wet Saturday afternoon traipsing around Yangon. 'Maybe moving is a mistake.'

He said nothing, but I was sure he agreed. Time was running out and our animals were counting on us to find them a suitable place to live.

'We might have to compromise on something,' I said. 'Maybe we should take the place in South Okkalapa with the small yard?'

'That wasn't a small yard, babe – that was no yard. The gap

between the front door and the fence was thirty centimetres. Plus it was right next to the main road, so Butters would probably be hit by a car and killed in less than a week.'

With just two weeks left until our lease expired, we were in full panic mode. Mercifully, one Saturday morning during that time we met an energetic young agent who seemed to be at the top of his game. He'd arrived at our gate in a red hatchback ten minutes early, and he wore a purple polo shirt with the agency's logo emblazoned across it. He held a clipboard in one hand and vigorously shook 'Mr Sherpa's' hand while introducing himself as Ko Ko Gyi.

'Let's do this,' he said, grinning.

We jumped into the back seat and headed east for Thingangyun Township. The first couple of places that Ko Ko Gyi showed us weren't far off the mark. We were on our way to a third place, which Ko Ko Gyi referred to as one of his 'special properties,' when he turned around to face Sherpa and me.

'Are you Muslims, Mr Sherpa?' he asked.

'No, we're not,' replied Sherpa.

'We're not religious,' I added hastily.

'That's good,' Ko Ko Gyi said, smiling brightly. 'Landlords don't like to rent to Muslims. But you won't have any problems if you're not.' He said this in the same cheerful way he might have told us what he'd been up to on the weekend.

Sherpa and I fell silent. My mind was racing. It never occurred to me that property owners would even turn their minds to whether we were Muslim. After all, this was a business transaction; it wasn't as though we would be living under the same roof. How much harder would such an assumption make our house hunt? Is this why it had already been hard?

'Here we are,' Ko Ko Gyi said as we rounded a bend off busy Thu Mingalar Road in Thingangyun Township. 'And here is the owner's son, ready to meet us with the keys.'

I sucked in my breath when I saw the house. This was our new home – I just knew it. The two-storey house had a fresh coat of sky-blue paint and an enormous yard that wrapped around the property. To the left of the driveway were neat rows of purple-leaved plants and a mango tree laden with fruit. The fence, also painted sky blue with dark-blue trimmings, looked solid and strong. Our current home suddenly seemed decrepit by comparison.

It was even lovelier inside, with polished wooden floorboards, lots of natural light and four well-proportioned bedrooms – not the closet-sized ones we'd so often seen. The kitchen looked about a hundred years old, but neither of us cared. The price was bang on budget.

'We'll take it,' Sherpa told Ko Ko Gyi, as I nearly choked up with relief.

We returned to the house with Ko Ko Gyi the following week to sign the lease, and planned to move in the following day. The owner looked to be in her sixties like Daw Kyi Kyi and she was already inside when we arrived, along with her son and a woman I presumed to be his wife. The husband and wife sat cross-legged on the floor, while the owner sat on a chair, smiling and at ease. The trio stood up and smiled kindly as we entered. The few Burmese landowners Sherpa and I had met were wealthy in a showy way, but not this family. To me, they looked friendly and refined.

After a few minutes of chitchat led by Ko Ko Gyi, the younger woman laid out some lacquer plates on the floor and retrieved three clear Seasons Bakery bags from a green plastic basket. She filled the first plate with sausages encased in glazed white buns, the second with mini pizzas and the third with a plaited bun that was topped with baked cheese and pink sausage pieces. It all looked pretty unappetising and it was far too much food, but it was a kind gesture all the same.

'Please, help yourself,' said Ko Ko Gyi. 'These are pork snacks.'

As he said this, the three family members looked at us intently.

Oh – now I understood. The food was a test: Muslims don't eat pork. Clearly our assurances to Ko Ko Gyi were insufficient. I forced myself to keep smiling despite the revelation hitting me like a punch to the stomach.

Sherpa eats like a sparrow and never usually eats in social situations, which I understand as being part of his shyness. Considering the circumstances we were in, his expression was remarkably neutral. Had he heard Ko Ko Gyi properly and twigged that we must eat the food? Or was he on the verge of politely refusing, as he usually would? I took the plate of mini pizzas from Ko Ko Gyi and offered it to Sherpa.

'Take one,' I said with imploring eyes and a fake smile still plastered across my face.

To my relief, he obliged. I took one for myself and passed the bowl back to Ko Ko Gyi. For good measure, I also took two glazed buns.

We chewed, swallowed and smiled, and my cheeks burnt with shame.

'Lovely,' I said to the group. 'Thank you very much.'

The house owners smiled back. Ko Ko Gyi was positively beaming. He would be getting a month's rent from us as his commission. He pulled out the paperwork and the owner and her son set about counting and recounting thirteen months' rent, which was mostly Sherpa's money. When that was done, Ko Ko Gyi handed us the keys and everyone left, with a dozen *cezu din ba deh*s exchanged.

As the cars pulled out of the driveway and disappeared along the quiet, palm-lined road, Sherpa and I did a little dance and hugged each other, then raced upstairs to look at the rest of the house.

I was elated that we'd found such a wonderful new home, but I felt awful about making Sherpa eat the pork. I'd debased him and myself – and, you could argue, all Muslims. I began searching for the words to apologise to him and as I did I thought how sad it was that Yangon was becoming a place where eating a particular meat mattered so much and two of the world's great religions couldn't seem to co-exist.

18

TEN CENTS A WORD

AUGUST 2014

I t was eating away at me that Sherpa had to stump up most of the rent money for our new home. I loved freelancing, but I was yet to solve a basic flaw in my career choice: earning an adequate income. I'd kept telling myself that things would be okay once I was really in the swing of things. That was until the day came, not long after we'd moved, that I was forced to admit just how dispiriting the financials of freelancing were.

My day had started off well. I was in a great mood because it was pay day. I sent off a couple of pitches from my sun-dappled, air-conditioned study and then headed off in a taxi for *Mizzima.*

I was doing most of my writing for *Mizzima*'s weekly magazine and although I'd never met its British editor, Julian Gearing, or even spoken to him on the phone, I enjoyed working with him. He lived across the border in northern Thailand, where he had been based throughout *Mizzima*'s years of exile. Although *Mizzima*'s other staff had returned to Yangon since the political reforms had begun, Julian had told me that he and his Thai wife had no plans to move. Thailand was their home, and the costs of living in Yangon were exorbitant compared with the cheap conveniences of Thailand. Julian and I were in regular contact over email and I found him unfailingly polite, responsive and straightforward – in short, he was everything Ross hadn't been.

Julian had emailed me the day before to say that my pay was ready to be collected from *Mizzima*'s office. Although ATMs with international banking facilities had recently become available in Myanmar after EU and US sanctions were eased, cash was still very much king. Only a minuscule number of people had bank accounts – the Burmese still preferred to stash their cash under a mattress, and home safes were also popular. The onus was on me to collect my pay each month, and it never crossed my mind to ask whether a bank deposit would be possible.

At the end of his email, Julian had said that as I had established myself as one of *Mizzima*'s regular contributors, I should introduce myself to the company's founding editor-in-chief, Soe Myint. I was excited by the suggestion because I'd long been curious to meet him. Soe Myint was a stalwart member of Myanmar's media scene, but what really intrigued me was the fact that he had once hijacked an aeroplane.

In 1990, and while still a teenager, Soe Myint and his accomplice used a fake bomb made of soap and wires to hijack a Thai Airways flight from Bangkok to Yangon. They forced the Airbus to divert to India and then held the passengers hostage for ten hours on the tarmac in Kolkata. The hijackers had two demands: for Aung San Suu Kyi to be released from house arrest and for military rule to be ended in Myanmar. Of course, neither came to pass, but some might say that the hijacking shone a light, however briefly, on the suffering of Myanmar's people. Others might say that two wrongs don't make a right. In any case, the hostages were released unharmed and the hijackers surrendered. Incredibly, rather than being charged, Soe Myint was granted asylum as a refugee in India and he launched *Mizzima* from Delhi, while his accomplice moved to Ireland.

Until I'd lived in Myanmar, I'd not had friends or

associates who had been in prison. Now I had quite a number of them. Of course, being a former political prisoner in Myanmar was completely different from being an ex-con in Australia or anywhere else. Far from carrying stigma, a political prisoner was a selfless hero who was brave enough to fight for a better future for Myanmar. But hijacking a plane, even as an act of political protest – as it had been in Soe Myint's case – was in a league of its own. What kind of a person possessed enough daring and ruthlessness to hijack a commercial airliner?

When Myanmar's quasi-civilian government started granting licences to privately run newspapers in 2011, this was all the encouragement Soe Myint needed to return home. He somehow had his name struck off the blacklist and arrived in 2012, the same year I did. His backstory intrigued me no end.

When I arrived at *Mizzima* the receptionist told me that Soe Myint had just popped out of the office but would be back soon, so I headed straight for the finance department. My usual contact U Myint Oo retrieved several bundles of kyat from a locked filing cabinet and began removing the elastic bands from each *lakh*, a term that originated in India to describe 100,000 units. My pay that month came to just over US$650, which was the equivalent of almost a million kyat. For reasons that weren't entirely clear to me, even though I invoiced all the local magazines in US dollars, I was paid in kyat. My pay could vary quite considerably according to how strong the kyat was against the dollar.

U Myint Oo used a calculator to show me that day's exchange rate and then switched on a money-counting machine, which looked a bit like a bulky fax machine. He then popped the 1000-kyat notes into the feeder at the top and the currency was spat out in a noisy blur below.

'One-thousand-kyat notes: eight hundred and forty-four,' he

read mechanically off the small screen. 'Five-hundred-kyat notes: one. One-hundred-kyat notes: four. Fifty-kyat notes: one.'

He repeated the counting process three times for good measure, and I then signed a document saying that I had received my pay. U Myint Oo gave me a plastic bag to carry my money in, which weighed at least half a kilogram.

On my way back to Soe Myint's office I bumped into Sonny Swe, who seemed especially ebullient. He told me that business was going well and there were hopes that his father would be released (he was, two months later). Sonny then excused himself with a grin and a wave and rushed off to a meeting with a prospective advertiser on the other side of Yangon. At his side was Thandar, who looked happier than I'd seen her in a long time. I then said hello to a few other former colleagues from *The Myanmar Times*, all of whom appeared cheerful and relaxed.

I wandered over to Soe Myint's office and tapped gently on the glass. He looked up from his papers and I introduced myself. He stared at me blankly.

'Er, Julian suggested I come and say hello when I came to pick up my pay. I write for the magazine,' I mumbled, suddenly unsure of myself.

'Ah yes, Julian. He has worked for me for many years from Thailand.'

Silence followed. It seemed unlike Julian not to have told Soe Myint that I was coming, yet he seemed not to register who I was. As I weighed up whether to fill the silence and racked my brains for something sensible to say, Soe Myint asked me whether I liked living in Myanmar.

'Very much,' I said brightly. 'It's the most fascinating country I've ever lived in. There are so many incredible stories to tell.'

'That's true,' he replied. 'But the Myanmar people need a better government. They have suffered for too long.'

'Absolutely,' I agreed, while wondering if I had come across as a self-serving journalist. I tried to correct myself by adding, 'I'm looking forward to the elections and I hope that Aung San Suu Kyi wins.'

'There is no question as to whether she will win. The question is whether the military will allow her to be president.'

I looked at Soe Myint, waiting for him to go on, at which point I realised that he wasn't looking at me. Disconcerted, I murmured, 'I hope so.'

There was an empty chair across from his desk but I dared not ask if I could sit in it, so I stood a few steps in from the doorway, awkwardly clutching my plastic bag full of cash.

'Do you speak Burmese?' Soe Myint asked me, changing the subject.

I hated this question. I knew that the degree to which I had mastered Burmese was taken as an indication of how sincere my commitment was to my adopted country. And my answer was a lousy one.

'I took lessons while I was working at *The Myanmar Times*,' I ventured. 'I'm not very good at it though – I can only speak at a transactional level.'

This was an exaggeration. I could order a taxi and ask it to turn right, left or stop – but that was about it.

'You should learn to speak Burmese,' said Soe Myint. 'Myanmar people will appreciate it.'

'I should, yes. I might start lessons again,' I said weakly.

We both fell quiet. I figured Soe Myint was a busy man so I excused myself, saying it was wonderful to meet him.

'Yes, it was,' he said, looking past me.

'Bye-bye,' I said, before backing out the door.

My fleeting conversation with Soe Myint had given me no insights whatsoever as to his character. I'd expected to see fire in his eyes but instead I found him polite but completely unreadable – vague, even. I'd been dying to ask him about the hijacking but the lack of any kind of rapport prevented me. I hoped I'd get my chance another day, but in the end I never did. That was the longest conversation Soe Myint and I ever had.

I glanced at my watch before heading down the stairs and back out onto the street. I'd been at *Mizzima* for nearly an hour. I jumped in a taxi and headed for a travel magazine uptown called *My Magical Myanmar*, which had been launched six months earlier by Sonny's wife, Yamin. I always looked forward to seeing her when I collected my pay, because she was sassy and fun, with a husky voice and a full-bodied laugh. Writing for *My Magical Myanmar* was also a great gig because I could turn my travels into paid work. My most recent assignment from Yamin had been a bar crawl through Yangon's newest drinking dens. I'd decided that it was a ridiculously fun way of earning money – even if Sherpa and I had spent more that night than I was actually paid for the story.

The taxi ride to Yankin Township shouldn't have taken more than twenty minutes, but we got stuck at a railway crossing for a full quarter of an hour before a creaking train lumbered past. I arrived at the multi-storey office building forty minutes after I'd set off, and also just as a power cut started, which meant that I had to walk up six flights of stairs.

After a cup of tea, a cigarette and a few laughs, I bundled my pay from Yamin into my plastic bag and grabbed yet another taxi. This time I was headed for a magazine called *Myanmore*. It had just moved its premises from the Strand Hotel building and, for the life of me, I couldn't find its new office. I wandered around and around a seemingly deserted, half-constructed office building. I was unsure if I was even on the right floor and was about to give up when a security guard spotted me and led me through a long, dark corridor with sawdust all over the floor. We turned a corner and arrived at the only office with a light on.

Myanmore's pretty young office assistant manually counted out a few hundred dollars' worth of kyat and I was on my way again.

It started to rain just as I headed back out onto the street and I realised with dismay that I must have left my umbrella in the last taxi. Unwilling to bargain lest I get completely saturated, I took an overpriced taxi to Citymart supermarket in upmarket Bahan Township. Citymart was Myanmar's largest supermarket chain and its branch on Dhammazedi Road had the best selection of international foods by a mile, so expats tended to do their grocery shopping there. On days when I was feeling cashed up, I liked to go there and just stand in front of the cheese section. Dairy products weren't widely consumed in Myanmar, nor had they been in Bangladesh, which is partly due to Asian populations having higher rates of lactose intolerance. As for me, I was crazy about cheese but ate it only once or twice a month. Today would be one of those days.

With a grumbling stomach, I sighed appreciatively at the scene before me. Basking under the glare of the bright lights were tautly wrapped triangles of parmesan, soft rounds of camembert, cheerful blocks of cheddar and snowball-shaped mozzarellas. I fondled a long log of goat's cheese and ran my hands over a square of crumbly feta. Many of these flavours were long forgotten to me, but upon seeing them again I was suddenly overcome with intense cravings.

I thought long and hard about which cheese I'd choose. I tried to factor in which would give me the most bang for my buck. The prices of imported goods in Myanmar were as eye-watering as the products were mouth-watering. I deliberated between goat's cheese and camembert, before settling on the former. Then I grabbed some crackers and a few longneck bottles of Myanmar Beer.

Sherpa was already back from work when I got home. He

was having a beer on the couch, with Ripley gnawing a broken sandal at his feet.

'Look what I have here,' I said delightedly, waving my shopping bag at Sherpa as I rushed towards the kitchen. 'Cheese and money!'

I carefully arranged the crackers in a half-circle on a plate and then tore open the foil around the goat's cheese.

'It's mouldy!' I wailed to Sherpa, staring at it in disbelief.

'Isn't goat's cheese meant to be mouldy?' said Sherpa.

'That's blue cheese,' I snapped.

'Can you eat around the mould?' asked Sherpa, who was never one to waste food. He also had no appreciation for cheeses, despite my best attempts to get him interested.

'I guess,' I whined miserably. 'But there's only a small amount that isn't mouldy. I can't believe it. This cheese cost me twelve dollars and I'll get one lousy bite!'

I popped the goat's cheese into my mouth. It had a sour, almost metallic taste.

'No wonder people call Citymart "Shittymart",' I fumed.

'Do you want a beer before we head out to the party?' said Sherpa, who padded into the kitchen while tucking his business shirt back in.

'Absolutely,' I said. 'Beer never lets me down.'

But rather than taking the edge off my annoyance, that first beer seemed to only spur on my grumblings in the taxi. I knew that I was winding myself up, but I couldn't seem to stop it.

'Today I spent the equivalent of thirty-two dollars on taxis and twelve dollars on cheese. Plus I lost my umbrella so I'll have to buy a new one. So I'm about fifty dollars down and I didn't earn a single kyat. I spent the entire day collecting my pay and buying mouldy cheese.'

'I'm sure you'll have a much more productive day tomorrow,' said Sherpa encouragingly, who was now fiddling with his tie.

'I guess so,' I said. 'But it's not just collecting my pay that is time-consuming. So many aspects of freelancing are. I have to do all my interviews face-to-face because the phone call quality is lousy, which means I spend ages in Yangon's terrible traffic and a huge amount on taxis. And if I need a translator, I have to pay Raj on top of that. Most magazines pay me ten cents a word, which means that to earn what I did at *The Myanmar Times* I'd have to write fifteen thousand words a month. Actually, I'd need to write twenty thousand words to cover my expenses. That's totally impossible.' I sighed. I wanted to cry.

'Why don't you try writing for international publications that would pay you more than local ones?' Sherpa asked.

'From time to time I do try, but most of my pitches go unanswered and then I get despondent. Plus those kinds of hard-hitting stories are harder to find, and riskier, too. I worry that if I write about really controversial things that would interest an international audience, it could get me into hot water and jeopardise us living here.'

'Fair enough,' said Sherpa.

'I'm so poor,' I concluded miserably.

Sherpa looked at me sympathetically. 'You'll work something out,' he said, adding, 'you always do.'

I didn't agree, but I lacked the energy to protest. No doubt to Sherpa's relief, we soon pulled up at our destination.

'Come on, babe,' said Sherpa, grabbing my hand after handing over a 5000-kyat note to the driver. 'This is going to be fun. Plus it's free drinks.'

From his jacket pocket he retrieved the invitation, which was printed on thick white paper, adorned with cursive script and had the blue-and-yellow flag of the European Union printed at the top.

Sherpa flashed the invitation at the security guards posted at a set of enormous gates. Sherpa Hossainy and his 'spouse' were duly checked off the list of RSVPs and we were waved along a pebbled path that led past one of the grandest homes I'd set eyes upon.

'Oh my god,' I whispered as we rounded the corner. 'This is something else.'

As the editor-in-chief of *Myanmar Business Today*, Sherpa had scored us invitations to some fantastic parties in Yangon. We'd been invited to receptions hosted by embassies as well as the opening of new businesses, and no expense ever seemed to be spared. But I hadn't seen anything as elegant as the garden party held to mark the opening of the EU ambassador's residence – it was like a scene out of *The Great Gatsby*. Dotted about the sloping manicured lawns and exquisite gardens were a couple of hundred people dressed to the nines. Halfway up the expansive outdoor area was a six-piece jazz band, who occupied a stage that was flanked by enormous terracotta pots and sprouting dramatic fronds. The property backed onto Inya Lake, where a full moon was reflected in the milky, calm waters. Tens of thousands of fairy lights were draped from palm trees and waiters in black silk vests darted from guest to guest with trays of drinks and finger foods. To my delight, my first glass of prosecco was topped up while it was still half full.

The residence itself was a vast, sumptuous villa. The side facing the lake was comprised almost entirely of glass panels, allowing guests to get a tantalising glimpse inside. Suspended from the ceiling of what was probably one of several living rooms were dramatic spherical light shades, which cast a warm glow on an all-white leather lounge suite below.

'One of my reporters told me that Ne Win's family owns this house, plus a few other properties along this road,' Sherpa told me quietly, referring to Myanmar's first dictator. 'Ne Win apparently used to live in the house next door and some of his relatives still live there.'

'Seriously? That's incredible. I wonder if the neighbours were invited to the party,' I joked.

'I'd say not,' replied Sherpa. 'It wouldn't be a good look to have the dictator's relatives mingling with guests at a party hosted by the EU.'

I knew that military high-ups owned vast amounts of Myanmar – from banks to airlines and five-star properties like this one, but even so, it was painfully ironic that the EU had finally eased sanctions on Myanmar just the year before, only to begin passing money directly into the hands of the family of the former dictator who was responsible for the sanctions being imposed in the first place. It wasn't chump change either. A few months later, a local news outlet revealed that the rent for this residence was somewhere between US$80,000 and $100,000 *per month* – a gross amount, by any measure.

We'd scarcely been at the party ten minutes when the EU ambassador came up and greeted Sherpa by name, shook both our hands and offered us his business card. Roland Kobia was Belgian and looked to be in his early fifties. He was bald and had a goatee, and when he smiled I noticed he had a slight gap between his two front teeth, which gave his face an interesting edge. He praised a recent article about the EU that had appeared in *Myanmar Business Today*, and which had been written by Sherpa's deputy editor, Oli. Then he asked me what I did for a living, and appeared genuinely interested. For someone of such high ranking, Kobia seemed delightfully down-to-earth. I wondered whether all high-ranking diplomats were this charming.

That night we met a number of people from the world of diplomacy, along with heads of mission at aid agencies and several European businesspeople. Sherpa also discreetly pointed out a couple of Burmese government ministers, who wore dark-green chequered *longyis* and a *taikpon*, a black mandarin collar, while their wives wore glittering gowns. After initially wondering whether I was the only person at the party who could scarcely afford the cost of the taxi home, by the time I had five wines in me, I'd forgotten the day's frustrations.

But when I woke up the next morning with a horrible wine headache and the realisation that my writing would be completely sub-par with a hangover, I fell back into despondency. It wasn't that I craved the riches I'd seen the night before – just some level of financial stability.

I got out of bed with a sigh, went downstairs and started pushing words around my laptop screen. I thought to myself once again that I needed to find a means of making more money.

It wasn't until a few months later that I thought I may have found it, or at least the possibility of it. I saw a post on the Google group Yangon Expat Connection advertising a six-month role at the British Embassy. The focus was on promoting British trade and investment opportunities in Myanmar – or rather, Burma, as the Brits still called it. The salary was twice what I had earned as a staffer at *The Myanmar Times* and the journalist in me was intrigued.

I spent an hour crafting an application, even though I didn't think I was in with a real chance. I figured that an embassy would steer clear of hiring a journalist. After hitting send, I took Ripley for a walk. As we came around the second bend in the quiet backstreets, a massive snake slithered across the road ahead, scaring the absolute bejesus out of both of us. It was only a few days later when I received a reply to my email that I remembered the Burmese superstition about snakes: if one crosses your path, it is a sign that your luck with money is about to change.

The first thing that struck me about the email I received from the British Embassy was the header – in capital letters it screamed: SECTION UNCLASSIFIED. Underneath was an invitation to come in for an interview the following week with the deputy ambassador. I screeched and phoned Sherpa as I jumped around my study.

'I knew that you would eventually work something out,' he said. 'I'm sure you'll get the job.'

And as it turned out, I did.

19

RANGOON DAYS

SEPTEMBER 2014

Within a month of applying for the job at the embassy, I found myself sitting next to the British ambassador, Andrew Patrick, in his resplendent dining room, being served a six-course meal and enjoying polite conversation with the celebrated film producer Lord Puttnam. Also at the dinner were Lord Puttnam's son, a talented classical musician called Sacha, the deputy ambassador, Matthew Hedges, and my new boss, Lisa Weedon. Lord Puttnam was visiting Myanmar on official business as the UK's trade envoy and one of my first tasks in the new job had been to help arrange his schedule. As Lord Puttnam regaled us with a witty anecdote about being on the set of *Chariots of Fire* and I simultaneously tried to guess which piece of cutlery I should use to spread butter on my dinner roll, I wondered what on earth I was doing there.

My sense of disbelief was compounded by the speed with which I'd taken up my new appointment. I had expected the embassy machine to move slowly as a result of copious protocols, but that wasn't at all the case – my first day on the job was only ten days after I was informed that I'd got it. I was hired as a 'local staff member' at the UK's Foreign Office, which is essentially someone of any nationality who is recruited outside the UK, isn't a member of the civil service and is subject to local employment conditions, just as my Burmese colleagues were. Our salaries were also more in keeping with local ones, while still being generous.

Another thing that sped up the process, I was told, was the fact that I was Australian. Australia belongs to an intelligence alliance called the 'Five Eyes', which is the world's oldest intelligence partnership, having been created in 1941. The other members are the United Kingdom, the United States, Canada and New Zealand. Thanks to my country's membership in the Five Eyes, my background check was completed in a mere matter of days – I presume because Australia happily and speedily handed over any relevant information it had on me.

Being a journalist wasn't a barrier to working at the embassy, as I thought it may have been, provided I agreed not to write any articles during the six months that I would be working there. In fact, having writing and research skills had worked in my favour as a job candidate, because part of the role involved producing reports on trade and investment opportunities in Myanmar.

Once I had my security clearance, I flew to Bangkok to get my embassy-sponsored business visa. With perfect paperwork in hand, I expected everything to go smoothly, so I was aghast when my visa was very nearly refused on a silly technicality. After a few phone calls were made by Tina May Thwin Oo, the British Embassy's ultra-efficient head of protocol in Yangon, my visa was duly granted. However, the delay made me miss my return flight and proved once and for all that no number of well-oiled connections can match the unpredictability of a Burmese visa department.

While in Bangkok, I had also taken the opportunity to buy some smart work clothes from one of the megacity's gleaming malls, and delighted in being able to browse racks of global brands. But I soon realised that I was totally outclassed by my new boss, Lisa, who was the epitome of refined British style. She turned up to work each morning in her chauffeured black Land Rover with a perfectly coiffed blonde bob and, most often, a sheath dress, which she accessorised with pearls, pumps and a beautiful handbag. Lisa was a couple of years younger than me, but the poise with which she carried herself, coupled with her Queen's English accent, made me feel very much her junior. Not to mention the fact that I was also – literally – her junior at UK Trade and Investment (UKTI) Burma, which she had single-handedly set up in the country the year before.

I tried to emulate Lisa's refinement by blow drying my hair one morning, but I got so sweaty that the make-up slid off my skin and dripped onto my top, leaving a stain. I also admired her gorgeous heels, but I stuck to ballet flats because I would have broken an ankle while scampering around Yangon's pothole-ridden pavements.

You do you, I told myself early on.

THE DINNER with Lord Puttnam was the first in a steady stream of surreal experiences at work. To be honest, simply turning up in the morning was surreal in the early days. I'd do a double-take when I caught sight of the British flag fluttering above the entrance of the grand, four-storey embassy building that overlooks Yangon River. Built in 1900 as the local headquarters of a Scottish firm, it's one of the oldest buildings on Strand Road, which is one of the few roads in Yangon that has retained its colonial name. Unlike the city's other colonial-era buildings, which are plentiful but mostly in a state of crumbling decay, the embassy was beautifully maintained. Its white exterior always looked freshly painted, and its elegant arched windows were free of the cobwebs and pigeon poop that obscured the view into others.

I got a good look at the building every morning because I approached it on foot, whereas the British staff and senior Burmese staff had their own vehicles and parked and entered around the back. For security reasons, traffic wasn't allowed to stop within fifty metres of the embassy's huge front doors, and the footpath was sealed off from the road with bollards and wire. So I'd leap out of the taxi and walk the last minute or so, which I liked because I got to take in everything.

Other highlights included giving a presentation to a trade delegation about Myanmar's abundant oil and gas reserves, and the time I oversaw the safe delivery of a couple of brand-new Land Rovers across the city for a British Embassy display. After I phoned up the new showroom in Insein Township and placed my order for the cars (which I'd originally hoped would be Jaguars, but was told they weren't available on the day), they were put on the back of a trailer and carefully transported to the British ambassador's residence in Ahlone Township, which has a number of quiet streets lined with embassies, diplomatic residences and the homes of families with old money.

The vehicles were displayed on the lawns of the residence to showcase excellence in British automotive manufacturing during an event in 2014 called the 'Great Day Out'. Hundreds of people attended, including young students from a local monastery. The embassy put on a traditional high tea of scones, sponge cake and cucumber sandwiches, as well as cobbling together old-fashioned fairground games like a coconut shy, which involves tossing a ball at a row of coconuts.

The Great Day Out was part of a global 'Great Britain'

campaign, which aimed to celebrate all things British and ultimately boost economic growth in the UK, but in the local context of Myanmar the elephant in the room (or on the lawn) was its status as a former British colony. Myanmar was part of the British Raj for 124 years until it gained its independence in 1948, so plastering the British flag everywhere – as bunting, on the cheeks of kids with face paint (which was my job), and on toothpicks poking out of the sandwiches – made the whole thing feel a bit awkward, at least to me.

Another minefield of awkwardness was the UK's insistence on referring to Yangon and Myanmar as Rangoon and Burma. Of course, it wasn't the only country to refuse to use the names adopted by Myanmar's military rulers in 1989. Many Western countries did so to avoid what they perceived as lending legitimacy to the regime; plus Aung San Suu Kyi always said Burma and Rangoon when she spoke in English, which added moral weight to that choice. However, on the streets of Yangon itself I very seldom heard either name uttered, so the decision by the UK government to stick with their original names was very noticeable. While most Burmese didn't seem to care what other people called their country, I wondered whether some people interpreted it as the UK clinging to Myanmar's colonial past. To avoid offending the reformist government, the British Embassy had started using two letterheads: if the recipient was a member of Myanmar's government it would say 'British Embassy Myanmar.' For everyone else the letterhead used was 'British Embassy Burma'. It was messy.

MY WORKING week passed quickly at the embassy, because there was often a lot going on. Lisa was a whirlwind of activity and usually had multiple projects on the go. One afternoon, she sent my colleague Nwe Nwe and me to the swanky Park Royal Hotel to taste-test canapés. The nibblies at the last few receptions hadn't been up to scratch, so Lisa was counting on us to choose alternatives that met two criteria: deliciousness and whether it could be eaten with one hand without making a mess. I undertook the task with earnest delight, but I didn't tell anyone that until a few weeks earlier, I hadn't known what a canapé was.

The new finger foods were served up at the frequent receptions hosted by UKTI, almost all of which were held at the ambassador's residence – either in the spacious and stately living room or, for large-scale events like the Great Day Out or Welsh National Day, on the lawns, which featured a pond as their centrepiece.

At the start of an event, my job was to stand under the arcaded marble verandah and welcome guests to the residence. I loved seeing newcomers' faces as they walked up the path and took in all the old-world grandeur. They'd gaze at the manicured hedges surrounding the statue of an admiralty officer before their eyes focused on the residence itself, which dates back to 1855. After a quick bit of chitchat, the guests would then walk through the arched doorway and into the reception room, where a waiter would be holding a tray of wine and beer. This room was the most like a museum to me, with its white columns, dark wooden floorboards, timber-panelled walls and a matching timber staircase that led up to the second floor, and which I never set foot upon because it was off-limits. On the walls of the reception room hung portraits of Lord Mountbatten and a young Queen Elizabeth II in all her finery, both in gilded frames. On an antique sideboard was a more recent photograph of the Queen, and on either side of her were crests mounted on shields, plus an antique clock and a tasselled table lamp. Guests would mingle around an enormous bouquet of fifty white roses in the centre of the room, before making their way into the living room or dining room at the function's appointed time.

Ambassador Andrew Patrick was a good sport about welcoming people into his home on any given night of the week – I personally would have found the lack of solitude a bit trying. He had also taken up learning Burmese with enthusiasm and often began and ended his speeches in Burmese. He had wispy, light-grey hair and spectacles with thick black frames. At well over six-foot tall, Andrew looked like a giant next to some of his Burmese guests, who are not a tall people. I also became very fond of the deputy ambassador Matthew Hedges, and his partner Liam, who was an actor and gave a few of us actual elocution classes ahead of various presentations. Myanmar could not have been an easy or straightforward diplomatic posting, but I was consistently impressed by Britain's diplomatic team. The previous British ambassador, Vicky Bowman, had remained in Myanmar and married a well-known painter and former political prisoner, Htein Lin. She spoke Burmese fluently and was razor sharp – her knowledge on Myanmar was truly encyclopedic.

While I myself wasn't cut out for life as a diplomat, I loved mingling with VIPs at Andrew's residence and amassed an impressive collection of business cards. In Myanmar, exchanging business cards is a vital part of social etiquette. Gone were the flimsy ones I'd handed out as a freelancer – my embassy business cards were extra thick and had my official Foreign and Commonwealth Office email address on the front and the Union Jack on the back. I'd also been given a leather pouch to keep my cards in, and the pouch was embossed with the royal coat of arms. I met so many people that soon after starting I had to place an order for a second batch.

∼

ONE OF THE people I came to know through my work at the embassy was a British entrepreneur called Mike. Lisa had initially asked me to interview him about his Myanmar-based investment company for the UKTI newsletter. I met Mike for a coffee at the Strand Hotel, which was just a couple of doors up from the embassy, and where I now had a staff discount. I liked Mike immediately. He seemed sharp, witty and kind, and talked a lot about his kids, who were a few years younger than me. When Sherpa and I met Mike and his wife, Patricia, at a cocktail reception at the ambassador's residence a few weeks later, we mentioned that we were excited about our upcoming trip to the annual Ubud Writers and Readers Festival in Bali.

Patricia clapped her hands and said, 'If you're going to Bali, you must stay at our holiday house.'

'Oh yes!' agreed Mike. 'You really must.'

And so we really did. I'd been expecting a rustic holiday home on Bali's quiet north coast, not a gigantic villa with a cook, gardener and driver. Out the back was an oversized aquamarine pool with a diving board and a cabana to the right of the shallow end. On the first day we arrived, Sherpa and I lounged about on the cabana as the sun began to set, idly gazing at the private beach and cracking open a couple of beers.

'Tough life,' I joked to Sherpa as we clinked our bottles.

I PASSED those first few months at the embassy very happily. My work was interesting, the setting was fascinating and my improved financial situation made life a whole lot more comfortable. Sherpa and I were even planning a trip home to Australia over Christmas, because for once I had enough money for the airfare. And I wasn't even missing journalism – or at least so I told myself.

But one morning my phone lit up with a text message from Sherpa that shattered my newfound contentment. He'd received a press release from the US Embassy and it contained news about something big.

'Obama is coming back to Myanmar,' he wrote. 'Next week. And this time he's going to give a public speech in Yangon.'

It was almost too much to take in – I thought I was going to lose it. Barack Obama is my all-time favourite speaker and over the years I'd watched dozens of his addresses. Whether he was calling out racial tensions in America, cracking jokes at the annual White House Correspondents' Association dinner or reaching out to the global Muslim community from Cairo University, I thought he gave the best speeches I had ever seen. He was funny, profound, bold and remarkable – to name but a few qualities I admired in him. And President Obama was once again showing that he believed in the reforms Myanmar was undertaking, and that they would create a more prosperous and democratic future. I loved him for showing that he cared.

'OMG. Can we go to his talk?' I fired back.

'The US Embassy is taking applications for media passes,' came Sherpa's swift reply. 'Students can also attend the talk.'

I began to write that this was amazing and unbelievable news, but stopped typing mid-sentence. I had momentarily forgotten that I wasn't allowed to work as a journalist for another two months, while I was still under contract to the embassy. That meant I wasn't eligible for a media pass.

As my excitement turned to despair, I thought about how cruel the timing of Barack Obama's visit was for me personally. Ever since I'd been accredited as a newspaper journalist in London in 2009, I'd pursued my career with passion and had given it everything I had, including moving countries twice. This was the first time I'd taken so much as a temporary break from it, and it just happened to be at the same time that Obama was visiting.

Of course, the sensible thing to do was to just keep on working at the embassy and miss the speech. But not being able to seize the once-in-a-lifetime opportunity was too painful to bear. I swallowed hard, realising I had a difficult decision to make.

20

BARACK COMES BACK

NOVEMBER 2014

I decided to sound out a couple of my editors about whether I could write an article about Obama's speech for their outlet. I figured I needed to know, at least hypothetically, whether it would be possible for me to go.

I went to the Strand Hotel for my lunch break and emailed Julian at *Mizzima* from my smartphone. He replied in a flash, saying that he couldn't give me the assignment. He had a long list of staff journalists who were vying for it, and one of *Mizzima's* in-house reporters would naturally be given priority over a freelancer like myself.

Then I tried Colin at *Democratic Voice of Burma*, but he too said no.

'I haven't even been able to get a pass for myself,' he added.

This last bit of information worried me. Maybe media spots were limited and had already been snapped up. Of course every journalist in town wanted to cover Obama's second visit to Myanmar.

I sighed. It seemed that even if I had been working as a journalist, I wouldn't have been able to see President Obama. In a sense, I was relieved. I didn't have to choose between his speech and my job at the embassy. But I still felt frustrated about not being able to see my idol.

Then I was struck by an idea. What if I applied for a spot as a blogger? Lisa had given me her blessing to continue publishing stories on my personal blog while I was working at the embassy, so there was no issue there. I reread the email from the US Embassy that Sherpa had forwarded me, which contained instructions on how to apply to be part of the White House press pool. Journalists were asked to provide their contact details, the name of the media outlet they worked for and their role within it. For me, the key sentence was this one: 'The US Embassy invites members of local and foreign media organisations to cover this event.'

My blog was getting several hundred hits a day and had even attracted some advertisers, but by no stretch could it be considered a 'media organisation'. The embassy's press team would probably laugh out loud when they read my application.

But I had nothing to lose, so that night after work I wrote a heartfelt email to the US Embassy's press officer, May Myat Noe. I talked up my blog and included links to the articles I'd written about Obama over the years, as well as a link to the special report about his 2012 visit that I'd put together for *The Myanmar Times*.

I have tried, I told myself, and started cooking dinner.

THE NEXT AFTERNOON, I left my desk to go and buy a cob of corn each for Nwe Nwe and me. The corn lady, as I called her, set up her portable stall of steamed and salted corn cobs on the pavement near our building most days, and I was a regular customer. I had just handed her 300 kyat when I felt my phone vibrate in my pocket. I was starving, so I took a few bites of the juicy corn before pulling out my phone. In my inbox was an email from the US Embassy. I stopped eating.

Thank you for registering to cover the Young Southeast Asian Leadership Initiative Town Hall with the President of the United States at the University of Yangon. This is a confirmation that you have been approved for a White House credential for the event on November 14, 2014.

My hands started shaking and I let out a massive whoop, startling the corn lady. I would see President Obama on Friday.

ON THE DAY of Obama's speech, I woke up with the same kind of butterflies in my stomach that I used to get on exam days at university. I couldn't concentrate, so I gave up trying to write and set off for the University of Yangon three hours before Obama was due to appear onstage. It was lucky I did, because the journey took much longer than it usually would have. An incredible number of Yangon's roads had been sealed off and thus became dead-ends, presumably to clear a route for the VIPs' cavalcade.

As the taxi approached the university along Pyay Road, I saw that crowds had formed on both sides of the road. They were no doubt hoping to catch a glimpse of the American president, just as I had when I turned up at Yangon International Airport two years ago. There was a heavy security presence, with hundreds – possibly even a thousand – policemen standing by in their blue-and-purple camouflage and netted hard hats. I made my way through the throng of people and gave my name to the security guard on the gate. I felt envious eyes upon me as I stepped inside the campus grounds, which were buzzing with activity.

It had been decades since the university had seen such crowds. Following pro-democracy demonstrations led by students in 1988, the regime shut all the country's universities for several years, and did so again when protests reignited in 1996. The University of Yangon was founded by the British in 1884 and it had once been the country's most prestigious learning institution, with alumni that included Aung San Suu Kyi's father, Aung San. However, to the junta, it simply had an irritating track record of attracting troublemakers. Its students had frequently played a central role in protest movements, be they against colonial rule or the military dictatorship. So the regime had kept the university closed to undergraduates for nearly twenty years, and had permitted them to return for the first time only this year.

I skipped up the steps leading to the arched entranceway of Diamond Jubilee Hall, whose enormous gilded pillars oddly brought back memories of the golden arches of McDonald's. Under the shade of a covered walkway, I went through an airport-style security screening where a group of staff and a sniffer dog were processing people as they entered. A man with a blond crewcut checked off my name and asked me to pass over my bag. He gave it to the dog handler standing behind him, who unzipped it and placed it under the nose of a German Shepherd in a harness. As the sniffer dog went to work, a man in beige slacks and a black polo shirt waved me through a metal detector. He gave me back my bag, plus a lanyard to wear around my neck. He grinned, showing a set of perfect pearly whites, and handed me two cookies in cling wrap.

'They're from the US Embassy,' he added when I looked at him, confused.

Once inside, I scanned the windowless conference room for Sherpa. It took a few seconds for my eyes to adjust to the harsh fluorescent lighting, which gave everything a greenish tinge. It was a much smaller space than I'd been expecting, which was fantastic. I'd envisioned the event as more of a stadium rock concert than an intimate acoustic session. There were only a few hundred people there.

I spotted Sherpa at one of the long tables set up for reporters in a cordoned-off area to the left of the stage. He too was twitching with excitement. Fortunately for Sherpa, as an editor-in-chief, there was never any doubt that he would get a media pass. We had our photo taken in front of the massive American and Burmese flags that were rigged up from the ceiling. After decades of sanctions and mutual suspicion, just seeing the two flags side-by-side felt historic. And it was only then that I noticed what they had in common: both featured stars and stripes. It was just the arrangement of them that was different: no doubt like much else.

'Do you think he's with the secret service?' I whispered to Sherpa, tilting my head in the direction of a man in an expensive-looking suit standing stock still beside a timber pillar.

'I'd say so,' said Sherpa. 'There's a few of them dotted around the room.'

We observed the man in silent fascination. He wore a discreet earpiece and every so often he said something under his breath, or gave the slightest of nods – to whom, I had no idea. His expression gave nothing away.

Scarcely ten minutes had passed when a couple of officials whipped around to tell the media to take their positions. I had just a few seconds to decide whether to remain with Sherpa or base myself from the photographers' section, which was directly in front of the stage. As much as I wanted to share the moment with my husband, I opted for the better view.

And what a view it was. I was less than fifteen metres from the stage. Next to me was my ex-colleague Kaung Htet, who was still a photographer for *The Myanmar Times*, and who I'd also recently collaborated with on a travel story for the Malaysian Airlines' inflight magazine.

'Have you seen this?' he asked me, pulling his smartphone out of his pocket.

On Kaung Htet's Facebook newsfeed was a series of photos that was quickly going viral. Obama and Aung San Suu Kyi had been caught in another awkward public display of affection during his visit to her home that morning. In one of the photos, Aung San Suu Kyi had her arm around the back of Obama's neck as he planted a kiss on her earlobe. In another, her nose was tickling his cheek. Their eyes were closed in all four photos, which made them look as though they were lost in the moment.

'Apparently this time it was Aung San Suu Kyi who kissed Obama,' said Kaung Htet with a shrug.

'They can't help themselves,' I replied, feigning exasperation.

At that moment the stage lights came on, causing a ripple of excitement to pass through the room. Thirty seconds later, the American national anthem began to play and a voice over the loudspeakers boomed, 'And now, the President of the United States, Barack Obama!'

Out strode a grinning Obama onto the stage. He waved hello to the audience, who were out of their seats and cheering. Once they'd quietened down, he began speaking, but I couldn't take anything in. I just stood there with my mouth open, completely awed. This person who was so familiar and yet not quite real was right in front of me. He was so close that I could make out the colour of his watchband. I'm not sure how much time had passed before I realised I was pointing my camera at the ceiling.

Get it together, I told myself, and began snapping away.

'When I took office nearly six years ago, I said the United States would extend our hand to any nation willing to unclench its fist,' said Obama, pausing for effect. 'And here, after decades of authoritarian rule, we've begun to see significant progress in just a few years. There is more of a sense of hope in Myanmar, that was once so closed to the world, about the role it can now play in the region and the world.'

Yes, I thought. *Just look at Myanmar now, hosting an American president and on the cusp of holding its first democratic elections in fifty years.*

I had never felt more optimistic about Myanmar's future than I did right then. It had proven that even the most repressive dictatorships are capable of change, and its journey to democracy would surely pave the way for the world's last remaining despots to fall like lonely dominoes.

But of course, Obama hadn't come to Myanmar just to shower praise on the reformist government. The country's political transition was still a work in progress, and arguably the biggest test – the elections – were yet to come. They were scheduled to be held in a year's time, but the highly partisan election commission had floated the idea of delaying them – for who knew how long. Many saw Obama's second visit, which was ostensibly to attend a regional conference, as a way of showing that the world was watching.

'We know that a journey to progress is not completed overnight,' he continued, holding his index finger aloft. 'There are setbacks and false starts, and sometimes even reverses. There are still attacks against journalists and against ethnic minorities. And America is still deeply concerned about the humanitarian situation in Rakhine State, and the treatment of minorities who endure discrimination and abuse.'

As he said this, a young Kachin woman in the audience wearing a striking shawl made of sterling silver discs and tassels caught my eye. She was vigorously nodding her head in agreement. The Kachin ethnic minority group are mostly Christians and they have been fighting the military for greater autonomy since 1961, in what has become one of the world's longest running civil wars. I wondered how her life had been impacted by the xenophobia of Myanmar's military regime. Did she know how to read and write in her own language? Possibly not. As part of the regime's policy known as 'Burmanisation', the only language taught in government schools was Burmese, and there were documented cases of ethnic minority language teachers being thrown into prison for conducting language classes outside of school hours.

Obama spoke beautifully – but then, to my dismay, he stopped. After just ten minutes, he invited the audience to ask him questions in what he referred to as a 'town hall'. I'd seen this term on the email from the US Embassy but I'd never encountered it before and had just thought it was another word for a public address. I was so disappointed. I'd been looking forward to witnessing Obama deliver one of his iconic speeches: to hear him draw historical parallels, to utter a poetic turn of phrase that would instantly become one of his quotable quotes, and to be left breathless with a rousing call to action that connected all the dots. I was glad that I hadn't quit my job for a question-and-answer session, even if it was with the American president.

A university student from Rakhine State asked the first question. He didn't say that he was a Rohingya, but he had darker skin than the majority Burman ethnic group typically do, and he said he'd witnessed sectarian and racial violence in his neighbourhood. He asked the president what he could do to promote tolerance and eradicate extremism.

With great prescience, Obama told the young man, 'There is no example of a country that is successful if its people are divided based on religion or ethnicity.' He added that Syria showed how terribly things can turn out if it is, then continued, saying, 'If you are Christian and you have a friend who says, "I hate Muslims," then it's up to you to say to that friend, "You know what? I don't believe in that. I think that's the wrong attitude and we have to be respectful of the Muslim population." If you are quiet, then the people who are intolerant will own the stage.'

I thought about our landlords feeding us pork snacks. I also thought about the taxi driver who had kicked out Sherpa when he told him that he was from Bangladesh, and how his colleagues had called him a *kalar* behind his back. I wished they could hear their behaviour being called out.

Obama took the next question from a girl and said he would alternate boy, girl, boy, girl, because 'societies that are most successful also treat their women and girls with respect'.

The students, however, were too excited to respect his wishes. Boys and girls wildly waved their hands in the air whenever Obama called out for the next question. I wondered whether the questions had been pre-approved by the embassy. Surely it would be too risky to chance it? But what happened next made me think that perhaps they hadn't vetted the questions.

Obama chose a young man to ask him the next question, but when he started reading out his notes from a piece of paper, Obama laughingly confiscated it.

'There are, like, twenty questions on here,' he said, turning the paper over. 'Why don't you just ask me one of them? I'll read the rest,' he assured him, folding the paper and putting it in his shirt pocket.

Over the next hour, the students gave Obama a good-natured grilling – and he clearly loved the exchange. No matter that he was the most powerful person in the world: even his pronunciation of 'Rakhine' was teased by the students for being off the mark. It was rare to see the president in such an informal setting, and the jokes were almost as frequent as the reflections. It was something very special to witness.

Obama wrapped up the session by saying he hoped the students would take up the mantle of reform from activists like Aung San Suu Kyi.

'And as you do,' he vowed, 'I promise you will have no better friend and partner than the United States of America.'

Obama's final words were in Burmese, and the applause that came afterwards was deafening. While flanked by the secret service, Obama came down from the stage to shake hands with a few lucky students. He most definitely got the rock-star treatment.

SHERPA and I went out to nearby Hledan for beers to celebrate our amazing day. Even before the alcohol hit my bloodstream, I felt drunk with happiness. I thought back to how I had almost lost it when I had found out that Obama was returning to Myanmar, only to be devastated that I couldn't see him, then to be elated when I had learnt that I'd been given a media pass. In the end, everything had worked out beautifully.

'I'm so happy that Myanmar is home,' I said to Sherpa after we'd ordered a second round of Tiger beers. 'I wouldn't have had these incredible experiences anywhere else. That goes for my job at the embassy too.'

'It's been incredible,' agreed Sherpa, looking starry-eyed.

'And next year we'll witness history being made when the elections are held.'

'If they are held,' said Sherpa, ever the realist.

'They will,' I replied. 'I'd put money on it.'

I HAD a ball writing the blog post that weekend. Unlike when I wrote an article for a magazine, I was free to write as many words as I wanted. I went on and on, describing everything from the taxi ride to the University of Yangon to the background music that was playing before Obama took to the stage. I wrote it for myself, as a way of helping me remember everything, as much as I did to create a public record of the event. By the time I'd finished, the blog post came to 2500 words, which was very long indeed. I broke up the text with twenty photos that I'd carefully selected from the hundreds I'd taken. After hitting the 'publish' button, I shared the blog post with my followers on social media and sent a link with a gushing thank-you note to May Myat Noe at the US Embassy.

Much later – long after I had returned to journalism – a young business leader I interviewed started following me on Twitter, which I didn't check very often.

He sent me the following message:

Hey Jess! Thanks again for the interview yesterday. I can't wait to see the article when it's published. By the way, I can't believe that Obama follows you on Twitter! How on earth did that come about?

This time, I did lose it.

21

THE MAN IN THE CLOUDS
AUGUST 2015

By August, I had been with the British embassy for the better part of a year. My contract had been extended, and after that I'd stayed on as a part-time consultant writing reports on investment opportunities in different sectors. This allowed me to freelance a few days a week. It was the perfect arrangement: my income was solid, I was writing articles again and I'd kept a foot in the door at the embassy.

So I wasn't looking for a new job, and certainly not a full-time one. But that was before I received an email from my friend Yuko, a fellow expat. She told me that the state-run newspaper, *The Global New Light of Myanmar*, was looking to hire its first foreign editor. Her friend Sean had been seconded there for six months by his employer in Japan, *Kyodo News,* as part of a two-year partnership that aimed to improve the look and feel of Myanmar's state-run newspaper. The partnership was coming to an end and Sean was returning to Tokyo, so *The Global New Light of Myanmar* was looking to hire a foreign editor to take his place. She thought I might be interested and asked if I would like to contact Sean about a possible job interview.

At first I thought Yuko's email was a joke. I was aware that the newspaper had made some changes in line with Myanmar's reform process, but it was hard to believe that those changes would extend to hiring a permanent foreign editor. It seemed too insular an enterprise.

For fifty years, the regime had used *The New Light*, as it was often called, as its propaganda tool, along with three Burmese-language state-run newspapers and some television stations. Most of the articles in *The New Light* covered select activities by the regime and its cronies, such as cutting the ribbon at a new monastery, and everything was cast in glowing terms – under the wisdom of junta rule, social ills like poverty and crime did not exist. International news was censored and there were also fillers of dubious news value – I once read an article about a refrigerator being found in a paddock.

Before the reforms began in 2010, *The New Light* was a truly nasty newspaper. Aung San Suu Kyi was namelessly depicted in cartoons and poems as being a sluttish slave to the west. Her marriage to the late British academic Michael Aris was frequently held up for contempt: it was implied, not very subtly, that only a loose Burmese woman would marry a foreigner. The back page had a banner across the top that ran xenophobic messages, such as accusing the BBC and Voice of America of 'sowing hatred among the people'. Another common mantra was: 'Crush all internal and external destructive elements as the common enemy'. A long-term expat I'd interviewed had witheringly referred to the newspaper as the 'The New Lies of Myanmar'.

And yet despite being widely loathed and ridiculed, *The New Light* had more readers than any other English-language publication in Myanmar. This was partly because it had the best distribution network, and government subsidies allowed it to undercut its rivals on price. *The New Light* also had a monopoly on breaking news from the government, so people were forced to read it to know what was going on. Privately owned media outlets like *The Myanmar Times* and *Mizzima* would pick up a piece of news and run it a day later with the oft-repeated phrase: 'as reported in state-run media ...'

In recent times, *The New Light* had been attempting to revamp its image, as the country itself was. The partnership with *Kyodo News* had seen the newspaper go from smudgy black and white to colour, and the word 'Global' was inserted into its already long title – a change that was presumably meant to convey a more international outlook for the former hermit nation. The accusations against the BBC were gone and Aung San Suu Kyi was nowadays simply ignored: her name and photograph never appeared in its pages. But *The New Light* was still very much the mouthpiece of the quasi-civilian ruling party, whom it never, ever criticised. And it still carried some laughably dull news stories.

Why on earth, then, would I want to work there? I wasn't sure that I did. I was curious, certainly, but also apprehensive about becoming an employee of the powerful Ministry of Information, which was responsible for Myanmar's state-run media. Virtually all of the members of Myanmar's reformist government had military backgrounds, including the information minister, U Ye Htut. The same people who had overseen one of the world's most brutal dictatorships would effectively be my employers. What would the consequences be if I made a mistake? What if I fell into disfavour, as I had at *The Myanmar Times*?

Despite my misgivings, curiosity won out. Working at *The New Light* was the closest I'd ever get to a real-life version of George Orwell's depiction of newspeak and the Ministry of Truth in *Nineteen Eighty-Four*. Propaganda had always fascinated me, and it sounded as though there was an opportunity to make positive changes at the newspaper, in order to reflect a more democratic Myanmar. I reasoned that I should at least go in for an interview. I could see whether the place had an ominous vibe and then weigh up things if I was offered the job.

THREE MEN STARED at me intently from across an enormous table. My job interview was taking place in a meeting room that was almost the size of a basketball court, and just outside the door we'd come through was a printing press worth several million dollars. If it had been switched on, I'd been told by the newspaper's personnel manager U Maung Maung Than, we wouldn't have been able to hear one another over the noise it made. But the hulking piece of machinery sat dormant until eleven o'clock at night, when it began pumping out newspapers.

'We are looking for someone who will help the newspaper become more people-focused,' said U Maung Maung Than, who smiled at me pleasantly.

For twenty minutes, he had been peppering his sentences with this term. He didn't say so explicitly, but I took 'people-focused' to mean less propaganda and more emphasis on something resembling the public interest. Sitting on either side of U Maung Maung Than was the Burmese, betel-chewing news editor, Wallace, and Sean, who was a thirty-something Australian-Japanese journalist.

I was told that *The New Light* was no longer completely state-owned: it had a private investor with a forty-nine per cent share, with the Ministry of Information owning the rest. U Maung Maung Than didn't tell me who the private investor was, and I sensed it prudent not to ask. They were looking for a foreign editor to continue Sean's work there, which included improving the quality of the newspaper – both cosmetically and editorially, as well as training journalists and sub-editing news stories. I could hire a couple of expat editors to help me and the salary was the same as I'd had while full-time at the embassy.

U Maung Maung Than asked me a couple of questions about my time in Myanmar: How long had I lived there and why had I come?

'Okay, very good,' he said, nodding as I wound up my answer. 'We'd like to offer you the job of Senior Editor. Can you start tonight?'

I was taken aback. So much for weighing up things. But nothing I'd seen or heard had frightened me and the remit was unlike anything I'd had before. So, after hesitating for a couple of heartbeats, I took the job. I proposed starting the following week so I could meet my pending freelance deadlines. It would take me longer to wrap up the project I was working on at the British Embassy, so for the next few weeks I would be working for two governments, neither of which was my own.

That night, I excitedly announced the news about my new job on Facebook. The comments came thick and fast. Colin from the *Democratic Voice of Burma* congratulated me and then remarked wryly, 'Maybe they'll publish today's weather instead of yesterday's.'

Most of my friends were happy for me, but a couple accused me of losing credibility. They said that I wasn't a real journalist if I worked at *The New Light*. With a touch of defensiveness, I said my new job involved improving the newspaper during a critical time for Myanmar, but they remained incredulous. No doubt others were too.

Never mind what other people think, I thought to myself. *Myanmar's first general elections in fifty years are three months away and I've got a ringside seat.*

❦

As I HELPED myself to a second slice of pizza from the box lying open on a table in the newsroom, I was feeling upbeat about my decision to join *The New Light*. My new colleagues and I had gathered for a 'pizza party' that had been arranged as a farewell for Sean and a welcome to me. So far everyone seemed friendly and no one had three heads. I noted to myself that I was getting a warmer welcome than I'd received at *The Myanmar Times*.

It looked like a typical newsroom, with reporters and translators huddled over their screens and dusty stacks of past editions lining the back wall. A TV played the rolling news on MITV, a state-run channel. It was obvious, though, that the government was miserly in its funding of the enterprise. We worked on uncomfortable plastic chairs and some of the desks and computers looked about a hundred years old.

When Wallace introduced me to the chief reporter, Ko Aye Min Soe, the first thing that came out of his mouth was, 'We must improve the paper.' Hearing this was encouraging, because it suggested that the team was keen to embrace further changes. Ko Aye Min Soe looked to be about thirty and he had an unmistakable twinkle in his eye, although he also looked weary. He wore a faded, short-sleeved shirt tucked into a *longyi*. He told me that the newspaper's managers wanted *The New Light* to emulate *The Straits Times* in Singapore. In other words – censored and pro-ruling party, but of respectable quality.

I returned to my desk feeling excited about the unusual opportunity I'd been given. But when I read the story that was sitting in my inbox waiting to be sub-edited, I suddenly felt overwhelmed. There was so much wrong with it that I didn't know where to start.

Low production of maize in some areas of Tatkon
TATKON—A lack of rain in some areas of Tatkon Township in Nay
Pyi Taw Council Area has decreased maize production this year,

according to a maize farmer in Naungthikha Anawyahta ward. But the farm hands processing maize from the '888-species' corn crop are in much supply and cheap, as the workers are keen to skin the corn husks which are much in demand to be used as filters for Myanmar cheroots. The current price of a basket (33.33 kg) of maize is K10,000 which is good, said the maize farmer, who cultivated 10 acres of maize. He added that maize brokers come to buy right to his house.

It was one thing to say that I was going to help *The New Light* become a better newspaper: making it happen would be another. I tried not to despair. Instead, I went over to Wallace's desk. Every shift, he sent me about ten news stories to sub-edit after they had been translated into English. The stories from our reporters outside Yangon mostly arrived by fax.

'Hey, Wallace,' I began. 'I don't think we should run the story about maize. It has no news value.'

'Alright,' he said, not sounding thrilled. 'I'll give you another one.'

There was no question that the next story Wallace sent me was newsworthy. Police had intercepted a baby elephant and two adult females being smuggled from the far northern state of Kachin. The problem was that vital bits of information were missing, and certain aspects of the story didn't make sense. Were the elephants being smuggled as part of the ivory trade in China? But if so, why were they heading to Bago, which was in the opposite direction? Was it really possible to fit three elephants onto a single truck, as the reporter claimed? What penalty were the smugglers facing? What would happen to the elephants now?

I went back over to Wallace's desk. He looked up from his screen and gave me a watery smile.

'Sorry to bother you again, Wallace. Can I get the translator to call the reporter and ask him a few questions about the elephant smuggling story?'

'We don't have phone numbers for our regional reporters,' he replied.

'Could we send him an email then?'

'They don't use email.'

'Ah, okay,' I said. 'I guess I'll work with what I've got.'

'Very good,' said Wallace. 'I'm just about to send you three more stories. I need them all back by 8 p.m.'

Unfortunately, the first story I opened read like a shopping list. It contained such an excruciating level of detail about the contents of a donation to monks that it would make a reader's eyes glaze over.

The Ministry of Religious Affairs presented donations to the monks that included 120 bags of rice, 60 viss [97 kilograms] of cooking oil, 535 sets of robes, 348 umbrellas, 348 pairs of slippers, 348 alms bowls, 348 fans, 700 steel bowls, 119 dozens of steel spoons, 119 packages of juice donated by the people to 119 monasteries in the township.

After thinking hard about what to do, I decided then and there to be pragmatic. The newspaper's pages had to be filled every day and our time to work on each edition was limited. If the best I could do was to improve the grammar in certain stories, so be it – for now. I made a note to discuss the 'five W's' of reporting during our next newsroom meeting, because it was already clear that the who, what, where, when and why were often missing from our stories. Decades of censorship and self-censorship had produced a misplaced focus on the mundane.

I also didn't want to drive Wallace completely nuts by taking issue with every article he sent me. He was already exhausted. He worked twelve-hour shifts seven days a week and got just three days off a year. I wasn't sure whether he even had any interest in journalism, as at no point had he mentioned wanting to work at a newspaper. He'd proudly told me about his years as a captain in the military, back when he was still a young man. While fighting against insurgent groups in the jungle, he'd contracted cerebral malaria and nearly died. When he recovered, he was transferred to *The New Light*. That was fifteen years earlier.

During my second week in the job, I walked into the newsroom and saw Wallace look at me with a face full of worry lines.

'Take a seat,' he said, extending a sinewy arm towards the empty chair on the other side of his desk.

I gulped and sat.

'I got a phone call from the information minister this morning about a story you edited yesterday. You inserted the name of the interfaith marriage bill into the article. He was very angry that you did that.'

I knew that the proposed law was contentious because it would make it difficult for Buddhist women to marry men from different religions. I had simply assumed that the reporter had missed out that detail, and that the obvious thing to do was include it. Wrong.

'I'm really sorry, Wallace,' I said. 'I'll check with you before adding in something that could be controversial.'

'Thank you,' he said, and stood up to go check the fax machine.

The exchange rattled me, so when Wallace emailed me half an hour later with a request to edit a public message from President Thein Sein, I nervously wondered whether I would get myself into hot water again.

Hi Jess!

This is the message of the president on International Teacher's

Day. Normally we do not exclude any line in Myanmar version. So, please edit it but not omit any line and understand me.
    Wallace

I OPENED the Word document with a sense of trepidation. To my dismay, I saw that it was riddled with grammatical errors. I wanted the president to sound – well – presidential, but I was worried that I might inadvertently change the meaning of his words, which I figured someone else had drafted on his behalf. I spent a long time deliberating every correction. To my relief, there was no call from the minister the following day, and Wallace often gave me the job of polishing the president's words.

I was thrilled when some of our readers noticed the improvements I'd helped bring about at *The New Light*. A foreign correspondent in Yangon took a photo of a page and shared it on social media, praising the newspaper for being more balanced in its coverage of the upcoming elections. That felt great. But I wasn't proud of everything I did. Sub-editing propaganda made me feel pretty terrible. The stories that came from the military-owned news agency, *Myawady Daily*, were always problematic. The news agency had been established in 2011, right after the quasi-civilian government was sworn in. It was part of the military's surprisingly extensive media portfolio and published by the distinctly Orwellian-sounding Directorate of Public Relations and Psychological Warfare. The stories we received were completely one-sided, and possibly untrue. For example, one day Wallace asked me to edit a story that claimed that the Kachin Independence Army (KIA) had breached the newly created ceasefire agreement and was 'harassing locals'. The Burmese military was therefore justified in attacking the KIA camp with 'air and artillery power'. Like all the stories from *Myawady Daily,* only the fatalities on the military's side were included. I hated editing these kinds of stories, but I never said anything to Wallace. It wasn't for me to pick and choose the stories I sub-edited, and there was no question that we would continue to run them. I'm not sure whether Wallace suspected my reluctance, but he would sometimes inform me in an email whether a story was a 'must' story – and it was often the ones I felt worst about.

As I got to know my colleagues better over time, I asked them how they felt about facilitating propaganda. Contrary to what outsiders assumed, none of them (other than Wallace) had supported the military regime. It was simply a job and a way of being able to use English in a professional context – and such opportunities were still in short supply. My colleagues were kind and thoughtful people. One wrote poetry in his spare time, while another was working on a novel. There was also a young fitness fanatic. A translator, who I'll call U Nyan Aung, was a former political prisoner. He'd spent eight years in prison after taking part in a pro-communist rally when he was twenty-three.

'At school I'd wanted to be a writer,' U Nyan Aung told me one night as we smoked a cigarette in the dimly lit outdoor space. 'But when I came out of prison, I had no skills. I hadn't graduated from university and I was too old to return. I was always opposed to military rule and I didn't want to work for the regime – no one did. But I got the job here very easily after sitting an English-language test.'

U Nyan Aung's prospective employer didn't ask him if he had been in prison, so he simply didn't disclose it. During his time behind bars he had contracted tuberculosis. He was often in poor health, especially during the rainy season. Because of that, he was sometimes allowed to work from home – the concession he was given to work flexibly surprised me.

Another colleague who had been with the newspaper for fifteen years said that *The New Light* was the only source of

English-language teaching material that tutors could afford to buy. So he saw his work not so much as aiding propaganda but as a way of helping his fellow Burmese to learn English.

'I always said to my teacher friends: "Ignore the message and focus on the language",' he explained.

I took my colleague's advice when I had to sub-edit propaganda, although it always sat uneasily with me.

THE FINAL TASK of my work day was my favourite: writing the front-page headlines. I got a kick out of seeing my words emblazoned across the newspaper the next day. But it was mortifying when a mistake was made.

One night, a story came in late about a fire at a warehouse that stored raw materials for Coca-Cola bottles. Despite 400 firefighters attending the blaze, virtually all the stock was destroyed. It was a blow for the soft drinks giant, who had only recently returned to Myanmar after an absence of fifty years (leaving North Korea and Cuba as the only Coke-free countries in the world). Ko Aye Min Soe phoned Coca-Cola's local office, but they declined to comment. We had another reporter on the ground who attended the blaze. Ko Aye Min Soe and I rearranged the contents of the front page to make it the next day's lead story. I penned the following headline: 'Fire Causes $1 Million Damage at Coca-Cola Warehouse'. It all seemed straightforward, if a bit uncreative.

I went home at 10 p.m. as usual, leaving the deputy news editor U Than Thaung and Ko Aye Min Soe behind. They were permitted to sign off only when the first newspaper had been printed. Both of them worked such long hours that they often slept at the office.

When I picked up my newspaper from the porch the next morning, I almost dropped my mug of coffee.

'What the hell ...?' I exclaimed.

Someone had changed the headline. Instead of stating that the damage was estimated at $1 million, it said it was only $100,000. And yet the references to a million dollars of damage in the actual story remained unchanged. It made no sense.

When I arrived at work that afternoon, I tried to keep my voice level as I asked Ko Aye Min Soe why my headline had been changed after I'd gone home.

He shrugged and said, 'One million dollars seemed like too much.'

I didn't know what to say to him. I was embarrassed, because it looked as though that day's newspaper had been put together by amateurs. The naysayers would have a field day laughing at me.

Other mistakes were the result of the language barrier. One night, for example, I asked a designer to put some headlines in red, but he thought I meant only the first letter of every word. As a colleague commented, the newspaper looked like a kids comic strip.

Sometimes changes were made to the newspaper's contents that mystified me. Stories that Wallace had sent me to edit didn't appear in the newspaper, or I'd find that paragraphs had been removed. When we lost an excellent story filed by one of our most experienced reporters, Ye Myint, I was frustrated. He had got some great quotes from primary sources about working conditions in Myanmar's garment factories, which were being used by the likes of Adidas. We had strong photos and Oxfam had just published a new report on the issue. We'd made it the lead story on the front page and I'd given it the headline 'Not a Pretty Picture', which I felt was safe because it was an understatement.

To my chagrin, I saw that the entire story had disappeared and in its place was an article that was six days old – an eternity in news – about UNESCO giving Inle Lake World Heritage List status. Why would our reporters bother taking my suggestions onboard to write better stories if their efforts were in vain? I went over to Wallace's desk to try to find out what had happened.

'Hi there, Wallace. I noticed that Ye Myint's story on the garment industry was spiked. I thought you'd said it was a great story?'

'Ah yes, that one. He told me not to run it.'

'Sorry. Who is *he*?'

Wallace mumbled something indiscernible about the Ministry of Information and began shuffling the documents in his in-tray. I didn't think it was the minister himself who had given the order, because he surely wouldn't have had the time – and when he'd called Wallace enraged about me mentioning the interfaith marriage bill, it was *after* the newspaper had been printed.

'Who was it who told you not to run it?'

Wallace averted my gaze and kept on chewing betel.

'Wallace? Is there a man in the clouds?'

Wallace's eyes lit up. 'Yes,' he said, with a chortle. 'You could say that: a man in the clouds. He knows everything. He tells me what to do.'

The nickname spread in the newsroom. Together we tried not to anger the man in the clouds. It was almost like a game, where winning meant keeping all of that day's content. However, trying to predict what would fall foul of him was impossible. I think that was partly because the newspaper was in the midst of change, and it was hard to know how far the changes extended. For example, crime was a new addition to the newspaper –

including it was part of what U Maung Maung Than meant by being 'people-focused'.

One night, Ko Aye Min Soe and I stood around a designer's screen, deliberating over which photo to use for a story about a major drugs haul. I wanted to use the one we had of a middle-aged woman who had discovered the drugs in a creek while fishing for recyclable plastics that she could sell.

'We won't be allowed to use that photo – the creek is filled with rubbish,' cautioned our young designer, Nyi Zaw Moe. 'How about the shot of the men in front of the drugs stash?' he said, referring to an image of two scrawny young men in hand-cuffs. They were standing in front of a table laid out with blocks of methamphetamines. But we went with the shot of the woman beside the littered creek, and the photo made its way into the newspaper. This would have been unthinkable just a couple of years earlier.

I often wondered what the man in the clouds thought of my work at *The New Light* – assuming he knew I was there. Or perhaps it had been his idea in the first place to hire a foreign editor. Was he happy with the changes I was making at the newspaper, or was I pushing things too far? Would he have me sacked if I made too many errors of judgement? It was by far the strangest work relationship I ever had.

22

A SEA OF GREEN

OCTOBER 2015

A big part of my job at *The New Light* was training journalists. It was something I loved doing, and when two expat sub-editors called Jacob and Alec were hired, I had more time to devote to it. I tried to pass on what I'd learnt while studying to become an accredited newspaper journalist in London and, as a team, we'd comb through the newspaper each day and identify what could be done better. I also introduced weekly awards for the best news stories, which was something we had done at *The Myanmar Times*. When a reporter called Khaing Thanda Lwin hit the streets and returned with a story about people facing difficulties in registering to vote, I was ecstatic (as I was when the story appeared in its entirety the next day). It may not seem like a big deal, but Khaing Thanda Lwin's article was such a departure from the types of stories *The New Light* had run for decades, with their positive spin on the ruling elite and no acknowledgement of the realities faced by the general public. It felt as if we were contributing to Myanmar's democratic future.

Wallace was less enthusiastic. After one meeting, he

bellowed, 'That meeting lasted seventeen minutes! I am a military man and I don't want to waste time with these processes.'

Until then I hadn't realised that Wallace had been keeping time in his notebook. I tried to appease him by running shorter meetings, but one thing we couldn't agree on was the value of trying to motivate staff with awards. He told me that he didn't see the point of it, as the work would be done regardless of whether or not they wanted to do it.

Although I believed that our stories were improving, when it came to the content we relied on from other state-run news organisations, such as Myanmar News Agency, the same issues were cropping up time and time again. Sub-editing those stories – which usually had vital bits of information missing – often felt like trying to solve a riddle. We couldn't simply use our reporters because the likes of Myanmar News Agency had exclusive access to government sources. It was also the only entity allowed to take photographs at government events and it was often the only one present, too.

It was frustrating, so I asked U Maung Maung Than if I could run a workshop in the capital city of Nay Pyi Taw, as Sean had done before me, for the handful of state-run publications based there. U Maung Maung Than said he'd check with the powers that be and, within a matter of days, a plane ticket appeared on my desk. I knew that the benefits of a one-off session would be limited, but I figured it was better than nothing – which appeared to be what journalists at Myanmar's state-run media were given in the way of training.

The following week, I boarded a Myanmar National Airline flight along with a young translator called Hay Mar, who had been assigned to help me with any language difficulties I might face. Sitting next to me and clasping a small bag of belongings on her lap, she yawned sleepily and closed her eyes. Though it wasn't yet 7 a.m., I was wide awake thanks to the pre-flight adrenaline that was coursing through my veins. Still a nervous flier, I was nonetheless grateful not to be travelling in a car. The stretch of road between Yangon and Nay Pyi Taw was known as 'Death Highway' because so many people had died on it in the few short years since it opened. The expressway was poorly constructed and had dozens of dangerous curves – and many Burmese also believed it was cursed. There was also a belief that people who died a sudden, violent death in something such as a car accident would not pass into the next life and would haunt the area as ghosts. So monks had been dispatched to recite exorcist prayers and sprinkle holy water on the asphalt to ward off the evil spirits. But people continued to lose their lives every week during the five-hour journey.

Thankfully, the flight was short and uneventful, and a driver in a black pick-up truck met Hay Mar and me at the airport and deposited us at a nondescript hotel. After dropping our overnight bags in our rooms, we were back inside the air-conditioned vehicle and cruising along an empty boulevard that shimmered with heat haze. Other than when we overtook a couple of motorcyclists, the only sign of life was a small collection of gardeners tending a verge. It was hard to tell whether they were men or women because they were stick-thin and draped in baggy clothing that included long-sleeved shirts, *longyis* and gloves. Their faces were hidden under the conical hats associated with Vietnam, while a scrap of material covered their necks and was tied in a knot beneath their chins. I think they wanted to avoid their skin being darkened by the sun because lighter skin was considered much more desirable in Myanmar, but the heat in all those clothes must have been suffocating. With their heads bowed, they made slow, mechanical movements, and in so doing reminded me of a chain gang.

As we pulled up in front of a Soviet-style building in the city's ministerial zone, I wondered what kind of a reception I was about to get. I would be giving a talk to journalists from three state-run newspapers, as well as the *Myawady Daily*, the military's newspaper. I was a bit wary of this last group. Once I'd got to know my colleagues at *The New Light*, I'd realised they weren't regime lackeys, but it was hard to see how those at *Myawady Daily* couldn't be at least a little bit pro-military. I was concerned they may not appreciate an outsider flying in and telling them how to do their jobs.

But as soon as the doors opened and people began filing into the conference room, I felt reassured by the shy smiles directed my way. They were an attentive audience and showed no impatience with my talk taking twice as long due to it being consecutively translated by Hay Mar. They were quick to laugh at even my corniest jokes, and when I opened the floor up for questions, several hands shot into the air.

'What do you think is the most important quality in a journalist?'

'Can you recommend any free online training materials?'

'What are your favourite international news websites?'

Afterwards, the chief editor and chief reporter of *Myanmar Alin* showed me around the various newsrooms, where I met more journalists. They struck me as no different from those I knew at *The Myanmar Times* and *Mizzima*, or really any other young people in Myanmar. Not for the first time, I wondered who was behind the frightening persona of Myanmar's state-run media if it wasn't driven by the journalists themselves. Perhaps there was not just one man but many men in the clouds.

Not long after we began the drive back to the hotel zone, Hay Mar pointed at a building on the left and said, 'That's the Ministry of Information.'

'Oh wow – really? Can you please ask the driver to pull over so that I can take a few photos?'

The ministry was smaller than I'd imagined, at just a couple of storeys high. Two thick concrete pillars flanked a curved front that was made up of reflective panels. The glass was tinted the bright blue of a swimming pool. That those inside the ministry could see out without being seen seemed fitting, given that power had historically been wielded with a total lack of transparency. I wasn't sure if people were staring at me as I trotted about on the lawn, so, feeling self-conscious, I took a few quick photos and a selfie before heading back to the pick-up truck. Before hopping inside, I turned and took one last look at the ministry. Surely the man in the clouds was in there somewhere. Could he even be looking out at me now? And if so, was he smiling or sneering?

TRUTH BE TOLD, I had an ulterior motive for wanting to visit Nay Pyi Taw. And that was to see Myanmar's parliament in action. I'd put in a request to U Maung Maung Than, who submitted a copy of my passport and wrote a letter on my behalf. And, voila, my wish was granted. Without government connections, such access would have been unthinkable. The closest most people got to parliament was hundreds of metres away, because it was never open to the public and the road in front was barricaded. During a previous visit to the capital city, I'd taken a few blurry photos of the building from behind a chain-link fence, half-expecting the soldiers stationed along it to tell me to move on.

But this time around, I passed through the barricade and into the complex, which is surrounded by an actual moat and spans 800 acres. After driving for a minute or so along a road lined with beautifully landscaped gardens, a final gate slid open for us, beyond which stood the utterly enormous Union Parliament, or *Pyidaungsu Hluttaw* as it is called in Burmese. With its tiered roof and gigantic columns, it looked part Chinese temple, part Roman mausoleum – though it was brand-spanking new. Dotted about the lawns were smaller buildings with the same clashing colour scheme of beige, mint, brown and red. Sumptuous and grand, it must have cost a huge sum to construct. With a third of Myanmar's population living below the poverty line, it seemed distinctly over the top.

I excitedly drummed my fingers on the window of the pick-up truck. I'd seen footage of Myanmar's parliament on television before, so I could visualise the scene I was about to witness. Both houses of parliament were laid out like a theatre, with rows of seats cascading down towards a stage where the speaker sat. Parliamentarians of the majority Bamar ethnic group wore an eye-catching hat called a *gaung baung* that was the colour of lemon sorbet. The country's most famous member of parliament, Aung San Suu Kyi, wore flowers in her hair, because women were not required to wear a hat when taking the floor. Next to the section of *gaung baungs* were several people wearing truly extraordinary hats that were made from feathers, claws and boar bones. These were parliamentarians representing Myanmar's ethnic minority groups. To the left of those was a sea of green, where the military sat in their uniforms. The armed forces were automatically allocated a quarter of parliament's 440 seats. They were unelected, yet they had veto powers over any constitutional amendment – and they had designed a constitution that suited their purposes by banning Aung San Suu Kyi from being president, among other things. The military had branded the arrangement 'disciplined democracy'.

I wasn't excited about seeing parliament as a spectacle in and of itself – unlike the parliaments I'd seen in London and Canberra, proceedings in Myanmar were usually staid, with little emotion on display. But with the country on the cusp of historic elections, parliament was poised to welcome its first democratically elected government in fifty years. That was provided, of course, that the military respected the will of the people this time around.

As we pulled up, an official greeted Hay Mar and I at the foot of the steps. Beaming, I followed him and Hay Mar past two golden lion statues, under a portico and inside a cavernous hall, where my ballet flats click-clacked across the smooth marble floor. As we approached the ornate double doors leading into parliament, the official took an abrupt left and stopped.

'This is the media section,' Hay Mar explained, pointing to a dozen or so people sitting in lacquered teak chairs beside the wall. 'He'll come back to get us in fifteen minutes,' she added, as the official glided away.

Young men in jeans and t-shirts sat hunched over their phones, playing Candy Crush. Behind them was a set of gold satin curtains that must have been forty feet tall. A container filled with drinking water seemed to be all there was in the way of facilities. There weren't even any tables, so it was difficult to take notes. At first I thought it was some kind of waiting area for journalists, so as to prevent a session in progress being disrupted while entering the media gallery. Then I noticed the small television. On its screen was the familiar sea of green. With this set-up, the journalists may as well have been in Yangon.

'We can't see parliament?' I asked Hay Mar in disbelief.

'No,' she said. 'This is where journalists must stay.'

At arm's length from democracy, I thought.

The Myanmar Foreign Correspondents' Club in 2013. Photo - Julian Ray

Street stalls in downtown Yangon, 2016.

Bagan at dusk.

The entrance to the Shwedagon Pagoda in Yangon.

*The colonial-era Government Telegraph Office in Yangon was
built in 1913.*

Ananda Temple, Bagan.

A Kayan woman in Bagan.

A mother and her child on Inle Lake.

The Big British Day Out at the Ambassador's Residence in 2015.

Waiting for US President Obama to speak at Yangon University in 2014.

President Obama jokingly confiscates a page of questions at Yangon University in 2014.

A selfie out the front of the Ministry of Information in 2015.

News editor Ko Aye Min Soe at The Global New Light of Myanmar.

With a Pact Microfinance source while on assignment with Lauren DeCicca.

Our final home in Myanmar, in Yangon's Botataung township.

23

PURPLE PINKIES

OCTOBER 2015

As the elections drew closer, security arrangements at *The New Light* were being stepped up. A gate was installed so that visitors could no longer casually stroll inside the premises, and our lone security guard donned a uniform over the faded white singlet he always wore. During a meeting with senior staff, U Maung Maung Than told us that management was deciding whether to purchase CCTV cameras, and that the drums of chemicals stored near the newsroom would be moved further away for our safety.

Chemicals? I thought nervously. *I didn't know there were chemicals.*

We were also receiving an increasing number of articles from Myanmar News Agency that read like edicts. For example, one article insisted that the partisan Union Election Commission was the only source of election news and results, and that informal opinion polls on the likes of Facebook should be ignored. Our reporters weren't even allowed to quote members of the public about who they thought would win. That was surely because pretty much everyone thought that the ruling party would lose.

Other articles warned the international community not to meddle in Myanmar's election process, using an accusatory tone that harked back to the dark days of *The New Light* under junta rule: 'The government requests diplomats and foreign election observers to refrain from activities that could be construed as being biased, or that may negatively impact the country's ability to hold free and fair elections.'

The messaging seemed somewhat ominous, as it was the military junta and its so-called political parties who had a track record of interfering. When it lost to Aung San Suu Kyi's party in 1990, it annulled the election and ruled Myanmar as the 'State Peace and Development Council' until 2011, whereupon it created the Union Solidarity and Development Party (USDP), which had been in charge ever since. It was as though the military was setting the stage for declaring the election flawed if it lost – which it almost undoubtedly would.

While having a few whiskies with some colleagues after work, an editor I'll call Tin Moe Zaw told us that a coup was looming. He said he knew someone close to a military high-up, and that the high-up had told his friend that the armed forces were preparing to storm Yangon.

'They will arrive in tanks and assume power by force, just as they did in 1988 and 1962,' he said in a hushed tone. We were sitting on a couple of benches in a room adjacent to the newsroom and couldn't be sure who might be listening.

My mind started whirling. A coup did seem possible – likely, even. There had been one within the USDP just a few months earlier – it had taken place on the day of my job interview. The military had surrounded the party's headquarters and removed its leader, Shwe Mann, from power. The reason? He was getting too cosy with Aung San Suu Kyi. He had dared to float the idea of allowing her to be president one day. At the time, Shwe Mann was also the most powerful member of parliament, as he was its speaker. His removal suggested that guns still had more might than votes.

'But Myanmar has made its reforms so deliberately, and so publicly,' I said, thinking out loud. 'Why would it risk losing the new business opportunities and international support that are conditional on it holding free and fair elections?'

'You are a very optimistic person, Jess,' said Tin Moe Zaw. 'But I am from Myanmar and I know that the people in charge of this country are deluded narcissists.' He took a swig of neat whisky as the others murmured in agreement, encouraging him to continue. 'They think they are going to win this election, just as they thought they would in 1990. They expect the public to be grateful to them for bringing democracy back. I know it's ironic, but they'll be furious when they lose.'

I went home feeling rattled and as soon as I walked in the door I told Sherpa what Tin Moe Zaw had said.

'But even if there is a coup, I don't think *The New Light* is likely to be targeted,' I said. 'Surely the military would need us to inform the public about them taking charge. Under that scenario, a publication like *The Irrawaddy* would be more likely to be attacked as a means of intimidation, because it's always been so critical of military rule.'

'I guess,' Sherpa said, sounding unconvinced. 'But remember that anything is possible. Please don't assume that you understand what's happening around you, or you might not read the situation correctly. Be careful, okay?'

'Always, babe,' I said, as I wandered off to take a shower. 'But I think everything is going to be fine. It just doesn't make sense for Myanmar to go backwards after all the progress it's made.'

As the cool water washed away the sweat and grime, I hoped that I was right.

~

TWO DAYS BEFORE THE ELECTION, I realised my bosses knew something about the potential for election violence that I didn't. I got an email from U Maung Maung Than that made my hair stand on end.

Dear Colleagues,

I would like to request you all taking care seriously on our newspaper contents, which must be clear from mentioning biased news or photos on the results of political parties in the general election. The responses from them, including comments from the international community, should not be included, except official announcements of the Government.

Do not mention any comments on the results of the general election. Doing so could have a big impact on us, with physical attacks on our office and people.

Best regards,
Maung Maung Than

I STEPPED OUTSIDE and phoned Lisa, my former boss at the British Embassy. In a lowered voice, I told her about U Maung Maung Than's email and the rumours of a coup, which she had probably heard already.

'I'm starting to worry about my safety,' I added.

'If you feel that you're in danger at work, leave straight away. Listen to your instincts and don't feel obliged to stay if something doesn't feel right,' Lisa suggested, sounding concerned.

She then gave me the number of an embassy-backed international helpline that I could phone in an emergency, but after we hung up I remembered that I couldn't make international calls using my local SIM card.

When I returned to my desk I found it difficult to concentrate and had to really steel myself to focus. I practically leapt out of my seat when our chief translator, U Kyaw Thura, rushed into the newsroom and said, 'There's a scorpion in the corridor!'

I went with a couple of others to take a look at it. Though it was small enough to fit into the palm of my hand, it was one of the most menacing creatures I'd ever laid eyes on. It had a rock-hard black shell, and lobster-like pincers that were almost as wide as its body was long. Its tail was curled in the shape of a roller-coaster loop that ended halfway in a red, teardrop-shaped barb. Eight spindly legs were pumping away furiously as it made steady progress towards the newsroom.

'I was having a cigarette over there, near the rubbish bin, and by the time I saw it I'd almost stepped on it,' U Kyaw Thura explained.

'That's so scary,' I said with a shudder. 'How bad is its bite?'

'Scorpions don't bite,' said Ko Aye Min Soe. 'They grab their prey with their pincers and inject venom from the tail. A scorpion sting can kill you – a boy in my hometown died a couple of years ago. And even if you don't die, you'll be in the worst pain you've ever experienced for several days.'

'Yikes,' I said, suddenly becoming conscious of my sandal-clad feet. In keeping with Burmese custom, we all left our shoes in a pile by the door and went barefoot inside the office. It was too risky to let a scorpion roam free in our workplace, but no one was willing to kill it because harming a living creature went against my colleagues' Buddhist beliefs. I had no religious qualms, but was too chicken to get close enough to kill it in case I missed and got stung.

'Let's go and ask Wallace,' said Ko Aye Min Soe. 'He's a Christian.'

With a grim nod, Wallace agreed to do the deed. He went out to the corridor carrying a broken chair leg. I winced as I heard three loud whacks.

~

WHEN I ENTERED the newsroom on election day on 8 November, my colleagues were so eager to share their experiences of voting that they practically pounced on me. For most, it was the first time they'd ever had a say in Myanmar's political process.

'I got to the polling station at 6 a.m.,' said a grinning Nyi Zaw Moe, who showed me the selfies he'd taken on his phone.

'I was there at 4 a.m.,' said a reporter called Nyein Thit Sar. 'I was worried that if there were too many people ahead of me in the line, I might lose my chance to vote. I didn't know whether the voting centres would be closed by a certain time.'

'I should have gone earlier,' said U Than Thaung. 'I waited three hours in the line. Voting itself only took a few minutes. After I dropped my ballot paper into a big bucket, an official dipped my finger in ink so that I couldn't vote a second time.'

He proudly held up a purple pinkie.

'How fantastic,' I said, admiring it. As they each showed me their ink-stained fingers, I saw U Kyaw Thura's eyes moisten. Then I noticed that a translator I'll call Khin Myat Thu was sitting alone at her computer. She looked glum.

I called across to her, 'Where's your purple pinkie, Khin Myat Thu?'

'I didn't vote,' she replied flatly.

'Why not?'

'My father didn't let me. He couldn't decide who to vote for, so no one in our family voted.'

'I'm sorry to hear that.'

'It's okay,' she said, although I was pretty sure it wasn't.

I was sad for Khin Myat Thu. I knew that her father was controlling because she'd told me that he had forbidden her from dating one of our graphic designers. Her father wouldn't hear of the lovebirds getting together because the graphic designer belonged to the Rakhine ethnic group, whereas her family were Bamars. Khin Myat Thu was almost thirty, yet she was powerless to make decisions about her life.

For the others, though, I was overjoyed. They had only positive stories to share about voting, and as news came in from across the nation, it was clear that it had been a remarkably peaceful day. I still wasn't sure why U Maung Maung Than had been so worried, or whether some sinister plan had been aborted at the last minute, but I was thankful that nothing had come to pass.

As the votes began to be counted, we gathered around the television to watch the live coverage. A female election official in a white vest removed a ballot paper from a plastic bucket and held it up to the camera. The box that was ticked was next to a picture of a peacock, which meant a vote for the National League for Democracy. There was cheering onscreen and off. Mesmerised, we watched as each individual vote was tallied by the beaming election official. The transparency of it amazed me. Just as I began wondering how the ruling party would react to the walloping they were getting, a story came in with a quote from the army's commander-in-chief, Min Aung Hlaing.

'Just as the winner accepts the result, so should the loser,' he'd told reporters after casting his vote in Nay Pyi Taw. It was a strong sign that the election results would be honoured this time around.

We cracked open a bottle of Mandalay Rum just after nine o'clock. Ko Aye Min Soe held up his glass and said, 'To the peacock!'

'To the peacock!' we shouted, laughing and hugging.

Then I sat down at the designer's computer to write the next day's front-page headline. I drummed my fingers on the desk, thinking hard. I couldn't say that Aung San Suu Kyi and her party had won, because official results weren't in yet. At any rate,

I couldn't mention her by name. What I could say – and what I thought more important anyway – was that Myanmar had just ended half a century of military rule. However, it was imperative that the headline was strictly factual as opposed to being construed as a comment, because U Maung Maung Than had warned us against that. I typed out 'Dawn of a New Era'. Then I sat back and looked at the words on the screen. Yes. That was it. At long last, Myanmar had moved out of the shadows of dictatorship. History had just been made.

FOR A WEEK AFTER THE ELECTION, the newsroom was filled with a sense of euphoria. But to my astonishment this feeling soon evaporated and was replaced by a gloomy silence. At first I was mystified, but then it hit me: we were all going to lose our jobs. Aung San Suu Kyi had campaigned with the promise to end all forms of state-run media, rightly saying that it had no place in a democracy. Our newspaper would become a relic of a bygone era and our source of income would disappear. There was no such thing as unemployment benefits to fall back on in Myanmar, so the loss of a job could mean plunging into poverty. To make matters worse, some of my colleagues were battling health conditions, which limited their employment prospects. There was the translator with tuberculosis and the deputy news editor who was afflicted with a mysterious potassium deficiency that made him unable to stand up in the mornings. He'd only recently gone on extended leave and we'd passed around an envelope for donations to help him cover his medical bills. Other colleagues had been hoping for a pension, and were very close to having worked at the newspaper for thirteen years, which was the length of government service required to be entitled to it. The outlook for these older workers had instead become pretty grim.

I had been so wrapped up in the election that I hadn't given much thought to what I would do afterwards. In the lead-up to 8 November, many of the stories I'd worked on felt exciting and important, but the focus had since reverted to crop harvests and religious ceremonies. It was also difficult to see the point of trying to improve the newspaper when it was about to cease publication.

I decided to leave the sinking ship when I was offered a lucrative short-term research contract with public relations firm Today Ogilvy, even though I had some doubts about whether the role would be a good fit for me, and the idea of yet another short-term consultancy left me feeling a little weary.

My last day at *The New Light* came a month after the election. A few of my colleagues also resigned. Those who remained gave me a wonderful send-off, with a couple of funny, touching speeches and a mud cake with 'Farewell Jessica' written in green icing on top. They were some of the kindest people I'd ever met.

24

NIRANJAN

JUNE 2016

On a wet Friday night in June, I was at the British ambassador's residence playing a parlour game with a few of my former embassy colleagues. My friends Sue and Martin were about to head to Pakistan for their next posting, so Ambassador Andrew Patrick was hosting a farewell dinner. The game that we were playing involved one person saying two things about themselves that were true, and one that was false. The others had to guess which statement was a lie. The more outrageous the three things were, the more entertaining the game became.

It was Martin's turn.

'I have met Queen Elizabeth,' he began with a grin. 'I have met Queen the band. And I met Princess Diana, who may one day have been queen.'

I searched his face for clues. Finding none, I looked to his wife, Sue, who was sitting beside me on the settee.

She laughed and said, 'I'd better sit this round out.'

'It's possible that you met members of the royal family through work,' I ventured. 'So my guess is that you haven't met the band.'

'I agree with that logic,' said Lisa, my former boss.

'I'm not so sure,' said Andrew. He smiled as he stroked his chin and looked Martin squarely in the eyes. 'You've never mentioned meeting the queen before and that's not something I'd forget. I think that is the lie.'

'That's correct!' said Martin, snapping his fingers. 'I've never met her. That was a good guess.'

'Alright Jess, your turn,' said Andrew. 'And shall I top up your glass?'

'Please do,' I said, tilting it towards him. 'Okay, here goes. I've hiked to Mount Everest base camp. I was an extra in a block-buster Bollywood film, and Cate Blanchett is my second cousin.'

There was laughter as they tried to work it out, before I admitted that the Australian actor was no relation.

After the game ended, Sue pulled a manila folder out of her bag and thumbed through its contents before handing it to me.

'I'm giving this to you for safekeeping, Jess,' she said. 'These are copies of Niranjan's important documents, like his passport and visa, along with some stills from the CCTV footage that will be used as evidence when his trial starts. And this is the statement he signed, giving you power of attorney.'

'Thanks, Sue,' I said.

She smiled back, but her eyes were filled with anguish.

As the embassy's vice consul, one of Sue's responsibilities was helping British citizens who found themselves in trouble in Myanmar. A young man called Niranjan Rasalingam was in a great deal of it. The accountant from London had been arrested on suspicion of using fake credit cards to withdraw the equivalent of US$25,000 from ATMs in Yangon. Once in police custody, he was denied access to a lawyer and the British consulate. He was also given nothing to eat, and after three days he agreed to sign what he assumed was a confession statement in Burmese. Then he was thrown into prison. That was eighteen months earlier, and Niranjan still hadn't been charged with a crime.

Sue had been alerted to Niranjan's arrest not by the Burmese authorities but by a missing person's report filed in the UK. She had eventually met him a month after his arrest, and Niranjan had told her that he was innocent. He was a broker for a hotel-booking website, he'd explained, and had come to Yangon to set up a local office. The police had searched his hotel room and found a lot of cash, but he'd needed it to pay a year's rent up front, as was standard in Myanmar. When Sue subsequently contacted police in the UK, they examined the first batch of ATM transactions in question and deemed them genuine, meaning no crime had been committed.

Sue had reached out to anyone who might be able to help free Niranjan, including the United Nations, the International Court of Justice, British and Burmese charities, and even his MP back in south London. Sue's appeals resulted in the UK's foreign office minister, Hugo Swire, writing to the Burmese government to express his concerns about the delay in starting Niranjan's trial and his recurring chest infections while in prison. But the British government could not intervene in Myanmar's legal system, and Myanmar didn't seem to give two hoots what the UK's foreign minister thought. As Sue had said to me before, Burmese prisoners endured gross injustices on a daily basis – the only difference was that Niranjan was a British citizen, so it was Sue's job to kick up a fuss.

A new vice consul hadn't yet been hired to replace Sue, so I'd offered to help Niranjan in her absence. I wasn't being employed by the embassy – I just felt awful for Niranjan and I knew that Sue was upset about leaving the country while he was still in prison.

'How is Niranjan holding up?' I asked her.

'He's doing fairly well most of the time, considering the situation he's in,' she replied. 'But some days he feels so low that he can't even really speak. The conditions in Insein Prison are appalling, as everyone knows. On the days that he doesn't have a remand hearing, he spends virtually all day inside his crowded cell. A few weeks ago he was attacked by another inmate.'

As I took in what Sue was saying, I became conscious of my luxurious surroundings. I was sitting on a settee as soft as a marshmallow and beneath my feet was a plush cream carpet. Art of great beauty hung on the walls. My stomach was bursting from the four-course meal I'd eaten and I was sipping a single-malt Scotch from a crystal tumbler. Later that night I'd fall asleep with my head resting on a downy pillow in my air-conditioned bedroom. I felt wretched. I hoped that when I met Niranjan, I'd have the strength not to dissolve into a puddle of tears.

NIRANJAN WAS ONLY ALLOWED visitors who were family members and embassy officials, so my opportunities to meet with him came when he was attending remand hearings at various local courts. Despite being forewarned about Niranjan's mistreatment, I was still shocked by my first encounter with Myanmar's criminal justice system.

I arrived at the remand centre in the middle of a heavy monsoon downpour. In one hand was my umbrella, and in the other were four containers filled with curries, rice and fruit. After giving my name and Niranjan's to the policeman on the front desk, he pointed me through to the back of the facility, where a set of steps descended into murky flood waters. About thirty metres away was an outhouse that contained a couple of dilapidated cells. I looked back at him incredulously, but he only scowled and turned away. I tried not to lose my balance as I began wading through the knee-deep waters towards the cells, and shuddered when I stood on something soft that squelched underfoot – possibly a drowned rat. The cells were on a higher bit of ground, but with the monsoon rain pounding down, it was likely the floor would soon be submerged too. I couldn't understand why such an inhospitable parcel of land was being used for the facility – unless it was deliberate. Inside the cells, there wasn't so much as a bench for the inmates to sit on.

I stood outside Niranjan's cell, which he shared with four other inmates. When he saw me, he stood up and brushed the dirt off the back of his trousers. He was a few years younger than me at twenty-nine, but he looked old for his years due to the dark circles underneath sunken eyes and a bedraggled appearance. He wore a stained t-shirt and baggy jeans, which I later learnt were the clothes he'd been arrested in.

'Hi, Jess. Thanks for coming to see me,' he said.

'You're welcome,' I replied. 'I'm just so sorry for what you're going through.'

At this he smiled sadly, as if to say, 'Me too.'

'Sue said she will continue to do what she can from Pakistan, and I'm here to bring you food and whatever else might help. Here – take this,' I said, passing through the food containers.

'Thanks so much. And for the books and magazines that came through the embassy. We got them a couple of days ago when the post was handed out.'

One of Niranjan's cellmates lay dozing on the floor and was so gaunt that his arms looked like matchsticks and his skull seemed far too big for his body. His hollowed cheeks were marked with weeping sores. By comparison, the three prisoners standing a pace behind Niranjan looked positively radiant. They were young and clean-cut, and had been listening attentively as we talked.

'These are your co-accused?' I asked Niranjan. I smiled at the men, and they smiled eagerly back.

'Yes,' said Niranjan. 'We are supposedly a gang of criminals who belong to an international credit card fraud syndicate. But I didn't even know these two guys before I was arrested.' He gestured to the men on his immediate left, who nodded vigorously as he spoke.

The shortest of the trio stepped forward.

'I am Pandiyan Balu,' he said. 'But you can call me Balu. And this is Mathiyalagan Raj Kumar and Muthaya Dinesh Kumar. We're from Tamil Nadu in India. We are so happy to meet you.'

'Nice to meet you too,' I said. 'Sue told me about you and the awful situation you're in. I really am so sorry.'

'It has been very difficult,' said Balu. 'Especially as every single one of us is innocent. Raj and I weren't even in Myanmar when the crime was supposedly committed. The arrival stamps in our passports clearly prove that we arrived two days later. The Indian government wrote to Myanmar's ministry of foreign affairs to defend us. But they never got a reply. And so here we are, still.'

I looked inquiringly at Dinesh, who seized the chance to tell me his story.

'I have no idea why the police think I had anything to do with the ATM withdrawals. I know Niranjan through a family friend, and I served him a meal at the Banana Leaf Restaurant, where I was a manager. The police arrested me two weeks after the others were arrested. But they didn't even bother trying to prove that I'd committed a crime. They see me as just another dark-skinned man. To them, we are lower than dogs.'

I'd wondered before my visit whether part of the reason why Niranjan was being treated so appallingly was because he was dark-skinned. He looked like a Rohingya.

'This must also be really upsetting for your families,' I said. 'Have they been able to visit you?'

'My uncle came last year,' said Raj. 'But we are not from rich families and they have already spent eight thousand dollars on our legal fees. My mother is suffering a lot. And I missed my sister's wedding last month.'

'I missed my own wedding,' added Balu helplessly. 'I came here with Raj to enjoy one last bit of travel before I became a married man. But I don't think my bride is willing to wait much longer for me.'

'What has happened to you is absolutely appalling,' I said. 'I hope you will be freed soon.'

'All we want is for our trial to start so that we can defend ourselves,' said Niranjan. 'We don't even know the details about what they think we've done wrong, because we haven't been charged.' His voice wavered and I could see that he was agitated.

I racked my brains for some words of comfort.

'Did you meet Phil Blackwood in prison?' I asked, thinking I'd hit on something. 'He was the guy from New Zealand who posted the photo on Facebook of Buddha wearing headphones.'

'Yeah, I did. He got out a few months ago,' said Niranjan.

'That's right,' I said. 'Phil was sentenced to two-and-a-half years but he ended up serving thirteen months before being released in a presidential amnesty. You have already served eighteen months. So hopefully you're closer to freedom than you realise.'

'Maybe,' said Niranjan, with the faintest flicker of a smile.

As I walked away from the courthouse, I wondered if I'd said the wrong thing. Was it irresponsible to be optimistic? Perhaps. But I hated the thought of the four men losing hope, because that was all they had left. I was confident that the trial wouldn't be delayed much longer now that Aung San Suu Kyi's government had come to power. Many of her government members were former political prisoners, so they understood how terrible it was to be unjustly detained.

I made a conscious decision to be upbeat whenever I was around Niranjan. Even if privately I felt like weeping.

THE NEXT REMAND hearing was at Lanmadaw Courthouse, where I arrived just in time to see the battered police truck from Insein Prison pull up. Inside, the prisoners would be straining to breathe in some fresh air through the narrow grates at the top, and their legs would be aching from being forced to stand throughout the journey, which was sometimes two hours long. Niranjan, Raj, Dinesh and Balu were transported to eight different courts every fortnight, because each township where an alleged ATM withdrawal took place was holding its own trial. This meant that there were going to be eight separate trials running concurrently, and eight separate sentences. Meanwhile, Niranjan and the men claimed they had never even set foot in some of the townships, and that the authorities were maliciously slapping them with fresh allegations.

When the back doors of the truck swung open Niranjan was the first of about a dozen prisoners to emerge. He blinked rapidly, his eyes adjusting to the sunlight, and hungrily took in a rare slice of public life. He was handcuffed to Dinesh and waved at me with his free hand. He also waved at the man standing next to me on the footpath. I soon learnt that this was Niloy, who had befriended the men while he had also been in prison. After Niloy was released, he came to their remand hearings to help them, specifically by translating, as he spoke Burmese and Tamil, the latter of which was a language they all shared. Niranjan and the others were very appreciative, as they had never been provided with a translator and had understood exactly zero of what anyone had said to them.

The final prisoners to exit the truck were two women. One

was middle-aged, and the other in the bloom of her youth. She had full lips and long, shiny hair that she wore in a plait. She looked so terrified that I thought she must have only very recently been arrested. She was handcuffed to the older woman, who moved slowly, as though in a fog. Three policemen carrying truncheons circled the prisoners like sheepdogs, barking at them if they fell out of step.

I trailed behind the miserable group and watched as they were shunted into a cage at the back end of the noisy courthouse. The door swung shut behind them and an enormous iron padlock was fastened with an old-fashioned barrel key. A policeman standing guard clipped it onto his hip, where it jangled enticingly against a few others.

I'd brought some food for the men. As it was forbidden to pass anything directly to those inside the cage, the policeman lifted a flap of an enclosure on the floor that was embedded into the cage. He put the containers inside and shut the flap, whereupon Niranjan opened the flap from his side. It was like feeding lions at the zoo. And they were hungry lions, because it was the only food they'd seen all day. They typically weren't fed anything on remand days.

We'd been talking for a couple of minutes when the policeman guarding the cage started to film us on his phone. I looked askance at Niranjan.

'They always filmed Sue when she visited me in prison,' he said quietly. 'I think it's their way of trying to intimidate you, because I'm pretty sure they can't speak English anyway.'

Just then a second police officer sidled up to the cage. After a short exchange with the men through Niloy, he muttered something and left. I assumed he had been explaining something about the day's proceedings, but Niranjan set me straight.

'He wanted a bribe,' he said, with a note of disgust in his voice. 'He's a witness for the prosecution, but he said he knows nothing about the accusations against us and would speak in our favour at the trial if we paid him fifty thousand kyat. When we refused, he got annoyed. He said he resents wasting his whole day in court and that the least we could do is pay his taxi fares.'

'That's so corrupt,' I said.

'Yeah, he was pretty blatant about it,' Niranjan replied. 'It's hard to see how we will get a fair hearing when stuff like this happens.'

I was mulling over how bizarre it was that a policeman had effectively filmed another one asking for a bribe when I noticed that the young female prisoner also had a visitor. Two, in fact. A girl who also looked to be in her twenties arrived carrying a baby on her hip. She knelt down beside the cage, then gently lifted the baby girl up against the bars. She obviously belonged to the young female prisoner, who ran her hand over the baby's cheeks and chubby thighs, all the while staring into her daughter's big brown eyes with great tenderness. But then the ruckus in the room upset the infant, who started to cry. The young mother kissed her baby's forehead through the bars, but she was unable to comfort her in her arms. As the little girl began to wail, the woman broke into a sob. On her face was an expression of unspeakable anguish.

With a lump in my throat, I said to Niranjan, 'That's heartbreaking to see.'

'Yeah, it's sad,' he said ruefully. 'I don't know what her story is, but she probably didn't do anything wrong. Maybe her husband was caught doing something illegal and she got arrested alongside him. You don't have to be guilty of a crime to end up in prison in Myanmar.'

I nodded grimly. I thought back to when I'd travelled to Kachin State to write about injecting-drug use as part of a consultancy for a branch of the United Nations called UNAIDS. I'd met a young mother who was struggling to stay afloat while her husband was in prison. He had been getting a lift home on the back of his friend's motorbike when the police pulled the pair over and searched them. A few grams of heroin were found on her husband's friend and although her husband wasn't carrying any drugs, he received an equally severe prison term of six years: one year more than the legal minimum for drug possession in Myanmar. Then of course there were the thousands of political prisoners whose only crime had been to demand democracy for Myanmar. The casual way in which innocent people could be imprisoned for years – or even decades – was nothing short of horrifying.

The men were called for the remand hearing, and the cage door swung open. As they were led towards the dock, I took a couple of photos of Niranjan to send to Sue. A policeman who seemed to come out of nowhere started wagging his finger at me and bellowed, 'No! No! No!'

'I'm sorry. Really sorry. I didn't know,' I said, flustered. He stood over me until he was satisfied that I had deleted the photos from my phone.

Within five minutes, the proceedings were over and the men were back inside the cage, where they would spend another five hours before being trucked back to the prison.

Although under Burmese law it was technically legal to keep re-remanding the men every fortnight, the legal recourse of habeas corpus – which prohibits prolonged detention without charge – had been reintroduced in Myanmar's 2008 constitution after the military regime had removed it some forty years earlier. Sue had drawn attention to habeas corpus in her correspondence with human rights organisations. But sadly, in reality there was little they could do.

Despite the bleakness of the men's situation, when I said goodbye they thanked me for coming with smiles and warm words. I left the courthouse feeling broken-hearted for them. How they must envy me being able to simply walk away from that hell pit. I turned back to look at the building, and as I did, I wondered if there was something I could do to set them free. If only I could get them onto a plane that would take them far away from Myanmar.

My thoughts were interrupted when I saw the policeman who had shouted at me for taking photos. He had been walking towards me but stopped as we locked eyes. He held my gaze and lit a cigarette. I started to weave my way past the trishaws and street hawkers towards the main road, and after a few paces I glanced behind me. The policeman was closer, and he had a horrible smirk on his face. When I realised that I was being followed, I broke into a jog. I didn't look behind me again until I was in the back of a taxi. On a street corner stood the policeman. Seeing me gone, he turned on his heel and strolled back towards the courthouse.

~

AT YET ANOTHER courthouse some weeks later in Mayangone township, I was met with a remand cell that deeply disturbed me.

'No visitors,' barked the policeman guarding the remand cells.

'I'm with the British Embassy,' I said. 'I need five minutes with Niranjan Rasalingham, please.'

At my bluster, he let me inside. Each remand facility I'd visited had been unpleasant, but this one was in a league of its own. The dark windowless room smelt of human excrement and was incredibly hot. The men were standing inside a narrow enclosure made of chain wire – the type that surrounds dogs in a pound. I told Niranjan that I almost wasn't allowed in to see him.

'The guards are in a foul mood today because that guy over there tried to escape as we were getting off the truck,' said Niranjan. 'They beat him up pretty badly afterwards.'

I hadn't noticed the human-shaped lump in the shadows until Niranjan pointed it out. A teenage boy was trembling uncontrollably on the filthy floor, almost as though he were having a spasm. His hands were bound behind his back with a plastic cable tie and his eyes were wild. His matted hair was encrusted with congealed blood.

'Is he intellectually disabled?' I asked, horrified by the cruelty.

'Yeah, he is,' replied Niranjan. 'But they only treat him worse because of it.'

I should have listened carefully as Niranjan started to tell me that he had just got a new lawyer after being 'fleeced' by the first one, but I was so upset by the sight of the teenager that I struggled to concentrate.

I was relieved when a guard indicated that my five minutes were up. I wanted to get as far away from that room as possible.

IN AUGUST, I was transcribing an interview in my study when my phone rang.

'Hey, Jess. It's Niranjan. I paid a prison warden to use their phone. I just called to tell you that the new lawyer got things moving for us. The eight separate trials have been merged into one and that trial will start in a couple of weeks.'

'That's fantastic news!' I said. 'You must be so relieved.'

'Well, yes and no. We've just found out that there are more than thirty charges against us. Some of them don't even make sense. They believe that the fifth member of our so-called gang is on the run. So we are being charged with him absconding. I'm also being charged with overstaying my visa. How could I leave Myanmar when I'm locked up in this prison? I'm scared, Jess. All these charges might add up to a long sentence.'

'Try not to be scared,' I said. 'The new government is trying to empty the prisons, not fill them up as they did in the old days. The judges know that. Plus the evidence against you is really weak. You might be found innocent.'

'I doubt it,' he replied. 'There is no justice in Myanmar.'

I paused, unsure of what to say next. Nothing I had seen of the legal system suggested that Niranjan's assessment was wrong.

'Let's stay hopeful,' I said weakly.

As the phone clicked silent, I prayed that his ordeal was about to come to an end.

A few weeks later at Yangon Divisional Court, Niranjan, Raj, Balu and Dinesh shuffled into the courtroom, their movements constricted by clunking leg irons. They were also handcuffed, and a long steel chain had been looped through each cuff to bind them together as a group. The draconian restraints created the impression that the four men at the dock were violent criminals – so much for the presumption of being innocent until proved guilty.

From the moment I gingerly trod on the sagging spiral staircase that hugged the court building's domed interior, I'd felt as if I'd stepped onto the set of a historical drama. Yangon Divisional Court was a grand but dilapidated colonial building on Pansodan Street, built around 1900, with a mint exterior that had been ravaged by a hundred years of monsoon rains. The courtroom was sparsely fitted out with a handful of teak benches, a commanding desk for the judge and his assistant, and a dock that looked like something you'd corral a horse in. Sunshine streamed in through a shattered window, where a pigeon was noisily putting the finishing touches to its nest. A rat darted across a rafter.

Some of the crimes the men were accused of were even older than the building, as the penal code hadn't been updated since it was enacted by the British in 1861. And nothing about the scene inspired confidence in the court's ability to examine evidence relating to a complex financial crime known as skimming, which involves stealing credit card information to withdraw money using a cloned card. Furthermore, the first ATM arrived in Myanmar only in 2012 and banking was still so underdeveloped that the general public preferred to rely wholly on cash. It was possible that the authorities had never encountered the prepaid travel money cards Niranjan said he'd used and, in their confusion, assumed the worst.

Racism was also undoubtedly at play. Sue had told me that during an early remand hearing, the judge had laughed derisively when he saw the CCTV footage stills of the men supposedly using the ATMs. It was obvious that the men in the footage were random men of Indian heritage and not the actual suspects. Nonetheless, Myanmar's judiciary was not independent. A judge would do what the government told it to – no matter how absurd.

As the first witness was called to the stand, I watched Niranjan straining to understand what was being said as his fate began to be decided. Once again, there was no English translator. I smiled at Niranjan whenever he looked my way, hoping that it would ease the anxiety that was written all over his face.

It wasn't until a policeman in the row in front of me turned around and clicked his tongue that I realised the judge was eyeballing me.

'Give the judge your passport,' he said gruffly.

'Mine?' I asked, baffled. 'Why does he need my passport?'

No explanation was forthcoming, but I didn't protest. I retrieved my passport from my backpack and handed it to the policeman, who walked through the middle of the courtroom and passed it up to the judge, who wore a traditional *gaung baung* hat with a satin sash draped around a black mandarin-collar blazer. His assistant dutifully copied out the details as the judge continued glaring at me, as though I were wasting his time. All eyes in the courtroom were on me. Niranjan smiled and ever so slightly shrugged, as if to say, 'What next?'

After five excruciating minutes, I took back my passport and proceedings resumed. From the occasional grimace the judge threw in my direction, it was clear that my presence at the trial was resented. I suspected that any form of oversight would have been a source of irritation to the judge, no matter how inconsequential. Most cases took place behind closed doors.

As well as attending court hearings, I'd been trying to obtain extra bits of evidence that could strengthen Niranjan's defence case. I contacted the travel company he said he worked for, and reached out to some of his Facebook friends. I asked them to write a statement in support of his alibi – but to my surprise, no one replied. When I told Niranjan, he said they were probably too scared to get involved.

I also met with staff from KBZ, which was one of the banks involved in the case. Over dumplings in a private room at the Sule Shangri-La Hotel, I urged them to drop the charges against the men. In another strange quirk of Myanmar's legal system, private banks were listed as the prosecution rather than the state, as you'd expect in a criminal case. But the five senior bank representatives I met – one of whom was Sonny Swe's sister, Marlar, a consultant – were adamant that a crime had been committed.

They urged me to speak to the BBC's foreign correspondent in Myanmar, Jonah Fisher, as he too had talked to them about the case and could provide an independent perspective. I knew Jonah, so I got in touch. I was floored when he said that after doing some digging, he'd begun to suspect that Niranjan was guilty, and that it was the three Indian men who had been unwittingly dragged into the mess. For that reason, he hadn't filed a story about Niranjan's plight. Only *The Guardian* and a couple of local London papers had been following the case outside Myanmar.

When I told Sue and Niranjan what Jonah had said, they retorted that he must have got his facts wrong. Really? A BBC journalist was mistaken? I began following up the leads Jonah had given me, until I realised that I was only tormenting myself. What I thought about Niranjan's guilt or innocence was irrelevant. A court of law, however flawed, would decide whether he would walk away as a free man or be punished. I had agreed to help him not as a journalist or some kind of investigator, but by offering moral support and practical help. And that included taking his increasingly frequent and frightened phone calls, even though I dreaded answering when an unknown number flashed up on the screen.

∼

I WISH I could say that I was there for Niranjan until the end. But after the judge took my passport details, I got scared. I had learnt that anyone could be locked up and the key thrown away, with due process simply ignored. I knew that the authorities were irritated by my interest in the case, being a foreigner as I was – what was to stop them from doing something terrible to me, or even to Sherpa? I also found the men's situation really distressing, and was at a loss as to how Sue and the new vice consul, Zara, were able to undertake such emotionally draining work without themselves developing mental health issues. With a heavy heart, when Niranjan phoned me up one afternoon, I told him that I couldn't continue to help him.

'It's okay,' he said. 'I understand. Thank you for what you've done for us.'

There was an unmistakable air of sadness in his voice, but he didn't try to change my mind. In fact, he was so good about me letting him down that I felt even worse about it.

IN JUNE 2017, Sue got in touch to say that Niranjan's trial had finally come to an end. At once, I understood that it was naive of me to think that a new government could erase decades of deficiencies and corruption in the criminal justice system.

All four men were found guilty. Dinesh, Raj and Balu were sentenced to prison terms that ranged from seven to nine years. The heaviest sentence was reserved for Niranjan, who got seventeen years. Seventeen years. My jaw fell to the floor. Niranjan was obviously beside himself, Sue informed me. Conditions in Insein Prison were so appalling that a term of that length could easily become a death sentence. Niranjan had been right: there was no justice in Myanmar.

25

GAME OVER

SEPTEMBER 2016

I was attending a farewell party for a *New York Times* photographer who was moving to Bangkok. Lauren DeCicca was talented, beautiful and a delight to work with as a freelancer; I was sad to see her go. She and her boyfriend, Andre, who I knew a little, had chosen a photogenic setting for their farewell. The Sapphire Lounge was a rooftop bar on Nawaday Street in Dagon Township, where a number of hip cafes and boutiques with some global brands had opened. The bar had a terrific view of the Shwedagon Pagoda. As I came up the last few steps of the stuffy corridor, I saw that an incredible sunset was taking shape. The sinking orange sun was enormous, while the sky around it was streaked with honey-coloured clouds that looked like wisps of wavy hair.

I gave Lauren a hug and went off to get a drink from the bar, which was nothing more than a trestle table covered with a frilly green tablecloth and a few bottles of liquor. I took a Chang beer from a crate on the ground filled with half-melted ice before scanning the crowd for a familiar face. Sitting around a cast-iron table were Jeremy and Jesse, both of whom I knew from my days at *The Myanmar Times*. I pulled up a seat next to Jesse, and he introduced me to their friend, a researcher called Matthew.

'Is Sherpa working late tonight?' Jeremy asked me.

'Nope – he's in Bangkok on a visa run,' I said. 'He'll be back by the weekend.'

'I'm going in the morning,' said Matthew. 'No doubt with a hangover, which I have to say is starting to feel permanent. This is my third farewell party in a week.'

'Is it just me or does it feel like a lot of expats are leaving Myanmar now the election is over?' asked Jesse.

'People have been leaving in droves,' I agreed. 'I think many people lingered here because they wanted to witness something historic, and now that the moment has passed, they're moving on. Up until recently, I was always confident I'd see someone I knew when I went out in Yangon. But there are definitely fewer familiar faces about nowadays.'

Matthew nodded. 'I'm sure you're right, but I've been an expat for ten years now and I find that it's always a bit of a revolving door of hellos and goodbyes,' he said. 'But that's what I like about it – there are always fresh faces to meet and you never really get sick of anyone.'

'And with sunsets like these,' said Jeremy, tilting his bottle of beer towards the horizon, 'there will always be a steady stream of people arriving in Yangon to replace those who have left.'

The sky was awash with peach and streaked with ribbons of mauve and violet. The contrast with the gritty buildings below made the sunset even more sublime.

'I used to find it exciting to meet new people all the time,' I said. 'But I've started to find it tiring, and Yangon has felt less fun since some of my favourite people left, like Bridget – and Lauren is another one. Sometimes I sense that expats put less effort into their friendships because they know they won't last forever.'

'That might be true,' said Jesse thoughtfully. 'Though of

course it depends on the individual. And not everyone is leaving Myanmar. I, for one, don't plan on going anywhere.'

'Me neither,' echoed Jeremy. 'I love it here.'

By the time the guests had gathered for a toast, the sun had dropped out of view and the entire banner of sky along the horizon was an improbable shade of bubble-gum pink. The clouds had turned a strange milky grey. The Shwedagon Pagoda, now lit up by floodlights, was glinting in its golden splendour. As I clinked my beer bottle against Jesse's in a toast to Lauren and Andre's next adventure, I looked around and wondered who would be next to leave.

I was fiddling with the first paragraph of a climate change article based on my ten-day UN mission when an email from Sherpa popped into my inbox. As usual, I opened it immediately, eager to see what he had to say, while not expecting anything in particular. As I read the second line, my heart seemed to stop completely.

Hey Babe

I just got back from the Myanmar embassy. I'm in shock. I can't get another business visa. They wouldn't say why they won't give me one – but of course it's got something to do with me being Bangladeshi. I begged and pleaded with the visa officer: I was actually on the verge of crying. I told him that my wife was in Myanmar and that she was waiting for me to come home. Do you know what his reply was to that? He sneered and asked me if you were Pakistani. I think he was trying to insinuate that Bangladeshis marry their 'Muslim cousins' in Pakistan or something.

So I can't come home to you. It's game over. I'm sitting here feeling so depressed and I really can't believe it.

I miss you and love you always.

Sherpa

MY HEAD WAS SPINNING. Had this happened in retaliation for me trying to help Niranjan? Or was it simply because Sherpa was a Bangladeshi journalist? The authorities may have tolerated his presence in their country in the past, but tensions had been escalating with Bangladesh over the Rohingya people, who neither country wanted to accommodate. Our Bangladeshi friend Alvi had also recently been denied a visa, and had to abruptly quit his job at a law firm in Yangon. He'd told us of other Bangladeshi expats having similar problems. Had a snap decision been made to rid Myanmar of all Bangladeshis? The fact was that we would never know why our time in Myanmar had come to an end, but ended it had.

I asked Sherpa to call me from Skype. Then I went to the fridge and took out a bottle of beer. I gulped it down.

'Moving to Australia will cost thousands of dollars, babe,' I began when our call connected, feeling the panic rise in my voice. 'I'm only halfway through the UN consultancy so I won't be paid until at least the end of the year.'

Sherpa and I had recently begun to execute a long-term exit strategy from Myanmar, which is why we had just moved to a cheaper apartment and had to rehome our beloved Ripley to the caretaker of the Yangon Animal Shelter. The decision made me cry an awful lot, but importing both her and Butters to Australia would cost $20,000 – a sum we simply couldn't afford. Sherpa and I had given ourselves a year to save for the expense of relocating. The suddenness of having to leave immediately was an incredibly stressful prospect. And I knew that Sherpa would be heartbroken to abruptly leave his team behind at *Myanmar Business Today* without ever having said goodbye.

'Take a couple of deep breaths,' Sherpa said. 'And then I need you to do something for me, okay? I have a surprise for you.'

'What is it?'

'If you go and look under our bed, you'll see a green storage container next to my guitar. At the back of it is a pink folder. Can you bring the folder here?' He waited as I padded off to the bedroom.

'Got it,' I said when I returned, holding up the folder.

'Great.' He smiled. 'Can you find the envelope inside that says "Misc 2016"?'

'Uh, yup.'

'Please open it.'

'There's money inside.'

'That's right. It's nine thousand dollars.'

'Oh my god. This is such a relief. You're amazing.'

Sherpa smiled again.

'Now, please go to the living room. In the cupboard to the right of the bookshelf is a green document case.'

I returned with the slim case and unzipped it.

'That's twelve thousand dollars right there,' Sherpa said.

'I don't know what to say, babe. I'm completely lost for words.'

'We haven't finished,' he replied.

Ten minutes later, I was sitting dumbfounded at my desk, with thirty-two thousand dollars in my hands.

'I always knew you were an amazing saver,' I said. 'But I didn't realise you were this good.'

'I figured a rainy day would come along sooner or later. Now you just need to come and meet me here in Bangkok, and we'll start planning a new life in Australia.'

'I'll be there as soon as I possibly can. Without you here, I just want to leave.'

THERE WAS an unexpected downside to being in possession of so much money: taking it outside Myanmar meant breaking the law. The most anyone was allowed to leave with was ten thousand dollars. Many countries have similar laws as a way of preventing money laundering, but what was different about Myanmar was that it still didn't have international banking facilities or outward Western Union transfers. I couldn't deposit cash at a bank inside the country that could be accessed once I'd left. Customs would simply confiscate the money if they discovered it on me – meaning that Sherpa's life savings would disappear in a puff of smoke. And, somewhat ironically, the money just kept piling up as I began selling our furniture and white goods, and even managed to get some of our advance rent money returned, as we had only moved into the small apartment in Botataung Township two weeks earlier. It was really stressing me out.

I waited until I had sold almost everything and therefore knew the size of the problem before phoning up Day Day, the friendly hotel manager who had transferred around six thousand dollars of my father's money when we first needed to pay a year's rent upfront. I met him on a building site in Chinatown, where construction on his new hotel was in full swing. I followed Day Day up a ladder and across a wobbly plank to a concrete platform, where I gave him twenty thousand dollars – the amount he had offered to move. I watched on as he and his chain-smoking father counted the money on an upturned milk crate, with his father somehow also managing to maintain a conversation with the man standing behind him. A couple of workmen in white singlets and *longyis* trudged past without so much as a second glance at the pile of cash, even though it was more money than they would ever make in their lifetimes.

'I'll get the transfer done by lunchtime tomorrow,' said Day Day, as he deftly divided the money into three envelopes and marked each with a pencil that he stuck behind his ear. 'I'm sorry to see you and Sherpa go,' he added.

'Thank you so much, Day Day. You've been good to us over the years.'

But the following day, lunchtime came and went. At two o'clock, I sent him a Facebook message.

'Is it still possible to do the transfer today? I'm flying out tomorrow.'

Day Day replied almost an hour later. 'I've got a friend with an Australian bank account, so it will be better for you if he does the transfer, as you'll save on fees. I'll ask him to send a transfer receipt later today.'

But no receipt came. Instead, Day Day went offline for the next two hours, sending me into a panic. I couldn't bring myself to tell Sherpa what was happening. Just thinking about admitting that I might have lost his money made me feel sick. I had to try to get it back.

By six o'clock, I still had no receipt. I was pacing around the apartment, feeling utterly beside myself. When I finally reached Day Day, I told him that I was coming to get the money back.

'OK,' was all he sent by way of a reply. I hoped it meant that the cash I'd given him on the building site hadn't yet changed hands.

'I'm sorry to ask for the money back,' I said when I met Day Day in the lobby of MGM Hotel, where we'd agreed to meet. 'I'm just freaking out right now.'

'It's okay,' he said, handing me the three envelopes. 'All the best to you and Sherpa, Jess.'

I was so relieved to have Sherpa's money back that I dared

not even put it in my bag, and instead kept a hold of it during the entire taxi ride home. Once back in our empty apartment, I posted an urgent callout on the Google group Yangon Expat Connection. The kind of help I needed was very specific: I needed someone with an Australian bank account who was owed money by someone outside Myanmar. I would give the person inside Myanmar the cash, and the person who owed them money would transfer it to my account instead.

After a few false starts, an Australian businessman contacted me and I made a beeline for his apartment. I gave Ian, who was a total stranger, eight thousand dollars and he got a receipt from his friend on the spot. He said it was the most he could arrange to have transferred. My friend Tom took another ten thousand dollars, which still left me with eighteen grand. I had run out of time to do anything about it.

I'D ALWAYS IMAGINED Sherpa and I having a big send-off, with hugs and maybe a few tears. Instead, there was no farewell party. I wasn't in the mood and it didn't seem fair to have one if Sherpa couldn't come. In fact, the only friend I told that I was leaving Myanmar was my German friend Marita, who I'd known since I'd first arrived. I'd spent many happy nights at amazing parties in her flash apartment. We met up at a beer station the night before my flight left.

'Sherpa and I had been starting to think about leaving Myanmar, but him being kicked out like this leaves a bitter taste in my mouth,' I said after we'd taken a seat at a table on the footpath.

'Visas are never easy in Myanmar,' Marita said sympathetically. She lit a cigarette. 'In a way, I'm amazed that Sherpa managed to stay here as long as he did, being both Bangladeshi and in the media.'

'That's true. We had a good run. And maybe it's for the best, anyhow. I thought Myanmar was going to make huge changes when Aung San Suu Kyi came to power. But if anything, it feels like it's been going backwards this year.'

'In what sense?'

'Well, for one, *The New Light* never closed down. It just switched its allegiance to Aung San Suu Kyi and her party. I'm obviously glad that my former colleagues didn't lose their jobs, but I was sure that state-run media would come to an end in Myanmar. Honestly, this country never ceases to surprise me. Or frustrate me.'

'I thought you loved Myanmar.'

'I do. Or at least, I did. I don't know how I feel anymore. The racism that Sherpa has faced has been awful. And I have no doubt it's connected to the appalling treatment of the Rohingya, which Aung San Suu Kyi is doing nothing about. It makes me so mad when she refers to them as "Bengalis", just like the military do to deny their claim to being Burmese.'

'It can't be easy for her, though. She's banned from being president and the military won't give up control of the important ministries. She still has to toe the line even though she's in government.'

'I know, I know. But it still feels like she could be doing so much more. Anyway, I don't want to become one of those whinging expats who can't say anything positive about the country they live in. And I think I'm starting to sound like one.'

'Oh yes,' said Marita with a mischievous smile. 'Those expats irritate me. When they're complaining, it's on the tip of my tongue to ask them, "Why don't you leave if you don't like it? No one is forcing you to stay."'

'I agree. They drive me nuts. And no one is forcing Sherpa and me to stay – quite the opposite, actually.'

Marita squeezed my shoulder. 'Well, I am going to miss you – even if you don't miss us back here in Myanmar,' she said.

'I will miss you. And I hope to see you again one day, somewhere else in the world.'

'You are always welcome to come to Berlin as my guest.'

We hugged goodbye. As I walked back to my apartment along busy Maha Bandula Road, whose every shopfront I knew by heart, I had the strangest sensation: it was as if I was looking backwards into my past. My body was still in Myanmar, but my mind had already left.

SINCE RECEIVING Sherpa's email about him being unable to come home, I'd finished the one outstanding freelance article due and asked my boss at the United Nations if I could take a break from the consultancy and finish what I could from outside Myanmar. He agreed, and so I devoted all my time to wrapping up our lives in Yangon. I'd made multiple trips to the Ministry of Agriculture, Livestock and Irrigation to get the paperwork I needed for Butters to be exported. I had couriered the back editions of Sherpa's newspaper to him in Bangkok, along with a small number of our possessions. Our plan was for Butters and me to meet Sherpa in Bangkok and then relocate to Australia and apply for Sherpa to get residency – which was far from being a sure bet.

Sixteen days had passed in a blur. I had collected my last pay from various magazines, bought plane tickets, cleaned the apartment and sold or thrown away our belongings, many of which had sentimental value. I felt bereft as I watched my big old desk being carried out the front door, and realised that I'd acquired things over the past four years without ever really acknowledging that one day we would leave.

What I hadn't been able to do was find someone who could take the last eight thousand dollars off my hands to prevent it being confiscated, as I had eighteen thousand to depart with in total. My only option was to hide it. I felt bad about it, but I had run out of time and options. I divided up the notes and slipped some inside the pages of a book, and then sticky-taped the book shut. I put a few hundred in my toiletry bag, and a bit more in my only pair of socks. I tucked the last two thousand dollars inside my bra, because I was almost certain that modesty would prevent a customs officer from combing the area. *This adds a new meaning to cash-strapped*, I thought wryly as I double-checked that the notes weren't bunching up.

I bundled Butters into her cage and dragged three suitcases down the stairs. Once at the airport, my heart beat wildly as I waited in line for the security screening. As soon as I stepped forward and passed Butters' cage to the security official, I realised that a travelling cat was the perfect decoy. The security staff turned their backs to me as they cooed and poked their fingers through the cage at Butters, who was meowing plaintively. I strode through the metal detector and was on my way.

Once onboard the plane, I breathed a sigh of relief. A stunning Thai Airways flight attendant in a figure-hugging purple dress and fuchsia lipstick approached me in my seat.

'Would you like a blanket, ma'am?' she crooned.

'That would be amazing,' I said, wondering whether I looked cold or sick. 'Yes please. And a white wine too.' It wasn't even close to being an appropriate time for a drink, but I didn't care. I'd successfully smuggled out Sherpa's money and that called for a celebration. It was also my farewell party in a cup. I smiled as I realised that my time in Myanmar had ended the way it began: by faffing about with cash.

As the plane rumbled along the tarmac and began its ascent into the clouds, I closed my eyes and snuggled into the soft blanket. I hoped Butters wasn't too terrified in the belly of the plane. As soon as the seatbelt sign was turned off, I went to the toilet and took the money out of my bra, as it was itching me. My wallet was already bursting with ten thousand dollars, but I stuffed the rest in anyway – it no longer mattered if the notes got a bit rumpled. It was the first step in decoupling myself from Myanmar and its quirks.

Suvarnabhumi Airport in Bangkok was teeming with travellers. People of all nationalities darted this way and that under the glare of bright lights. Those with time to spare riffled through racks of luxury clothing labels or had a bite to eat from American fast-food chains, none of which was available in Myanmar. I had returned to the land of global capitalism.

A wave of grief hit me as I realised what I had left behind: a country more unique than anything I would again encounter.

But then I caught sight of Sherpa, whose big brown eyes were scanning the crowd for me. We grinned and ran to each other, and within a matter of seconds I was back in his arms and breathing in his familiar scent.

'My god, I've missed you,' I said.

'You too, babe,' he said, holding my hands in his. 'Very much.'

We stood there for a bit, just smiling at one another and letting the relief wash over us.

I didn't know what our future held. There was no guarantee that Sherpa would even be allowed into Australia; we could encounter yet more visa problems. But I knew in that moment that wherever we did end up, we would start all over again, building a new home together.

EPILOGUE
APRIL 2021

One of the great tragedies in Myanmar's recent history took place in October 2016, a month after Sherpa and I left Myanmar. The military launched attacks on Rohingya villages in troubled Rakhine State. Houses were torched, women were gang raped and families were murdered – including children. The genocide prompted one of the greatest exoduses in living memory, with hundreds of thousands of persecuted Rohingya people fleeing to neighbouring Bangladesh. Aung San Suu Kyi fell from grace on the international stage for failing to do anything to prevent the horrors. Five years later, almost a million stateless Rohingya still live in the world's largest refugee camp in Bangladesh. I suspect that Sherpa's inability to get another visa was because anti-Bangladesh and anti-Muslim sentiment was reaching a crescendo around the same time.

And then, as I was writing the final chapter of this book, news broke of a military coup in Myanmar. It took place on 1 February 2021, which was the day before the 2020 election winners were due to be sworn into parliament. Instead, parliament was suspended and State Counsellor Aung San Suu Kyi and President U Win Myint were detained, along with twenty-four ministers and deputies. Airports and banks were closed and sporadic internet blackouts began. Tanks rolled into major cities. My friend and former source, Australian academic Sean Turnell, was also arrested in February, and he faces a fourteen year sentence under a colonial-era law called the Official Secrets Act. Sean has been accused of trying to flee Myanmar with secret documents – a charge he refutes.

The pretext for the coup was patently absurd. The military, led by General Min Aung Hlaing, claimed that electoral fraud made the 2020 elections invalid, and demanded a recount of votes. Aung San Suu Kyi has won by a landslide every election she has ever participated in. If there were a recount, the military would probably only lose by more. After the elections of 2015, Min Aung Hlaing conceded electoral defeat and promised to respect the will of the people. Yet notwithstanding reality, he has declared a state of emergency for a year, after which time he promises to hold fresh elections. It is highly doubtful that the military leadership will keep its word. Tragically, Myanmar's decade-long experiment with democracy appears to be over.

Or is it? Hundreds of thousands of Burmese people have taken to the streets, day after day, to express their collective outrage. Doctors, engineers, railway workers, teachers and nurses have protested in their uniforms, along with bare-chested muscle men, beauty queens, and people dressed in superhero costumes and wedding dresses. I saw a photo of a teenage girl holding up a placard that said: 'I don't want a dictatorship – I just want a boyfriend.' The catch-cry among the young protesters is, 'You messed with the wrong generation', and they wield the three-finger salute from *The Hunger Games*. Their creativity, humour and peacefulness make me feel alternately hopeful and heartbroken. Seeing the streets of Yangon turned into a battlefield is deeply upsetting.

At the time of writing in mid-April, more than 700 people

have been killed for resisting military rule. The military shot 82 protesters on 10 April in the city of Bago. It is a repeat of the atrocities of 1988, when the military killed thousands of mostly student protesters. In recent weeks, the military have used tear gas on children, beaten up unarmed medics, and pushed a teenage girl off a balcony to her death. They behave as though they are sub-human.

Several analysts have warned that Myanmar is on the brink of civil war and that it may become a failed state.

Myanmar's sudden return to a dictatorship means that I have inadvertently written a history book. It documents a brief window of time when the country opened up to the world and embraced democracy. So much for my 'Dawn of a New Era' headline in *The Global New Light of Myanmar* the day after the elections in 2015. What we're seeing is a tragic case of history repeating itself.

The following is an account of what happened to some of the people who loomed large in my life in Myanmar.

In mid 2018, my former boss at *The Myanmar Times*, Ross Dunkley, was arrested in his home, alongside his business partner John McKenzie and five Burmese women, for using and possessing drugs. A stash of crystal meth, heroin and marijuana were seized alongside drug paraphernalia. In August 2019, Ross and John were sentenced to thirteen years in prison, while the five women received eleven-year sentences. On 18 April 2021, Ross was released in a Burmese new year presidential amnesty. His relief must be immense.

Niranjan Rasalingam was also released in the amnesty, after spending more than seven years in prison. I am absolutely thrilled for him and hope that he is able to rebuild his life. Balu, Dinesh and Raj were released a couple of months earlier. I believe the men's freedom should be credited to a large degree to the former British Embassy vice consul Sue Garbutt, who remained Niranjan's power of attorney all this time. She kept fighting for the men's release for years after her official duties in Myanmar ended.

The co-founder of *The Myanmar Times,* Sonny Swe, runs the award-winning *Frontier Magazine*. Each year, he has written a heartfelt Facebook post to mark the day that he was released from prison in 2013. Sonny must be extremely worried by the recent turn of events in his country, and he has left Facebook.

The Myanmar Times has been suspended for three months and its website is down. A friend told me that several senior journalists walked off the job after being told they would have to cooperate with the military. Other local publications are still bravely putting out news, though of course the future of independent media is uncertain, along with everything else. Thiri remains working at another publication in Yangon, but does so remotely. She told me that she has been too frightened to leave her apartment since the coup began.

As for Sherpa and me, we made it into Australia, along with our cat Butters. We rented a studio apartment in Sydney and I got a job at a homewares store to make ends meet until we were more settled. I found it difficult to adjust to life back home and suffered from quite a severe case of reverse culture shock. Australia felt so rule-oriented and sanitised.

But as the months passed, things improved. Sherpa got a job as a news curator at Twitter and I returned to freelance journalism. In December 2018, our daughter Olivia was born. Sherpa was granted permanent residency just before he became a father. Our second daughter, Claire, was born in August 2020. Sadly, Claire was only nine weeks old when Sherpa and I separated, after almost ten years of marriage. Maybe I'll write about it one day – but I don't think it will be any time soon.

Although this is a work of non-fiction, I have taken certain storytelling liberties, particularly as it relates to the timing of events. There were periods when so many things were happening almost simultaneously that I have had to separate them for narrative flow. Dialogue can be tricky – I would hate to ever put words in people's mouths – so wherever it was possible, I have used comments that are based on my interviews with them, or their published words. Aliases have sometimes been used to protect the identity of the source. Ultimately, this book is a collection of my memories, true as I hold them. Any errors are mine.

People say that writing a book can be a lonely endeavour, but I found the opposite to be true with *Our Home in Myanmar*. It has been my steady companion throughout a defining and turbulent period of my life, involving changes in my relationship, raising small children and getting through the COVID-19 pandemic. Returning to Myanmar, in my mind at least, was a great distraction and consolation when so much else was challenging. I hope that the enjoyment I derived from writing my first book is passed on to you as its reader.

ACKNOWLEDGMENTS

My thanks go to the people of Myanmar, who are among the kindest and most genuine people I have ever met. You are in my thoughts every day as you bravely fight for democracy. I hope that this is the last battle you have to fight against such a brutal regime. The military has overplayed its hand in your lives for far too long.

My profound thanks go to Lauren Finger, who was the first person to say that my idea for a book had legs. You were firstly my editor and then – to my delight – my friend. The care with which you edited the manuscript was indispensable to me, and your judgement so sound that I never once doubted it. Your cheerful flexibility enabled me to finish the job long after I hoped it would be completed.

Thank you also for recommending a team of talented individuals to assist with other aspects of book production, including designer Kirby Young, who made the beautiful cover. Another was Jo Lyons, who provided really excellent input. My 'triple layer of defence,' as I like to call it, was my dear friend 'Agent' (Aye Chan Wynn). Thank you, Agent, for reading the manuscript and providing such perceptive and thoughtful feedback. It was only after your eagle eye had passed over it that I felt confident in presenting it to the world.

My former colleague at *The Myanmar Times*, Kaung Htet, took the photo on the cover, which is just how I remember Yangon. At the time of writing, Kaung Htet is taking powerful, inspiring, yet often disturbing, photographs of the protests.

Thanks to Sherpa for sharing this adventure with me, and ten years of our lives. It is wonderful to also be able to share the joy of watching our girls grow, play and learn. I am thankful that we are able to do so amicably.

My parents, Simon and Margaret Mudditt, provided me with every opportunity and so much love, and always encouraged me to pursue my writing dreams. You even came to visit Sherpa and me in Myanmar, and were enthusiastic about every single thing we showed you, big or small.

A big thanks to my beautiful daughters Olivia and Claire – had you not been the wonderful sleepers that you were from day one, this book may never have been written. I feel like I won the lottery with you two – and that's not only because of the sleeping. Thank you for making me smile every day, and I hope that you enjoy reading this book one day when you're older.

Made in the USA
Middletown, DE
25 January 2022